32 BASIC Programs

for

the Apple Computer

Tom Rugg

and

Phil Feldman

dilithium Press
Beaverton, Oregon

ISBN: 0-918398-34-7
Library of Congress catalog card number: 80-68533

Printed in the United States of America.

dilithium Press
11000 SW 11th Street
Beaverton, OR 97005

Acknowledgements

Our thanks to the following for their help and encouragement:
Our wives and families, John Craig, Merl and Patti Miller,
Asenatha McCauley, Herb Furth, Freddie, Wayne Green, and
Al Outhier. Special thanks to everyone at ComputerWorld in
Van Nuys, California.

AN IMPORTANT NOTE

Preface

You have bought yourself an Apple computer (or maybe you just have access to one at school or work). You will soon find that the most frequent question you are asked goes something like this: "Oh, you got a computer, eh? Uh . . . what are you going to do with it?"

Your answer, of course, depends on your own particular situation. Maybe you got it for mathematical work, or for your business, or for home usage, or to enable you to learn more about computers. Maybe you got it for a teaching/learning tool or for playing games.

Even if you got the computer specifically for only one of these reasons, you should not neglect the others. The computer is such a powerful tool that it can be used in many different ways. If it is not being used for its "intended" function right now, why not make use of it in some other way?

The Apple is so small and portable that you can, say, take it home from work over the weekend and let the kids play educational games. They will have fun *and* learn a lot. After they go to bed, you can use it to help plan your personal finances. Or, you can let your guests at a party try to outsmart the Apple (or each other) at some fascinating games. The possibilities go on and on.

All these things can be done with the Apple, but it cannot do any of them without the key ingredient— a computer program. People with little or no exposure to computers may be in for a surprise when they learn this. A computer without a program is like a car without a driver. It just sits there.

So you ask, "Where can I get some programs to do the things I want my computer to do?" Glad you asked. There are several alternatives.

1. Hire a computer programmer. If you have a big budget, this is the way to go. Good programmers are expensive and hard to find (and you will not know for sure if they're really good until after the job is finished). Writing a couple of programs that are moderately complex will probably cost you more than you paid for the Apple itself.

2. Learn to program yourself. This is a nice alternative, but it takes time. There are lots of programming books available – some are good, some not so good. You can take courses at local colleges. If you can afford the time and you have a fair amount of common sense and inner drive, this is a good solution.

3. Buy the programs you want. This is cheaper than hiring your own programmer because all the buyers share the cost of writing the programs. You still will not find it very cheap, especially if you want to accumulate several dozen programs. Each program might cost anywhere from a few dollars to several hundred dollars. The main problem is that you cannot be sure how good the programs are, and, since they are generalized for all possible buyers, you may not be able to easily modify them to do exactly what *you* want. Also, they have to be written in a computer language that *your* computer understands. Even if you find a program written in the BASIC language, you will soon learn that the Apple's BASIC is not the same as other versions. Variations between versions of the same language typically result in the program not working.

This book gives you the chance to take the third alternative at the lowest possible cost. If you divide the cost of the book by the number of programs in it (use your computer if you like), you will find that the cost per program is amazingly low. Even if there are only a few programs in the book that will be useful to you, the cost is pretty hard to beat.

Just as important is the fact that these programs are written specifically for your Apple. If you type them in exactly as shown, they will work! No changes are needed. In addition, we show you exactly what to change in order to make some simple modifications that may suit your taste or needs. Plus, if you have learned a little about BASIC, you can go even further and follow the suggestions about more extensive changes that can be made. This approach was used to try to make every program useful to you, whether you are a total beginner or an old hand with computers.

But enough of the sales pitch. Our main point is that we feel a computer is an incredibly flexible machine, and it is a shame to put it to only one or two limited uses and let it sit idle the rest of the time. We are giving you a pretty wide range of things to do with your Apple, and we are really only scratching the surface.

So open your eyes and your mind. Play a mental game against the computer (WARI, JOT). Evaluate your next financial decision (LOAN, DECIDE). Expand your vocabulary or improve your reading speed (VOCAB, TACHIST). Solve mathematical equations (DIFFEQN, SIMEQN).

But please, don't leave your Apple asleep in the corner too much. Give it some exercise.

How to Use This Book

Each chapter of this book presents a computer program that runs on an Apple II or Apple III computer with Applesoft BASIC. Most will run on a 16K Apple II (see Appendix 1). Each chapter is made up of eight sections that serve the following functions:

1. **Purpose**: Explains what the program does and why you might want to use it.
2. **How To Use It**: Gives the details of what happens when you run the program. Explains your options and the meanings of any responses you might give. Provides details of any limitations of the program or errors that might occur.
3. **Sample Run**: Shows you what you will see on the screen when you run the program.
4. **Program Listing**: Provides a "listing" (or "print-out") of the BASIC program. These are the instructions to the computer that you must provide so it will know what to do. You must type them in extremely carefully for correct results.
5. **Easy Changes**: Shows you some very simple changes you can make to the program to cause it to work differently, if you wish. You do not have to understand how to program to make these changes.
6. **Main Routines**: Explains the general logic of the program, in case you want to figure out how it works. Gives the BASIC line numbers and a brief explanation of what each major portion of the program accomplishes.
7. **Main Variables**: Explains what each of the key variables in the program is used for, in case you want to figure out how it works.

8. **Suggested Projects**: Provides a few ideas for major changes you might want to make to the program. To try any of these, you will need to understand BASIC and use the information provided in the previous two sections (Main Routines and Main Variables).

To use any of these programs on your Apple computer, you need only use the first four sections. The last four sections are there to give you supplementary information if you want to tinker with the program.

RECOMMENDED PROCEDURE

Here is our recommendation of how to try any of the programs in this book:

1. Read through the documentation that came with the Apple to learn the fundamentals of communication with the computer. This will teach you how to turn the computer on, get into Applesoft, enter a program, correct mistakes, run a program, etc.

2. Pick a chapter and read Section 1 ("Purpose") to see if the program sounds interesting or useful to you. If not, move on to the next chapter until you find one that is. If you are a beginner you might want to try one of the short "Miscellaneous Programs" first.

3. Read Sections 2 and 3 of the chapter ("How To Use It" and "Sample Run") to learn the details of what the program does.

4. Enter the NEW command to eliminate any existing program that might already be in your Apple's memory. Using Section 4 of the chapter ("Program Listing"), carefully enter the program into the Apple. Be particularly careful to get all the punctuation characters right (i.e., commas, semicolons, colons, quotation marks, etc.).

5. *After the entire program is entered into the Apple's memory, use the LIST command to display what you have entered so you can double check for typographical errors, omitted lines, etc.* Don't mistake a semicolon for a colon, or an alphabetic I or O for a numeric 1 or 0 (zero). Take a minute to note the differences in these characters before you begin.

6. Before trying to RUN the program, use the SAVE command to save the program temporarily on cassette or disk. This could prevent a lot of wasted effort in case something goes wrong (power failure, computer malfunction, etc.).
7. Now RUN the program. Is the same thing happening that is shown in the Sample Run? If so, accept our congratulations and go on to step 9. If not, stay cool and go to step 8.
8. If you got a SYNTAX ERROR in a line, LIST that line and look at it closely. Something is not right. Maybe you interchanged a colon and a semicolon. Maybe you typed a numeric 1 or 0 instead of an alphabetic I or O. Maybe you misspelled a word or omitted one. Keep looking until you find it, then correct the error and go back to step 7.

   If you got some other kind of error message, consult the Apple documentation for an explanation. Keep in mind that the error might not be in the line that is pointed to by the error message. It is not unusual for the mistake to be in a line immediately preceding the error message line. Another possibility is that one or more lines were omitted entirely. In any event, fix the problem and go back to step 7.

   If there are no error messages, but the program is not doing the same thing as the Sample Run, there are two possibilities. First, maybe the program isn't *supposed* to do exactly the same thing. Some of the programs are designed to do unpredictable things to avoid repetition (primarily the game programs and graphic displays). They should be doing the same *types* of things as the Sample Run, however.

   The second possibility is that you made a typing error that did not cause an error message to be displayed, but simply changed the meaning of one or more lines in the program. These are a little tricky to find, but you can usually narrow it down to the general area of the problem by noting the point at which the error takes place. Is the first thing displayed correct? If so, the error is probably after the PRINT statement that caused the first thing to be displayed. Look for the same types of things mentioned before. Make the corrections and go back to step 7.
9. Continue running the program, trying to duplicate the Sample Run. If you find a variation that cannot be accounted for in the "How To Use It" section of the chapter, go to step 8.

Otherwise, if it seems to be running properly, SAVE the program on cassette or disk.
10. Read Section 5 of the chapter ("Easy Changes"). Try any of the changes that look interesting. If you think the changed version is better, SAVE it on cassette or disk, too. You will probably want to give it a slightly different title in the first REM statement to avoid future confusion.

A NOTE ON THE PROGRAM LISTINGS

A line on the screen of the Apple is 40 characters wide, The printer that was used to create the Program Listing section of each chapter prints lines up to 80 characters long. For best reproduction in this book, it was preferable that each published line be no longer than 56 characters. This combination of facts might cause you a little confusion when you are entering the programs into your Apple. Here's the way it works.

Wherever there is a line in a program that is longer than 56 characters, it has been divided into two lines that are each no more than 56 characters. You can recognize this easily because the second part has no line number at the left-hand side. This division is only for the purpose of printing the book. You should think of a divided line like this as one long line and enter it into your Apple as a single line. Usually, this division is made in such a way that the first part of the line ends with a colon or semicolon so you can notice it more easily.

Don't be fooled by the fact that the cursor on your Apple jumps down to the next line after you enter the 40th character —it's just one long line until you press **RETURN.**

Also, you should be aware that Applesoft "reformats" each line of your program when you LIST it by adding extra spaces. To improve readability and shorten the listings, the listings in this book are formatted without most of these spaces. You should key in each program as it is shown here, but be aware that Applesoft will add spaces when you LIST it. *The only places where it is critical that the number of spaces be the same are between quotation marks and in DATA statements.*

Contents

Section 6—MISCELLANEOUS PROGRAMS

Section 1

Applications Programs

INTRODUCTION TO APPLICATIONS PROGRAMS

Good practical applications are certainly a prime use of personal computers. There are a myriad of ways the Apple can help us to do useful work. Here are six programs for use around the home or business.

Financial considerations are always important. LOAN will calculate interest, payment schedules, etc. for mortgages, car loans, or any such business loan. Do you every have trouble balancing your checkbook(s)? CHECKBOOK will enable you to rectify your monthly statements and help you find the cause of any errors.

Fuel usage is a constant concern for those of us who drive. MILEAGE will determine and keep track of a motor vehicle's general operating efficiency.

The tedium of analyzing questionnaires and examinations can be greatly relieved with the aid of your computer. In particular, teachers and market researchers should find QUEST/EXAM useful.

Often we are faced with difficult decisions. DECIDE transforms the Apple into a trusty advisor. Help will be at hand for any decision involving the selection of one alternative from several choices.

Before anything else, you might want to consult BIORHYTHM each day. Some major airlines, and other industries, are placing credence on biorhythm theory. If you agree, or "just in case," simply turn on your Apple and load this program.

BIORHYTHM

PURPOSE

Did you ever have one of those days when nothing seemed to go right? All of us seem to have days when we are clumsy, feel depressed, or just cannot seem to force ourselves to concentrate as well as usual. Sometimes we know why this occurs. It may result from the onset of a cold or because of an argument with a relative. Sometimes, however, we find no such reason. Why can't we perform up to par on some of those days when nothing is known to be wrong?

Biorhythm theory says that all of us have cycles, beginning with the moment of birth, that influence our physical, emotional, and intellectual states. We will not go into a lot of detail about how biorhythm theory was developed (your local library probably has some books about this if you want to find out more), but we will summarize how it supposedly affects you.

The physical cycle is twenty-three days long. For the first 11½ days, you are in the positive half of the cycle. This means you should have a feeling of physical well-being, strength, and endurance. During the second 11½ days, you are in the negative half of the cycle. This results in less endurance and a tendency toward a general feeling of fatigue.

The emotional cycle lasts for twenty-eight days. During the positive half (the first fourteen days), you should feel more cheerful, optimistic, and cooperative. During the negative half, you will tend to be more moody, pessimistic, and irritable.

The third cycle is the intellectual cycle, which lasts for thirty-three days. The first half is a period in which you should have greater success in learning new material and pursuing creative, intellectual activities. During the second half, you are supposedly better off reviewing old material rather than attempting to learn difficult new concepts. The ups and downs of these cycles are relative to each individual. For example, if you are a very self-controlled, unemotional person to begin with, your emotional highs and lows may not be very noticeable. Similarly, your physical and intellectual fluctuations depend upon your physical condition and intellectual capacity.

The day that any of these three cycles changes from the plus side to the minus side (or vice versa) is called a "critical day." Biorhythm theory says that you are more accident-prone on critical days in your physical or emotional cycles. Critical days in the intellectual cycle aren't considered as dangerous, but if they coincide with a critical day in one of the other cycles, the potential problem can increase. As you might expect, a triple critical day is one on which you are recommended to be especially careful.

Please note that there is quite a bit of controversy about biorhythms. Most scientists feel that there is not nearly enough evidence to conclude that biorhythms can tell you anything meaningful. Others believe that biorhythm cycles exist, but that they are not as simple and inflexible as the 23, 28, and 33 day cycles mentioned here.

Whether biorhythms are good, bad, true, false, or anything else is not our concern here. We are just presenting the idea to you as an interesting theory that you can investigate with the help of your Apple computer.

HOW TO USE IT

The program first asks for the birth date of the person whose biorhythm cycles are to be charted. You provide the month and day as you might expect. For the year, you only need to enter the last two digits if it is between 1900 and 1999. Otherwise, enter all four digits.

Next the program asks you for the start date for the biorhythm chart. Enter it in the same way. Of course, this date cannot be earlier than the birth date.

After a delay of about a second, the program clears the screen and begins plotting the biorhythm chart, one day at a time. The left side of the screen displays the date, while the right side displays the chart. The left half of the chart is the "down" (negative) side of each cycle. The right half is the "up" (positive) side. The center line shows the critical days when you are at a zero point (neither positive nor negative).

Each of the three curves is plotted with an identifying letter — P for physical, E for emotional, and I for intellectual. When the curves cross, an asterisk is displayed instead of either of the two (or three) letters.

Eighteen days of the chart are displayed on one screen, and then the program waits for you to press a key. If you press the E key, the current chart ends and the program starts over again. If you press the **SPACE** key (or any other key except **RESET** or **SHIFT**), the program clears the screen and displays the next eighteen days of the chart. Pressing the **ESCAPE** key will end the program.

The program will allow you to enter dates from the year 100 A.D. and on. We make no guarantees about any extreme future dates, however, such as entering a year greater than 3000. We sincerely hope that these limitations do not prove to be too confining for you.

SAMPLE RUN

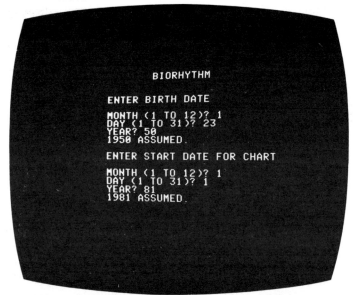

The operator enters his or her birth date and the date for the beginning of the chart.

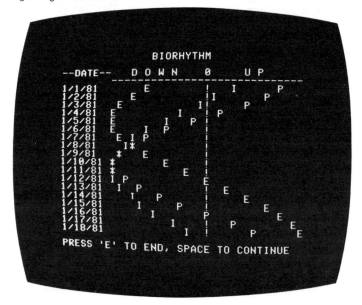

The program responds with the first 18 days of the operator's biorhythm chart, then waits for a key to be pressed.

PROGRAM LISTING

```
100 REM: BIORHYTHM
110 REM: COPYRIGHT 1980 BY TOM RUGG AND PHIL FELDMAN
120 L=0:Z=.99999:T=14:P=3.14159265
130 TEXT:HOME:PRINT TAB(8);"BIORHYTHM"
140 GOSUB 1200:PRINT:PRINT
150 PRINT"ENTER BIRTH DATE"
160 GOSUB 500
170 GOSUB 600
180 JB=JD
190 PRINT:PRINT"ENTER START DATE FOR CHART"
200 GOSUB 500
210 GOSUB 600
220 JC=JD
230 IF JC>=JB THEN 270
240 PRINT"CHART DATE CAN'T BE EARLIER"
250 PRINT"THAN BIRTH DATE.  TRY AGAIN."
260 GOTO 140
270 FOR J=1 TO 1000:NEXT
280 GOSUB 700
300 N=JC-JB
310 V=23:GOSUB 800:GOSUB 850
320 V=28:GOSUB 800:GOSUB 850
330 V=33:GOSUB 800:GOSUB 850
340 GOSUB 1000
350 PRINT TAB(1);C$;TAB(9);L$
360 JC=JC+1:L=L+1:IF L<18 THEN 300
370 PRINT:PRINT"PRESS 'E' TO END, SPACE TO CONTINUE";
380 GET R$:IF ASC(R$)=27 THEN END
390 IF R$="E" THEN 120
400 L=0:GOTO 280
500 PRINT
505 INPUT"MONTH (1 TO 12)? ";M
510 M=INT(M):IF M<1 OR M>12 THEN 505
520 INPUT"DAY (1 TO 31)? ";D
530 D=INT(D):IF D<1 OR D>31 THEN 520
540 INPUT"YEAR? ";Y
550 Y=INT(Y):IF Y<0 THEN 540
560 IF Y>99 THEN 580
570 Y=Y+1900:PRINT Y;" ASSUMED."
580 RETURN
600 W=INT((M-14)/12+Z)
610 JD=INT(1461*(Y+4800+W)/4)
620 B=367*(M-2-W*12)/12
```

```
630 IF B<0 THEN B=B+Z
640 B=INT(B):JD=JD+B
650 B=INT(INT(3*(Y+4900+W)/100)/4)
660 JD=JD+D-32075-B
670 RETURN
700 HOME
710 PRINT TAB(15);"BIORHYTHM"
720 PRINT:PRINT TAB(1);"--DATE--";TAB(12);
730 PRINT"D O W N";TAB(23);"0";TAB(29);"U P"
740 PRINT TAB(9);U$
750 RETURN
800 W=INT(N/V):R=N-W*V
810 RETURN
850 IF V<>23 THEN 900
855 L$=CHR$(32):FOR J=1 TO 4
860 L$=L$+L$:NEXT
870 L$=L$+LEFT$(L$,13)
880 L$=LEFT$(L$,T)+CHR$(33)+RIGHT$(L$,T)
890 IF V=23 THEN C$="P"
900 IF V=28 THEN C$="E"
910 IF V=33 THEN C$="I"
920 W=R/V:W=W*2*P
930 W=T*SIN(W):W=W+T+1.5
940 W=INT(W):A$=MID$(L$,W,1)
950 IF A$="P" OR A$="E" OR A$="*" THEN C$="*"
955 IF W=1 THEN 980
957 IF W=T+T+1 THEN 990
960 L$=LEFT$(L$,W-1)+C$+RIGHT$(L$,T+T+1-W)
970 RETURN
980 L$=C$+RIGHT$(L$,T+T):RETURN
990 L$=LEFT$(L$,T+T)+C$:RETURN
1000 W=JC+68569:R=INT(4*W/146097)
1010 W=W-INT((146097*R+3)/4)
1020 Y=INT(4000*(W+1)/1461001)
1030 W=W-INT(1461*Y/4)+31
1040 M=INT(80*W/2447)
1050 D=W-INT(2447*M/80)
1060 W=INT(M/11):M=M+2-12*W
1070 Y=100*(R-49)+Y+W
1080 A$=STR$(M)
1090 C$=A$+"/"
1100 A$=STR$(D)
1110 C$=C$+A$+"/"
1120 A$=STR$(Y):W=LEN(A$)
1130 C$=C$+MID$(A$,W-1,2)
```

```
1140 RETURN
1200 U$="-":FOR J=1 TO 4
1210 U$=U$+U$:NEXT
1220 U$=U$+LEFT$(U$,13)
1230 RETURN
```

EASY CHANGES

1. Want to see the number of days between any two dates? Insert this line:

305 PRINT "DAYS=";N: END

Then enter the earlier date as the birth date, and the later date as the start date for the chart. This will cause the program to display the difference in days and then end.
2. To alter the number of days of the chart shown on each screen, alter the 18 in line 360.

MAIN ROUTINES

120 - 140	Initializes variables. Displays titles.
150 - 180	Asks for birth date and converts to Julian date format (i.e., the number of days since January 1, 4713 B.C.
190 - 220	Asks for start date for chart and converts to Julian date format.
230 - 260	Checks that chart date is not sooner than birth date.
270	Delays about one second before displaying chart.
280	Displays heading at top of screen.
300	Determines number of days between birth date and current chart date.
310 - 330	Plots points in L$ string for each of the three cycles.
340	Converts Julian date back into month-day-year format.
350	Displays one line on the chart.
360 - 400	Adds one to chart date. Checks to see if the screen is full.
500 - 580	Subroutine to ask operator for month, day, and year. Edits replies.
600 - 670	Subroutine to convert month, day, and year into Julian date format.
700 - 750	Subroutine to clear screen and display headings.

800 - 810   Subroutine to calculate remainder R of N/V.
850 - 990   Subroutine to plot a point in L$ based on V and R.
1000 - 1140 Subroutine to convert Julian date JC back into
                      month/day/year format.
1200 - 1230 Subroutine to create U$.

MAIN VARIABLES

L	Counter of number of lines on screen.
T	Number of characters on one side of the center of the chart.
P	Pi.
JB	Birth date in Julian format.
JD	Julian date calculated in subroutine.
JC	Chart start date in Julian format.
K	Loop and work variable.
N	Number of days between birth and current chart date.
V	Number of days in present biorhythm cycle (23, 28, or 33).
C$	String with date in month/day/year format.
L$	String with one line of the biorhythm chart.
R$	Reply from operator after screen fills up.
M	Month (1 - 12).
D	Day (1 - 31).
Y	Year (100 or greater).
W, B	Work variables.
R	Remainder of N/V (number of days into cycle).
A$	Work variable.
U$	String of 29 dashes.

SUGGESTED PROJECTS

Investigate the biorhythms of some famous historical or athletic personalities. For example, are track and field athletes usually in the positive side of the physical cycle on the days that they set world records? Where was Lincoln in his emotional and intellectual cycles when he wrote "The Gettysburg Address"? Do a significant percentage of accidents befall people on critical days?

CHECKBOOK

PURPOSE

Many people consider the monthly ritual of balancing the checkbook to be an irritating and error-prone activity. Some people get confused and simply give up after the first try, while others give up the first time they cannot reconcile the bank statement with the checkbook. Fortunately, you have an advantage—your computer. This program takes you through the necessary steps to balance your checkbook, doing the arithmetic for you, of course.

HOW TO USE IT

The program starts off by giving you instructions about how to verify that the amount of each check and deposit are the same on the statement as they are in your checkbook. Sometimes the bank will make an error in reading the amount that you wrote on a check (especially if your handwriting is not too clear), and sometimes you will copy the amount incorrectly into your checkbook. While you are comparing these figures, make a check mark in your checkbook next to each check and deposit listed on the statement. A good system is to alternate the marks you use each month (maybe an "x" one month and a check mark the next) so you can easily see which checks and deposits came through on which statement.

Next, the program asks for the ending balance shown on the bank statement. You are then asked for the *check number* (not the amount) of the most recent check shown on the statement.

This will generally be the highest numbered check the bank has processed, unless you like to write checks out of sequence. Your account balance after this most recent check will be reconciled with the statement balance, so that is what the program asks for next—your checkbook balance after the most recent check.

The program must compensate for any differences between what your checkbook has in it prior to the most recent check and what the statement has on it. First, if you have any deposits that are not shown on the statement before the most recent check, you must enter them. Generally, there are none, so you just enter "END."

Next you have to enter the amounts of any checks that have not yet "cleared" the bank and that are prior to the most recent check. Look in your checkbook for any checks that do not have your check mark next to them. Remember that some of these could be several months old.

Next you enter the amount of any service charges or debit memos that are on the statement, but which have not been shown in your checkbook prior to the most recent check. Typically, this is just a monthly service charge, but there might also be charges for printing new checks for you or some other adjustment that takes money away from you. Credit memos (which give money back to you) are not entered until later. Be sure to make an entry in your checkbook for any of these adjustments so that next month's statement will balance.

Finally, you are asked for any recent deposits or credit memos that were *not* entered in your checkbook prior to the most recent check, but that *are* listed on the bank statement. It is not unusual to have one or two of these, since deposits are generally processed by banks sooner than checks.

Now comes the moment of truth. The program tells you whether or not you are in balance and displays the totals. If so, pack things up until next month's statement arrives.

If not, you have to figure out what is wrong. You have seven options of what to do next which allow you to review the numbers you entered in case of a typing error. If you find an error, go back to the beginning and try again. Of course, if it is a simple error that precisely accounts for the amount by which you are out of balance, there is no need to go through the whole thing again.

If you entered everything correctly, the most likely cause of that out-of-balance condition is an arithmetic error in your checkbook. Look for errors in your addition and subtraction, with subtraction being the most likely culprit. This is especially likely if the amount of the error is a nice even number like one dollar or ten cents.

Another common error is accidentally adding the amount of a check in your checkbook instead of subtracting it. If you did this, your error will be twice the amount of the check (which makes it easy to find).

If this still does not explain the error, check to be sure you subtracted *last* month's service charge when you balanced your checkbook with the previous statement. And, of course, if you did not balance your checkbook last month, you cannot expect it to come out right this month.

The program has limitations of how many entries you can make in each category (checks outstanding, deposits outstanding, etc.), but these can be changed easily. See "Easy Changes" below.

NOTE: SEE DISCLAIMER IN FRONT PART OF BOOK.

SAMPLE RUN

```
            CHECKBOOK BALANCER

FIRST, COMPARE THE BANK STATEMENT
WITH YOUR CHECKBOOK.
MAKE SURE THE STATEMENT AND THE
CHECKBOOK SHOW THE SAME FIGURES
FOR EACH CHECK AND DEPOSIT.

MAKE A MARK IN THE CHECKBOOK NEXT TO
EACH CHECK AND DEPOSIT LISTED
ON THE STATEMENT.

WHAT'S THE ENDING BALANCE SHOWN
ON THE STATEMENT?
?520.16

NOW FIND THE MOST RECENT CHECK THAT
IS SHOWN ON THE BANK STATEMENT.
```

WHAT IS THE CHECK NUMBER OF THIS CHECK?
?1652

WHAT BALANCE DOES YOUR CHECKBOOK
SHOW AFTER CHECK NO. 1652
?480.12

ENTER THE AMOUNT OF EACH DEPOSIT
THAT IS SHOWN IN YOUR CHECKBOOK
PRIOR TO CHECK NO. 1652
BUT IS NOT ON THE STATEMENT.
WHEN NO MORE, SAY 'END'
?END

TOTAL = 0

NOW ENTER THE AMOUNTS OF ANY CHECKS
THAT ARE IN YOUR CHECKBOOK PRIOR
TO CHECK 1652 BUT THAT
HAVE NOT BEEN SHOWN ON A BANK
STATEMENT YET.

WHEN NO MORE, SAY 'END'
?35.04
?10
?END

TOTAL = 45.04

NOW ENTER THE AMOUNTS OF ANY
SERVICE CHARGES OR DEBIT MEMOS.

WHEN NO MORE, SAY 'END'
?2.35
?2.65
?END

TOTAL = 5

ENTER THE AMOUNT OF EACH DEPOSIT
THAT IS SHOWN IN YOUR CHECKBOOK
AFTER CHECK NO. 1652 THAT IS
ALSO LISTED ON THE STATEMENT.

```
WHEN NO MORE, SAY 'END'
?END

TOTAL = O

CONGRATULATIONS! IT BALANCES.

STATEMENT BALANCE + CHECKS OUTSTANDING
+ SERVICE CHARGES = 525.16

CHECKBOOK BALANCE + CHECKS OUTSTANDING
+ RECENT DEPOSITS = 525.16

DIFFERENCE = O

PRESS ANY KEY TO CONTINUE

NEXT ACTION:
  1 - LIST CHECKS OUTSTANDING
  2 - LIST DEPOSITS OUTSTANDING
  3 - LIST SERVICE CHARGES
  4 - START OVER
  5 - END PROGRAM
  6 - DISPLAY BALANCING INFO
  7 - LIST DEPOSITS AFTER LAST CHECK
?5
```

PROGRAM LISTING

```
100 REM: CHECKBOOK
110 REM: COPYRIGHT 1980 BY TOM RUGG AND PHIL FELDMAN
120 TEXT:HOME
130 PRINT"CHECKBOOK ANALYZER"
140 PRINT:PRINT
150 MC=20:MD=10:MS=10:MR=10
155 L$="NO MORE ROOM"
160 DIM C(MC),D(MD),S(MS),R(MR)
170 TC=0:TD=0:TS=0:TR=0:NC=0:ND=0:NS=0:NR=0
180 E$="ERROR. RE-ENTER, PLEASE."
190 PRINT"FIRST, COMPARE THE BANK STATEMENT"
200 PRINT"WITH YOUR CHECKBOOK."
210 PRINT
```

```
220 PRINT"MAKE SURE THE STATEMENT AND THE"
230 PRINT"CHECKBOOK SHOW THE SAME FIGURES"
240 PRINT"FOR EACH CHECK AND DEPOSIT."
250 PRINT:PRINT"MAKE A MARK IN THE CHECKBOOK NEXT TO"
260 PRINT"EACH CHECK AND DEPOSIT LISTED"
270 PRINT"ON THE STATEMENT."
280 PRINT:PRINT"WHAT'S THE ENDING BALANCE SHOWN"
290 PRINT"ON THE STATEMENT?":INPUT SB
300 PRINT:PRINT"NOW FIND THE MOST RECENT CHECK THAT"
310 PRINT"IS SHOWN ON THE BANK STATEMENT."
320 PRINT
330 PRINT"WHAT IS THE CHECK NUMBER OF"
340 PRINT"THIS CHECK?":INPUT LC
350 IF LC=INT(LC) THEN 380
360 PRINT"NO, NOT THE AMOUNT OF THE CHECK."
370 GOTO 300
380 PRINT
390 PRINT"WHAT BALANCE DOES YOUR CHECKBOOK"
400 PRINT"SHOW AFTER CHECK NO. ";LC
410 INPUT CB
420 PRINT:PRINT
430 PRINT"ENTER THE AMOUNT OF EACH DEPOSIT"
440 PRINT"THAT IS SHOWN IN YOUR CHECKBOOK"
450 PRINT"PRIOR TO CHECK NO. ";LC
460 PRINT"BUT IS NOT ON THE STATEMENT."
470 A$="WHEN NO MORE, SAY 'END'":PRINT:PRINT A$
480 INPUT R$
490 IF R$="END" THEN 545
500 IF VAL(R$)>0 THEN 520
510 PRINT:PRINT E$:GOTO 470
520 ND=ND+1:D(ND)=VAL(R$):TD=TD+D(ND)
530 IF ND<MD THEN 480
540 PRINT:PRINT L$
545 PRINT:PRINT"TOTAL = ";TD:PRINT
550 PRINT"NOW ENTER THE AMOUNTS OF ANY CHECKS"
560 PRINT"THAT ARE IN THE CHECKBOOK PRIOR"
570 PRINT"TO CHECK ";LC;" BUT THAT"
580 PRINT"HAVE NOT BEEN SHOWN ON A BANK"
590 PRINT"STATEMENT YET."
600 PRINT:PRINT A$
610 INPUT R$
620 IF R$="END" THEN 690
630 IF VAL(R$)>0 THEN 660
640 PRINT:PRINT E$
650 GOTO 600
```

```
660 NC=NC+1:C(NC)=VAL(R$):TC=TC+C(NC)
670 IF NC<MC THEN 610
680 PRINT:PRINT L$
690 PRINT:PRINT"TOTAL = ";TC:PRINT
700 PRINT"NOW ENTER THE AMOUNTS OF ANY"
710 PRINT"SERVICE CHARGES OR DEBIT MEMOS."
720 PRINT:PRINT A$
730 INPUT R$
740 IF R$="END" THEN 800
750 IF VAL(R$)>0 THEN 770
760 PRINT:PRINT E$:GOTO 720
770 NS=NS+1:S(NS)=VAL(R$):TS=TS+S(NS)
780 IF NS<MS THEN 730
790 PRINT:PRINT L$
800 PRINT:PRINT"TOTAL = ";TS:PRINT
805 GOSUB 2000
810 W=SB+TD+TS-CB-TC-TR:W=ABS(W)
815 IF W<.001 THEN W=0
817 IF W<>0 THEN 840
820 PRINT:PRINT"CONGRATULATIONS!  IT BALANCES."
830 GOTO 850
840 PRINT:PRINT"SORRY, ITS OUT OF BALANCE."
850 PRINT
860 PRINT"STATEMENT BALANCE + DEPOSITS OUTSTANDING"
870 PRINT"+ SERVICE CHARGES = ";SB+TD+TS
880 PRINT
890 PRINT"CHECKBOOK BALANCE + CHECKS OUTSTANDING"
900 PRINT"+ RECENT DEPOSITS = ";CB+TC+TR
910 PRINT
920 PRINT"DIFFERENCE = ";W
925 PRINT:PRINT"PRESS ANY KEY TO CONTINUE"
930 GET R$
935 PRINT
940 PRINT"NEXT ACTION:"
950 PRINT" 1 - LIST CHECKS OUTSTANDING"
960 PRINT" 2 - LIST DEPOSITS OUTSTANDING"
970 PRINT" 3 - LIST SERVICE CHARGES"
980 PRINT" 4 - START OVER"
990 PRINT" 5 - END PROGRAM"
1000 PRINT" 6 - DISPLAY BALANCING INFO"
1010 PRINT" 7 - LIST DEPOSITS AFTER LAST CHECK"
1020 INPUT R$:R=VAL(R$)
1030 IF R<1 OR R>7 THEN 1050
1040 ON R GOTO 1100,1200,1300,1400,1500,850,1700
1050 PRINT:PRINT E$:GOTO 935
```

```
1100 PRINT:PRINT"CHECKS OUTSTANDING"
1110 FOR J=1 TO NC
1120 PRINT C(J):NEXT
1130 GOTO 925
1200 PRINT:PRINT"DEPOSITS OUTSTANDING"
1210 FOR J=1 TO ND
1220 PRINT D(J):NEXT
1230 GOTO 925
1300 PRINT:PRINT"SERVICE CHARGES"
1310 FOR J=1 TO NS
1320 PRINT S(J):NEXT
1330 GOTO 925
1400 CLEAR:GOTO 120
1500 END
1700 PRINT:PRINT"RECENT DEPOSITS"
1710 FOR J=1 TO NR
1720 PRINT R(J):NEXT
1730 GOTO 925
2000 PRINT
2010 PRINT"ENTER THE AMOUNT OF EACH DEPOSIT"
2020 PRINT"THAT IS SHOWN IN YOUR CHECKBOOK"
2030 PRINT"AFTER CHECK NO. ";LC;" THAT IS"
2040 PRINT"ALSO LISTED IN THE STATEMENT."
2050 PRINT:PRINT A$
2060 INPUT R$
2070 IF R$="END" THEN 2130
2080 IF VAL(R$)>0 THEN 2100
2090 PRINT:PRINT E$:GOTO 2050
2100 NR=NR+1:R(NR)=VAL(R$):TR=TR+R(NR)
2110 IF NR<MR THEN 2060
2120 PRINT:PRINT L$
2130 PRINT:PRINT"TOTAL = ";TR:PRINT
2140 RETURN
```

EASY CHANGES

Change the limitations of how many entries you can make in each category. Line 150 establishes these limits. If you have more than 20 checks outstanding at some time, change the value of MC to 50, for example. The other three variables can also be changed if you anticipate needing more than 10 entries. They are: the number of deposits outstanding (MD), the number of service charges and credit memos (MS), and the number of recent deposits and credit memos (MR). You'll need more than 4100 bytes free to make these changes. (See Appendix 1.)

MAIN ROUTINES

120 - 290	Initializes variables and displays first instructions.
300 - 370	Gets most recent check number.
380 - 410	Gets checkbook balance after most recent check number.
420 - 545	Gets outstanding deposits.
550 - 690	Gets outstanding checks.
700 - 800	Gets service charges and debit memos.
805	Gets recent deposits and credit memos.
810 - 920	Does balancing calculation. Displays it.
925 - 1050	Asks for next action. Goes to appropriate subroutine.
1100 - 1130	Subroutine to display checks outstanding.
1200 - 1230	Subroutine to display deposits outstanding.
1300 - 1330	Subroutine to display service charges and debit memos.
1400	Restarts program.
1500	Ends the program.
1700 - 1730	Subroutine to display recent deposits.
2000 - 2140	Subroutine to get recent deposits.

MAIN VARIABLES

MC	Maximum number of checks outstanding.
MD	Maximum number of deposits outstanding.
MS	Maximum number of service charges, debit memos.
MR	Maximum number of recent deposits, credit memos.
C	Array for checks outstanding.
D	Array for deposits outstanding.
S	Array for service charges and debit memos.
R	Array for recent deposits and credit memos.
TC	Total of checks outstanding.
TD	Total of deposits outstanding.
TS	Total of service charges and debit memos.
TR	Total of recent deposits and credit memos.

NC   Number of checks outstanding.
ND   Number of deposits outstanding.
NS   Number of service charges and debit memos.
NR   Number of recent deposits and credit memos.
E$ Error message.
SB   Statement balance.
LC   Number of last check on statement.
CB   Checkbook balance after last check on statement.
R$ Reply from operator.
W   Amount by which checkbook is out of balance.
R   Numeric value of reply for next action.
A$ Message showing how to indicate no more data.
L$ Message indicating no more room for data.
J   Loop variable.

SUGGESTED PROJECTS

1. Add more informative messages and a more complete introduction to make the program a tutorial for someone who has
   never balanced a checkbook before.
2. Allow the operator to modify any entries that have been
   discovered to be in error. This could be done by adding
   another option to the "NEXT ACTION" list, which would
   then ask the operator which category to change. This would
   allow the operator to correct an error without having to
   re-enter everything from the beginning.
3. If the checkbook is out of balance, have the program do an
   analysis (as suggested in the "How To Use It" section) and
   suggest the most likely errors that might have caused the condition.
4. Allow the operator to find arithmetic errors in the checkbook. Ask for the starting balance, then ask for each check or
   deposit amount. Add or subtract, depending on which type
   the operator indicates. Display the new balance after each
   entry so the operator can compare with the checkbook entry.

DECIDE

PURPOSE

"Decisions, decisions!" How many times have you uttered this lament when confronted by a difficult choice? Wouldn't a trusty advisor be helpful on such occasions? Well, you now have one – your Apple computer of course.

This program can help you make decisions involving the selection of one alternative from several choices. It works by prying relevant information from you and then organizing it in a meaningful, quantitative manner. Your best choice will be indicated and all of the possibilities given a relative rating.

You can use the program for a wide variety of decisions. It can help with things like choosing the best stereo system, saying yes or no to a job or business offer, or selecting the best course of action for the future. Everything is personalized to your individual decision.

HOW TO USE IT

The first thing the program does is ask you to categorize the decision at hand into one of these three categories:
1) Choosing an item (or thing),
2) Choosing a course of action, or
3) Making a yes or no decision.
You simply press **1**, **2**, or **3** and then press **RETURN** to indicate which type of decision is facing you. If you are choosing an item, you will be asked what kind of item it is.

If the decision is either of the first two types, you must next enter a list of all the possibilities under consideration. A question mark will prompt you for each one. When the list is complete, type "END" in response to the last question mark. You must, of course, enter at least two possibilities. (We hope you don't have trouble making decisions from only one possibility!) After the list is finished, it will be re-displayed so that you can verify that it is correct. If not, you must re-enter it.

Now you must think of the different factors that are important to you in making your decision. For example, location, cost, and quality of education might govern the decision of which college to attend. For a refrigerator purchase, the factors might be things like price, size, reliability, and warranty. In any case, you will be prompted for your list with a succession of question marks. Each factor is to be entered one at a time with the word "END" used to terminate the list. When complete, the list will be re-displayed. You must now decide which single factor is the most important and input its number. (You can enter 0 if you wish to change the list of factors.)

The program now asks you to rate the importance of each of the other factors relative to the most important one. This is done by first assigning a value of 10 to the main factor. Then you must assign a value from 0 - 10 to each of the other factors. These numbers reflect your assessment of each factor's relative importance as compared to the main one. A value of 10 means it is just as important; lesser values indicate how much less importance you place on it.

Now you must rate the decision possibilities with respect to each of the importance factors. Each importance factor will be treated separately. Considering *only* that importance factor, you must rate how each decision possibility stacks up. The program first assigns a value of 10 to one of the decision possibilities. Then you must assign a relative number (lower, higher, or equal to 10) to each of the other decision possibilities.

An example might alleviate possible confusion here. Suppose you are trying to decide whether to get a dog, cat, or canary for a pet. Affection is one of your importance factors. The program assigns a value of 10 to the cat. Considering *only* affection, you might assign a value of 20 to the dog and 6.5 to the canary. This means *you* consider a dog twice as affectionate as a cat but a canary only about two-thirds as affectionate as a cat. (No slighting of bird lovers is intended here, of course. Your actual ratings may be entirely different.)

Armed with all this information, the program will now determine which choice seems best for you. The various possibilities are listed in order of ranking. Alongside each one is a relative rating with the best choice being normalized to a value of 100.

Of course, DECIDE should not be used as a substitute for good, clear thinking. However, it can often provide valuable insights. You might find one alternative coming out surprisingly low or high. A trend may become obvious when the program is re-run with improved data. At least, it may help you think about decisions systematically and honestly.

SAMPLE RUN

```
                    DECIDE

     I CAN HELP YOU MAKE A DECISION.  ALL
 I NEED TO DO IS ASK SOME QUESTIONS AND
 THEN ANALYZE THE INFORMATION YOU GIVE.


         ------------------------------


 WHICH OF THESE BEST DESCRIBES THE TYPE
 OF DECISION FACING YOU?

     1) CHOOSING AN ITEM FROM VARIOUS
        ALTERNATIVES.

     2) CHOOSING A COURSE OF ACTION FROM
        VARIOUS ALTERNATIVES.

     3) MAKING A 'YES' OR 'NO' DECISION.

 WHICH ONE (1, 2, OR 3)? 1

 WHAT TYPE OF ITEM MUST YOU DECIDE UPON
 ? VACATION
```

    I NEED TO HAVE A LIST OF EACH
VACATION UNDER CONSIDERATION.

    INPUT THEM ONE AT A TIME
IN RESPONSE TO EACH QUESTION MARK.

    THE ORDER IN WHICH YOU INPUT THEM
HAS NO PARTICULAR SIGNIFICANCE.

    TYPE THE WORD 'END' TO INDICATE
THAT THE WHOLE LIST HAS BEEN ENTERED.

? MOUNTAIN CAMPING
? AFRICAN SAFARI
? TRIP TO WASHINGTON D.C.
? END

O.K. HERE'S THE LIST YOU'VE GIVEN ME:

    1)   MOUNTAIN CAMPING
    2)   AFRICAN SAFARI
    3)   TRIP TO WASHINGTON D.C.

IS THIS LIST CORRECT (Y OR N) ? YES

    NOW, THINK OF THE DIFFERENT FACTORS
THAT ARE IMPORTANT TO YOU IN CHOOSING
THE BEST VACATION.

    INPUT THEM ONE AT A TIME IN RESPONSE
TO EACH QUESTION MARK.

    TYPE THE WORD 'END' TO TERMINATE
THE LIST.

? RELAXATION
? AFFORDABILITY
? CHANGE OF PACE
? END

HERE'S THE LIST OF FACTORS YOU GAVE ME:

    1)   RELAXATION
    2)   AFFORDABILITY
    3)   CHANGE OF PACE

    DECIDE WHICH FACTOR ON THE LIST IS
THE MOST IMPORTANT AND INPUT ITS NUMBER.
(TYPE 0 IF THE LIST NEEDS CHANGING.)

? <u>2</u>

    NOW LET'S SUPPOSE WE HAVE A SCALE OF
IMPORTANCE RANGING FROM 0-10.

    WE'LL GIVE AFFORDABILITY A
VALUE OF 10 SINCE AFFORDABILITY
WAS RATED MOST IMPORTANT.

    ON THIS SCALE, WHAT VALUE OF
IMPORTANCE WOULD THE OTHER FACTORS HAVE?

RELAXATION
? <u>5.5</u>

CHANGE OF PACE
? <u>9</u>

    EACH VACATION
MUST NOW BE COMPARED WITH RESPECT TO
EACH IMPORTANCE FACTOR.

    WE'LL CONSIDER EACH FACTOR
SEPARATELY AND THEN RATE
EACH VACATION IN TERMS
OF THAT FACTOR ONLY.

    LET'S GIVE MOUNTAIN CAMPING
A VALUE OF 10 ON EVERY SCALE.

    THEN EVERY OTHER VACATION
WILL BE ASSIGNED A VALUE HIGHER OR
LOWER THAN 10. THIS VALUE DEPENDS ON
HOW MUCH YOU THINK IT IS BETTER OR
WORSE THAN MOUNTAIN CAMPING.

    CONSIDERING ONLY RELAXATION AND
ASSIGNING 10 TO MOUNTAIN CAMPING ;
WHAT VALUE WOULD YOU ASSIGN TO

AFRICAN SAFARI? <u>3</u>

TRIP TO WASHINGTON D.C.? <u>9</u>

   CONSIDERING ONLY AFFORDABILITY AND
ASSIGNING 10 TO MOUNTAIN CAMPING ;
WHAT VALUE WOULD YOU ASSIGN TO

AFRICAN SAFARI? <u>1</u>

TRIP TO WASHINGTON D.C.? <u>8</u>

   CONSIDERING ONLY CHANGE OF PACE AND
ASSIGNING 10 TO MOUNTAIN CAMPING ;
WHAT VALUE WOULD YOU ASSIGN TO

AFRICAN SAFARI? <u>60</u>

TRIP TO WASHINGTON D.C.? <u>25</u>

TRIP TO WASHINGTON D.C. COMES OUT BEST
BUT IT'S VERY CLOSE.

HERE IS THE FINAL LIST IN ORDER.

TRIP TO WASHINGTON D.C. HAS BEEN
GIVEN A VALUE OF 100 AND THE OTHERS
RATED ACCORDINGLY.

----

100   TRIP TO WASHINGTON D.C.
98.6587184   MOUNTAIN CAMPING
78.8375559   AFRICAN SAFARI

PROGRAM LISTING

```
100 REM: DECIDE
110 REM: COPYRIGHT 1980 BY PHIL FELDMAN AND TOM RUGG
150 TEXT
160 DIM L$(10),F$(10),V(10),C(10,10),D(10),Z(10)
180 E$="END"
200 GOSUB 2000
210 PRINT"   I CAN HELP YOU MAKE A DECISION.  ALL"
220 PRINT"I NEED TO DO IS ASK SOME QUESTIONS AND"
```

```
230 PRINT"THEN ANALYZE THE INFORMATION YOU GIVE.":PRINT
240 PRINT"          --------------------------------":PRINT
250 PRINT"WHICH OF THESE BEST DESCRIBES THE TYPE"
260 PRINT"OF DECISION FACING YOU?":PRINT
270 PRINT"  1) CHOOSING AN ITEM FROM VARIOUS"
280 PRINT"     ALTERNATIVES.":PRINT
290 PRINT"  2) CHOOSING A COURSE OF ACTION FROM"
300 PRINT"     VARIOUS ALTERNATIVES.":PRINT
310 PRINT"  3) MAKING A 'YES' OR 'NO' DECISION.":PRINT
320 PRINT"WHICH ONE (1, 2, OR 3)";
330 INPUT"? ";R$
340 T=INT(VAL(R$)):IF T<1 OR T>3 THEN 320
350 GOSUB 2000
400 ON T GOTO 410,440,470
410 PRINT"WHAT TYPE OF ITEM MUST YOU DECIDE UPON"
420 INPUT"? ";T$:GOTO 500
440 T$="COURSE OF ACTION":GOTO 500
470 T$="'YES' OR 'NO'"
480 NI=2:L$(1)="DECIDING YES":L$(2)="DECIDING NO"
490 GOTO 750
500 GOSUB 2000:NI=0
510 PRINT"   I NEED TO HAVE A LIST OF EACH"
520 PRINT T$;" UNDER CONSIDERATION.":PRINT
530 PRINT"   INPUT THEM ONE AT A TIME"
540 PRINT"IN RESPONSE TO EACH QUESTION MARK.":PRINT
550 PRINT"   THE ORDER IN WHICH YOU INPUT THEM"
560 PRINT"HAS NO PARTICLULAR SIGNIFICANCE.":PRINT
570 PRINT"   TYPE THE WORD '";E$;"' TO INDICATE"
580 PRINT"THAT THE WHOLE LIST HAS BEEN ENTERED.":PRINT
590 NI=NI+1:INPUT"? ";L$(NI)
600 IF L$(NI)<>E$ THEN 590
610 NI=NI-1
620 IF NI>=2 THEN 650
630 PRINT:PRINT"YOU MUST HAVE AT LEAST 2 CHOICES":PRINT
640 PRINT"TRY AGAIN":GOSUB 2100:GOTO 500
650 GOSUB 2000:PRINT
    "O.K. HERE'S THE LIST YOU'VE GIVEN ME:":PRINT
660 FOR J=1 TO NI:PRINT"   ";J;") ";L$(J):NEXT:PRINT
670 PRINT"IS THIS LIST CORRECT (Y OR N) ? ";
680 GET R$
690 IF R$="Y" THEN PRINT"YES":GOTO 750
700 IF R$="N" THEN PRINT"NO"
710 IF R$="N" THEN PRINT:PRINT
    "THE LIST MUST BE RE-ENTERED"
720 IF R$="N" THEN GOSUB 2100:GOSUB 500
```

```
730 GOTO 680
750 GOSUB 2000
760 PRINT"   NOW, THINK OF THE DIFFERENT FACTORS"
770 IF T<3 THEN PRINT
    "THAT ARE IMPORTANT TO YOU IN CHOOSING"
780 IF T<3 THEN PRINT"THE BEST ";T$;"."
790 IF T=3 THEN PRINT
    "THAT ARE IMPORTANT TO YOU IN DECIDING":PRINT
    "YES OR NO"
800 PRINT:PRINT"   INPUT THEM ONE AT A TIME IN RESPONSE"
810 PRINT"TO EACH QUESTION MARK.":PRINT
820 PRINT"   TYPE THE WORD '";E$;"' TO TERMINATE"
830 PRINT"THE LIST.":PRINT:NF=0
840 NF=NF+1:INPUT"? ";F$(NF)
850 IF F$(NF)<>E$ THEN 840
860 NF=NF-1:PRINT
870 IF NF<1 THEN PRINT
    "YOU MUST HAVE AT LEAST ONE! - REDO IT"
880 IF NF<1 THEN GOSUB 2100:GOTO 750
890 GOSUB 2000:PRINT
    "HERE'S THE LIST OF FACTORS YOU GAVE ME:":PRINT
900 FOR J=1 TO NF:PRINT"   ";J;") ";F$(J):NEXT:PRINT
910 PRINT"   DECIDE WHICH FACTOR ON THE LIST IS"
920 PRINT"THE MOST IMPORTANT AND INPUT ITS NUMBER."
930 PRINT"(TYPE 0 IF THE LIST NEEDS CHANGING.)":PRINT
940 INPUT"? ";A:A=INT(A):IF A=0 THEN 750
950 IF A<0 OR A>NF THEN 890
1000 GOSUB 2000:IF NF=1 THEN 1200
1010 PRINT"   NOW LET'S SUPPOSE WE HAVE A SCALE OF"
1020 PRINT"IMPORTANCE RANGING FROM 0-10.":PRINT
1030 PRINT"   WE'LL GIVE ";F$(A);" A"
1040 PRINT"VALUE OF 10 SINCE ";F$(A)
1050 PRINT"WAS RATED THE MOST IMPORTANT.":PRINT
1060 PRINT"   ON THIS SCALE, WHAT VALUE OF"
1070 PRINT"IMPORTANCE WOULD THE OTHER FACTORS HAVE?"
1080 FOR J=1 TO NF:Q=A:IF J=Q THEN 1110
1090 PRINT:PRINT F$(J):INPUT"? ";V(J)
1100 IF V(J)<0 OR V(J)>10 THEN PRINT
    " IMPOSSIBLE VALUE - TRY AGAIN":GOTO 1090
1110 NEXT
1200 V(A)=10:Q=0:FOR J=1 TO NF:Q=Q+V(J):NEXT:FOR J=1 TO
    NF
1210 V(J)=V(J)/Q:NEXT:GOSUB 2000
1220 IF T<>3 THEN PRINT"   EACH ";T$
1230 IF T=3 THEN PRINT"   DECIDING YES OR DECIDING NO"
```

```
1240 PRINT"MUST NOW BE COMPARED WITH RESPECT TO"
1250 PRINT"EACH IMPORTANCE FACTOR.":PRINT
1260 PRINT"  WE'LL CONSIDER EACH FACTOR"
1270 PRINT"SEPARATELY AND THEN RATE"
1280 IF T<>3 THEN PRINT"EACH ";T$;" IN TERMS"
1290 IF T=3 THEN PRINT
     "DECIDING YES OR DECIDING NO IN TERMS"
1300 PRINT"OF THAT FACTOR ONLY.":PRINT
1310 PRINT"  LET'S GIVE ";L$(1)
1320 PRINT"A VALUE OF 10 ON EVERY SCALE.":PRINT
1330 IF T<>3 THEN PRINT"  THEN EVERY OTHER ";T$
1340 IF T=3 THEN PRINT"  THEN DECIDING NO"
1350 PRINT"WILL BE ASSIGNED A VALUE HIGHER OR"
1360 PRINT"LOWER THAN 10.  THIS VALUE DEPENDS ON"
1370 PRINT"HOW MUCH YOU THINK IT IS BETTER OR"
1380 PRINT"WORSE THAN ";L$(1)
1390 PRINT:FOR J=1 TO NF
1400 PRINT"    --------------------"
1410 PRINT"   CONSIDERING ONLY ";F$(J);" AND"
1420 PRINT"ASSIGNING 10 TO ";L$(1);" ;"
1430 PRINT"WHAT VALUE WOULD YOU ASSIGN TO"
1440 PRINT:FOR K=2 TO NI
1450 PRINT L$(K);:INPUT"? ";C(K,J):PRINT:IF C(K,J)>=0
     THEN 1470
1460 PRINT"  --NEGATIVE VALUES NOT LEGAL--":GOTO 1450
1470 NEXT:PRINT:C(1,J)=10:NEXT
1500 FOR J=1 TO NF:Q=0:FOR K=1 TO NI
1510 Q=Q+C(K,J):NEXT:FOR K=1 TO NI
1520 C(K,J)=C(K,J)/Q:NEXT:NEXT
1530 FOR K=1 TO NI:D(K)=0:FOR J=1 TO NF
1540 D(K)=D(K)+C(K,J)*V(J):NEXT:NEXT
1550 MX=0:FOR K=1 TO NI
1560 IF D(K)>MX THEN MX=D(K)
1570 NEXT:FOR K=1 TO NI:D(K)=D(K)*100/MX:NEXT
1600 FOR K=1 TO NI:Z(K)=K:NEXT:NM=NI-1
1610 FOR K=1 TO NI:FOR J=1 TO NM:N1=Z(J):N2=Z(J+1):IF D(
     N1)>D(N2) THEN 1630
1620 Z(J+1)=N1:Z(J)=N2
1630 NEXT:NEXT:J1=Z(1):J2=Z(2):DF=D(J1)-D(J2):GOSUB
     2000
1700 PRINT L$(J1);
1710 PRINT" COMES OUT BEST"
1720 IF DF<5 THEN PRINT"BUT IT'S VERY CLOSE.":GOTO 1800
1730 IF DF<10 THEN PRINT"BUT IT'S FAIRLY CLOSE.":GOTO
     1800
```

```
1740 IF DF<20 THEN PRINT"BY A FAIR AMOUNT.":GOTO 1800
1750 PRINT"QUITE DECISIVELY."
1800 PRINT:PRINT"HERE IS THE FINAL LIST IN ORDER.":PRINT
1810 PRINT L$(J1);" HAS BEEN"
1820 PRINT"GIVEN A VALUE OF 100 AND THE OTHERS"
1830 PRINT"RATED ACCORDINGLY.":PRINT
1840 PRINT"   --------------------":PRINT
1850 FOR J=1 TO NI:Q=Z(J):PRINT D(Q);TAB(16);L$(Q):NEXT
1860 END
2000 FOR J=1 TO 500:NEXT
2010 HOME:PRINT TAB(16);"DECIDE":PRINT:RETURN
2100 FOR J=1 TO 3000:NEXT:RETURN
```

EASY CHANGES

1. The word "END" is used to flag the termination of various input lists. If you wish to use something else (because of conflicts with items on the list), change the definition of E$ in line 180. For example, to use the word "DONE," change line 180 to

180 E$="DONE"

2. Line 2100 contains a timing delay used regularly in the program. If things seem to change too fast, you can make the number 3000 larger. Try

2100 FOR J=1 TO 5000:NEXT:RETURN

3. The program can currently accept up to nine decision alternatives and/or nine importance factors. If you need more, increase the dimensioning in line 160. Each dimension value is one more than the number the program will actually allow. Thus, to use 14 values, line 160 should be

160 DIM L$(15),F$(15),V(15),C(15,15),D(15),Z(15)

MAIN ROUTINES

150 - 180	Initializes and dimensions variables.
200 - 350	Determines category of decision.
400 - 490	Gets or sets T$.
500 - 730	Gets list of possible alternatives from user.
750 - 950	Gets list of importance factors from user.
1000 - 1110	User rates each importance factor.
1200 - 1470	User rates the decision alternatives with respect to each importance factor.

MAIN VARIABLES

NI	Number of decision alternatives.
L$	String array of the decision alternatives.
NF	Number of importance factors.
F$	String array of the importance factors.
V	Array of the relative values of each importance factor.
A	Index number of most important factor.
C	Array of relative values of each alternative with respect to each importance factor.
T	Decision category (1=item, 2=course of action, 3= yes or no).
T$	String name of decision category.
E$	String to signal the end of an input data list.
J,K	Loop indices.
R$	User reply string.
Q, N1, N2	Work variables.
D	Array of each alternative's value.
MX	Maximum value of all alternatives.
DF	Rating difference between best two alternatives.
Z	Array of the relative rankings of each alternative.

SUGGESTED PROJECTS

1. Allow the user the review the numerical input and modify it if desired.
2. Insights into a decision can often be gained by a sensitivity analysis. This involves running the program a number of times for the same decision. Each time, one input value is changed (usually the one you are least confident about). By seeing how the results change, you can determine which factors are the most important. Currently, this requires a complete re-running of the program each time. Modify the program to allow a change of input after the regular output is produced. Then recalculate the results based on the new values. (Note

that many input arrays are clobbered once all the input is given. This modification will require saving the original input in new arrays so that it can be reviewed later.)

LOAN

PURPOSE

One of the most frustrating things about borrowing money from a bank (or credit union or Savings and Loan) is that it's not easy to fully evaluate your options. When you are borrowing from a credit union to buy a new car, you might have the choice of a thirty-six or a forty-eight month repayment period. When buying a house, you can sometimes get a slightly lower interest rate for your loan if you can come up with a larger down payment. What option is best for you? How will the monthly payment be affected? Will there be much difference in how fast the principal of the loan decreases? How much of each payment will be for interest, which is tax-deductible?

You need to know the answers to all these questions to make the best decision. This program gives you the information you need.

HOW TO USE IT

The program first asks you the size of the loan you are considering. Only whole dollar amounts are allowed – no pennies. Loans of ten million dollars or more are rejected (you can afford to hire an investment counselor if you want to borrow that much). Then you are asked the yearly interest rate for the loan. Enter this number as a percentage, such as "10.8." Next, you are asked to give the period of the loan in months. For a five year loan, enter 60. For a thirty year mortgage, enter 360. The program then displays this information for you and calculates the monthly payment that will cause the loan to be paid off with equal payments each month over the life of the loan.

At this point you have four options, First, you can show a monthly analysis. This displays a month-by-month breakdown, showing the state of the loan after each payment. The four columns of data shown for each month are the payment number (or month number) of the loan, the remaining balance of the loan after that payment, the amount of that payment that was interest, and the accumulated interest paid to date. Sixteen lines of data are displayed on the screen, and then you can either press the T key to get the final totals for the loan, or any other key to get the data for the next sixteen months of the loan.

The second option is overriding the monthly payment. It is a common practice with second mortgage loans to make smaller monthly payments each month with a large "balloon" payment as the final payment. You can use this second option to try various monthly payments to see how they affect that big payment at the end. After overriding the monthly payment, you will want to use the first option next to get a monthly analysis and final totals using the new monthly payment.

The third option is to simply start over. You will generally use this option if you are just comparing what the different monthly payments would be for different loan possibilities.

The fourth option ends the program.

By the way, there is a chance that the monthly payment calculated by your lender will differ from the one calculated here by a penny or two. We like to think that this is because we are making a more accurate calculation.

NOTE: SEE DISCLAIMER IN FRONT PART OF BOOK

SAMPLE RUN

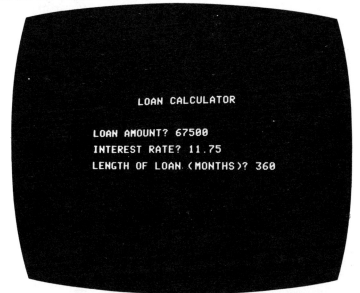

```
                    LOAN CALCULATOR

          LOAN AMOUNT? 67500
          INTEREST RATE? 11.75
          LENGTH OF LOAN (MONTHS)? 360
```

The operator enters the three necessary pieces of information about his or her loan.

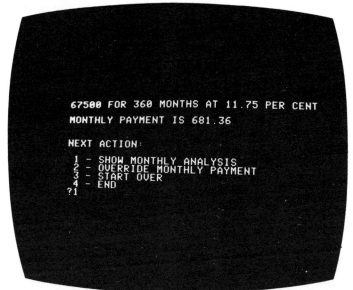

```
     67500 FOR 360 MONTHS AT 11.75 PER CENT
     MONTHLY PAYMENT IS 681.36

     NEXT ACTION:
       1 - SHOW MONTHLY ANALYSIS
       2 - OVERRIDE MONTHLY PAYMENT
       3 - START OVER
       4 - END
     ?1
```

The program responds with the monthly payment that will pay off the loan with equal payments over its life, then asks the operator what to do next. The operator asks for the monthly analysis.

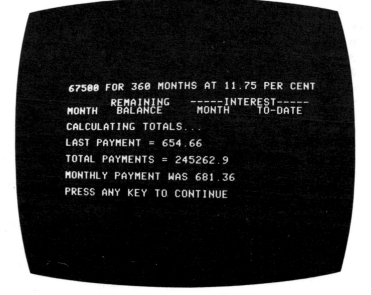

```
67500 FOR 360 MONTHS AT 11.75 PER CENT
            REMAINING       -----INTEREST-----
MONTH       BALANCE         MONTH       TO-DATE
1           67479.58        660.94      660.94
2           67458.96        660.74      1321.68
3           67438.14        660.54      1982.22
4           67417.11        660.33      2642.55
5           67395.88        660.13      3302.68
6           67374.44        659.92      3962.60
7           67352.79        659.71      4622.31
8           67330.93        659.50      5281.81
9           67308.85        659.28      5941.09
10          67286.56        659.07      6600.16
11          67264.05        658.85      7259.01
12          67241.32        658.63      7917.64
13          67218.36        658.40      8576.04
14          67195.18        658.18      9234.22
15          67171.77        657.95      9892.17
16          67148.13        657.72      10549.89

PRESS 'T' FOR TOTALS, OR
ANY OTHER KEY FOR NEXT SCREEN
```

The program responds with information about the first 16 months
of the loan, then waits.

```
67500 FOR 360 MONTHS AT 11.75 PER CENT
            REMAINING       -----INTEREST-----
MONTH       BALANCE         MONTH       TO-DATE

CALCULATING TOTALS...

LAST PAYMENT = 654.66

TOTAL PAYMENTS = 245262.9

MONTHLY PAYMENT WAS 681.36

PRESS ANY KEY TO CONTINUE
```

The operator presses "T", and after a few seconds the program
displays totalling information about the loan.

PROGRAM LISTING

```
100 REM: LOAN CALCULATOR
110 REM: COPYRIGHT 1980 BY TOM RUGG AND PHIL FELDMAN
120 BL$="            ":TEXT:HOME
130 PRINT TAB(8);"LOAN CALCULATOR"
140 PRINT:PRINT:PRINT
150 INPUT"LOAN AMOUNT? ";A
155 GOSUB 1000:IF A=0 THEN 150
160 PRINT:INPUT"INTEREST RATE? ";R
170 PRINT:INPUT"LENGTH OF LOAN (MONTHS)? ";N
180 R=ABS(R):N=INT(N):M=R/1200:PRINT
190 GOSUB 800
199 REM:'UP ARROW' IS SHIFTED N
200 W=(1+M)^N
210 P=A*M*W/(W-1)
220 P=INT(P*100+.99):P=P/100
230 PRINT"MONTHLY PAYMENT IS ";P
240 FP=P:PRINT:PRINT
250 PRINT"NEXT ACTION:"
260 PRINT
270 PRINT" 1 - SHOW MONTHLY ANALYSIS"
280 PRINT" 2 - OVERRIDE MONTHLY PAYMENT"
290 PRINT" 3 - START OVER"
300 PRINT" 4 - END"
310 INPUT C
320 ON C GOTO 440,400,120,370
330 PRINT"CHOICES ARE 1, 2, 3, AND 4"
340 GOTO 250
370 END
400 PRINT:INPUT"MONTHLY PAYMENT? ";P
410 GOTO 240
440 GOSUB 450:GOTO 510
450 GOSUB 800
460 PRINT TAB(8);"REMAINING";TAB(20);
470 PRINT"-----INTEREST-----"
480 PRINT"MONTH";TAB(9);"BALANCE";TAB(21);
490 PRINT"MONTH     TO-DATE"
500 RETURN
510 B=A*100:TT=0:TP=0:L=0:P=P*100:R$=""
520 FOR J=1 TO N
530 T=M*B
540 T=INT(T+.5)
550 IF J=N THEN P=B+T
560 TP=TP+P:B=B-P+T:TT=TT+T
```

```
565 IF B<0 THEN GOSUB 2000
570 IF R$="T" THEN 660
580 W=B:GOSUB 900:B$=S$
590 W=T:GOSUB 900:T$=S$
600 W=TT:GOSUB 900:TT$=S$
610 PRINT J;TAB(5);B$;T$;TT$
615 IF B=0 THEN J=N:GOTO 630
620 L=L+1:IF L<16 THEN 660
630 PRINT:PRINT"PRESS 'T' FOR TOTALS, OR"
640 PRINT"ANY OTHER KEY FOR NEXT SCREEN"
650 GET R$:IF R$="" THEN 650
655 L=0:GOSUB 450:IF R$="T" THEN PRINT:PRINT
    "CALCULATING TOTALS..."
660 NEXT
670 PRINT:PRINT"LAST PAYMENT = ";P/100
680 PRINT:PRINT"TOTAL PAYMENTS = ";TP/100
690 PRINT:PRINT"MONTHLY PAYMENT WAS ";FP
710 PRINT:PRINT"PRESS ANY KEY TO CONTINUE"
720 GET R$
730 P=FP:GOTO 240
800 HOME
810 PRINT A;" FOR ";N;" MONTHS AT ";R;" PER CENT"
820 PRINT
830 RETURN
900 W=INT(W)
905 S$=STR$(W):K=LEN(S$)
910 IF K=1 THEN S$=BL$+".0"+S$:RETURN
920 IF K=2 THEN S$=BL$+"."+S$:RETURN
930 D$="."+RIGHT$(S$,2)
950 S$=LEFT$(S$,K-2)+D$
960 S$=LEFT$(BL$,10-K)+S$
970 RETURN
1000 A=ABS(A):A=INT(A)
1010 IF A<100000000 THEN RETURN
1020 PRINT"TOO LARGE"
1030 A=0:RETURN
2000 P=P+B:TP=TP+B:B=0
2010 RETURN
```

EASY CHANGES

1. The number of lines of data that are displayed on each screen
   when getting a monthly analysis can be changed by altering
   the constant 16 in statement 620.

2. To include the monthly payment in the heading at the top of each screen of the monthly analysis, insert the following line:

815 IF FP <> 0 THEN PRINT"MONTHLY PAYMENT IS";FP

MAIN ROUTINES

120 - 170	Displays title. Gets loan information.
200 - 230	Calculates and displays monthly payment.
250 - 370	Asks for next action. Goes to corresponding routine.
400 - 410	Gets override for monthly payment.
440 - 730	Calculates and displays monthly analysis.
800 - 830	Subroutine to clear screen and display data about the loan at the top.
900 - 970	Subroutine to convert integer amount to fixed-length string with aligned decimal point.
1000 - 1030	Edits loan amount (size and whole dollar).
2000 - 2010	Subroutine to handle early payoff of loan.

MAIN VARIABLES

A	Amount of loan.
R	Interest rate (percentage).
N	Length of loan (number of months).
M	Monthly interest rate (not percentage).
W	Work variable.
P	Monthly payment (times 100).
FP	First monthly payment.
C	Choice of next action.
B	Remaining balance of loan (times 100).
TT	Total interest to date (times 100).
TP	Total payments to date.
L	Number of lines of data on screen.
R$	Reply from operator at keyboard.
J	Work variable for loops.
T	Monthly interest.
B$	String format of B.
T$	String format of T.
TT$	String format of TT.
S$	Work string.
D$	Work string.
K	Work variable.

SUGGESTED PROJECTS

1. Display a more comprehensive analysis of the loan along with the final totals. Show the ratio of total payments to the amount of the loan (TP divided by A), for example.
2. Modify the program to show an analysis of resulting monthly payments for a range of interest rates and/or loan lengths near those provided by the operator. For example, if an interest rate of 9.5 percent was entered, display the monthly payments for 8.5, 9.0, 9.5, 10.0, and 10.5 percent.

MILEAGE

PURPOSE

For many of us, automobile operating efficiency is a continual concern. This program can help by keeping track of gasoline consumption, miles driven, and fuel mileage for a motor vehicle. DATA statements are used to hold the vehicle's "data file." Thus a master file can be retained and updated by merely resaving the program after adding new information. The program computes mileage (miles per gallon or MPG) obtained after each gasoline fill-up. A running log of all information is maintained, allowing trends in vehicle operation efficiency to be easily checked.

HOW TO USE IT

Before running the program, you must enter a chronological history of your vehicle's gasoline consumption. This is accomplished by the use of DATA statements beginning at line 1000. For each gasoline fill-up, a record of the date, odometer reading, and number of gallons purchased is needed.

The form of each DATA statement should be:

line number DATA date, odometer value, number of gallons.

Some comments are in order here: the line number of each statement should increase as the information becomes more recent. We recommend starting with line number 1000 and incrementing each new line by five or ten. This allows later insertion to correct mistakes or to add previously missing data. The word DATA must be typed exactly as is.

The remainder of each DATA line contains the three pieces of information needed by the program. They must be separated by commas. The first item is the date of the gasoline fill-up. It can be comprised of any keyboard characters but should not contain commas, colons, or quotation marks. Only the leftmost eight characters will be used if more than eight are entered. We recommend that you use the general form typified by 12/25/80. However, you might want to use other notations, such as JAN 23, or WEEK 5 or something else. A comma must be typed after the date. The odometer reading and number of gallons purchased are then entered as numeric values separated by a comma. (See the Sample Run for an example of typical data entry.)

If you do not know part of the information for a particular DATA line you can do one of two things: make your best guess for the unknown item(s) or leave the entry for the unknown item(s) blank. You can leave a blank entry as follows: for an unknown date, place a comma as the first nonblank character after DATA; for an unknown odometer reading, leave two consecutive commas in the DATA statements after the date; for an unknown number of gallons, leave a comma as the last character in the DATA statement. The program will recognize these special input forms. However, *in all cases*, each DATA statement that you enter must contain *precisely* two commas.

Once your data is entered, you can retain it by saving the program on cassette tape or disk. Then, as new data becomes available, you can load the old program, add the new data to it, and save the program again to preserve the entire data file.

Having entered the appropriate data, you are ready to run the program. It operates from a central command mode. The operator branches to one of three available subroutines. When a subroutine completes execution, control returns to the command mode for additional requests. A brief description of each subroutine now follows.

Verify DATA Statements

This scans the DATA statements to look for possible problems with the data. It will test to see if any odometer values are too big or too small (they are presumed to be between 0 and 999999), or if any gallons values are too big or too small (they are presumed to be between 0 and 9999). It will look to see that the odometer values increase with each successive entry. Also, it will make sure that you have entered some data. If any of these problems are found, an appropriate error message will be displayed. If a bad data record is found (usually more or less than three items on a DATA line, or perhaps a string value for one of the numeric quantities), it will indicate the line at which it detected the error. The offending statement is usually either the line indicated or the line immediately preceding it. If all data is in the correct form the subroutine will display the beginning and ending dates for the data and the total number of data records found. It will then ask that you hit any key to re-enter the command mode.

Display Mileage Information

This subroutine computes mileage (miles per gallon) from the available data. It formats all information and displays it in tabular form. Numbers are rounded to the nearest tenth so that four columns of information can be displayed on one line. When data fills the screen, the user is prompted to hit any key to continue the listing. When all data is displayed, pressing any key will re-enter command mode. An error message will be printed and the program will terminate if a fatal error is found in the DATA records.

Terminate Program

This subroutine ends program execution and returns the computer to direct BASIC.

SAMPLE RUN

```
]1000 DATA 9/28/79,51051.1,14.6

]1010 DATA 10/6/79,51299.7,13.8

]1020 DATA 10/17/79,51553.8,13.1

]1030 DATA 10/29/79,51798,13.7
```

]1040 DATA 11/5/79,52041.9,13.3

]RUN

                        MILEAGE

COMMANDS
  1 - VERIFY DATA STATEMENTS
  2 - DISPLAY MILEAGE INFORMATION
  3 - TERMINATE PROGRAM

ENTER COMMAND BY NUMBER? 1

DATA FILE DISPOSITION

DATE OF FIRST DATA RECORD: 9/28/79
DATE OF LAST DATA RECORD: 11/5/79

5 DATA RECORDS FOUND

ALL DATA PROCESSED
HIT ANY KEY TO RESUME COMMAND MODE
(a key is duly pressed)

                        MILEAGE

COMMANDS
  1 - VERIFY DATA STATEMENTS
  2 - DISPLAY MILEAGE INFORMATION
  3 - TERMINATE PROGRAM

ENTER COMMAND BY NUMBER? 2

DATE	ODOMETER	GALLONS	MPG
9/28/79	51051.1	14.6	0
10/6/79	51299.7	13.8	18
10/17/79	51553.8	13.1	19.4
10/29/79	51798	13.7	17.8
11/5/79	52041.9	13.3	18.3

ALL DATA PROCESSED
HIT ANY KEY TO RESUME COMMAND MODE

MILEAGE

COMMANDS
1 - VERIFY DATA STATEMENTS
2 - DISPLAY MILEAGE INFORMATION
3 - TERMINATE PROGRAM

ENTER COMMAND BY NUMBER? 3

]

PROGRAM LISTING

```
100 REM: MILEAGE
110 REM: COPYRIGHT 1980 BY PHIL FELDMAN AND TOM RUGG
200 TEXT:HOME
210 PRINT:PRINT TAB(16);"MILEAGE"
220 PRINT:PRINT"COMMANDS"
230 PRINT" 1 - VERIFY DATA STATEMENTS"
240 PRINT" 2 - DISPLAY MILEAGE INFORMATION"
250 PRINT" 3 - TERMINATE PROGRAM"
260 PRINT:INPUT" ENTER COMMAND BY NUMBER? ";C
270 C=INT(C):IF C<1 OR C>3 THEN 200
280 ON C GOTO 300,700,290
290 END
300 HOME:PRINT:RESTORE
310 PRINT"DATA FILE DISPOSITION":PRINT
320 N=0:DD=-.001
330 ONERR GOTO 500
340 READ A$,D,G
350 POKE 216,0:N=N+1
360 IF N=1 THEN PRINT"DATE OF FIRST DATA RECORD: ";A$
370 IF D>=0 AND D<=999999 THEN 400
380 PRINT"--BAD ODOMETER VALUE OF ";D
390 PRINT"    AT DATE: ";A$
400 IF D>DD THEN 440
410 PRINT"--INCONSISTENT ODOMETER VALUES"
420 PRINT"    ODO READS ";D;" AT DATE: ";A$
430 PRINT"    YET READS ";DD;" AT PREVIOUS DATE"
440 IF G>=0 AND G<=9999 THEN 470
450 PRINT"--BAD GALLONS VALUE OF ";G
460 PRINT"    DETECTED AT DATE: ";A$
```

```
470 DD=D:GOTO 330
500 LN=PEEK(218)+256*PEEK(219)
510 EC=PEEK(222):POKE 216,0
520 IF EC=16 THEN 560
530 IF EC=42 THEN 590
540 PRINT:PRINT"--ERROR # ";EC;" HAS BEEN DETECTED"
550 PRINT"    AT LINE ";LN:END
560 PRINT"--BAD DATA RECORD DETECTED"
570 PRINT"    AT OR BEFORE LINE ";LN
580 PRINT"--PROGRAM ABORTED":END
590 IF N>0 THEN 620
600 PRINT:PRINT"--NO DATA FOUND"
610 PRINT"--PROGRAM ABORTED":END
620 IF C=2 THEN 650
630 PRINT"DATE OF LAST DATA RECORD: ";A$
640 PRINT:PRINT N;" DATA RECORDS FOUND"
650 PRINT:PRINT"ALL DATA PROCESSED"
660 PRINT"HIT ANY KEY TO RESUME COMMAND MODE"
670 GET T$:GOTO 200
700 GOSUB 820:RESTORE:DD=-1:N=0
710 ONERR GOTO 500
720 READ A$,D,G:POKE 216,0:N=N+1:A$=LEFT$(A$,8)
730 R=D:GOSUB 860:D=R:LD=18-L:IF INT(D)=D THEN LD=LD-2
740 R=G:GOSUB 910:G=R:LG=27-L:IF INT(G)=G THEN LG=LG-2
750 IF DD<0 OR G=0 THEN M=0:GOTO 770
760 M=(D-DD)/G
770 R=M:GOSUB 960:M=R:LM=38-L:IF INT(M)=M THEN LM=LM-2
780 DD=D:GOSUB 790:GOTO 710
790 PRINT TAB(1);A$;TAB(LD);D;TAB(LG);G;TAB(LM);M
800 K=K+1:IF K<20 THEN RETURN
810 PRINT:PRINT"HIT ANY KEY TO CONTINUE";:GET T$:PRINT
820 HOME:PRINT
830 PRINT TAB(1);"  DATE     ODOMETER    GALLONS     MPG"
840 K=0:RETURN
860 IF R>=0 AND R<=999999 THEN 890
870 PRINT:PRINT"ERROR IN ODOMETER DATA AT DATE:";A$
880 END
890 R=R*10+.5:R=INT(R)/10
900 L=LEN(STR$(R)):RETURN
910 IF R>=0 AND R<=9999 THEN 940
920 PRINT:PRINT"ERROR IN GALLONS DATA AT DATE: ";A$
930 END
940 R=R*10+.5:R=INT(R)/10
950 L=LEN(STR$(R)):RETURN
```

```
960 IF R<0 OR R>9999 THEN R=0
970 R=R*10+.5:R=INT(R)/10
980 L=LEN(STR$(R)):RETURN
```

EASY CHANGES

1. If you would like to give a name to the data file and have that name print out with the command mode, change line 210 and add line 205 as follows:

   205 B$="VOLVO 1979"
   210 PRINT:PRINT"MILEAGE FOR:";B$

   Just set B$ in line 205 to whatever file name you wish to use.
2. This program uses Applesoft ONERR GOTO statements to detect certain expected errors. Should an unexpected one occur, the program may abort after printing out a message like:

   – – ERROR # 255 HAS BEEN DETECTED AT LINE 340

   These error numbers and their meanings can be found in your Applesoft manual with the explanation of ONERR GOTO. Should you get one and not understand what has happened, re-run the program after making the following changes in order to get normal BASIC error messages:

   330 REM
   710 REM

MAIN ROUTINES

200 - 280	Command mode. Displays available subroutines and branches to the operator's choice.
290	Subroutine to terminate execution.
300 - 470	Subroutine to verify DATA statements.
500 - 670	Processes errors in reading DATA statements.
700 - 780	Subroutine to display mileage information.
790 - 840	Subroutine to print results.
860 - 900	Subroutine to round odometer values.
910 - 950	Subroutine to round gallons values.
960 - 980	Subroutine to round mileage values.
1000 -	User-created DATA statements.

MAIN VARIABLES

C	Command flag (1=verify DATA, 2=display mileage, 3=terminate execution).
N	Number of data records read.
A$	Date of current data record.
DD	Previous odometer value.
D	Current odometer value.
G	Current gallons value.
M	Current MPG value.
LD	Print position for odometer value.
LG	Print position for gallons value.
LM	Print position for mileage value.
T$	Temporary string variable.
L	Length of string.
R	Pre-rounded numbers.
K	Number of lines printed since HOME.
EC	Error code.
LN	Line number of detected error.

SUGGESTED PROJECTS

1. Calculate and print the average MPG over the whole data file. This will be the total miles driven divided by the total gallons purchased. The total miles driven is the difference between the odometer values of the last and first DATA statements. The total gallons used is the sum of all the gallons values from the second DATA statement to the last DATA statement.
2. Add an option to do statistical calculations over a given subset of the data. The operator inputs a beginning and ending date. He is then shown things like average MPG, total miles driven, total gallons purchased, etc., all computed over the range requested.
3. Write a subroutine to graphically display MPG. A bar graph might work well.
4. Add a new parameter in each data record—the cost of each fill-up. Then compute things like the total cost of gasoline, miles/dollar, etc.

QUEST/EXAM

PURPOSE

If you've ever had to analyze the results of a questionnaire, or grade a multiple-choice examination, you know what a tedious and time-consuming process it can be. This is particularly true if you need to accumulate statistics for each question showing how many people responded with each possible answer.

With this program, you provide the data, and the computer does the work.

HOW TO USE IT

First, enter the number of questions on the questionnaire or exam. The maximum is 35. Then enter the number of choices per question. This is an integer from 2 through 9. Each answer will be a digit from one to this number or left blank.

Next enter the maximum number of entries (exam papers) that you are going to analyze. Be sure to enter a number at least as large as the number of papers that you will be evaluating.

Finally, you are asked if you want to input names for each entry. This is especially useful when grading exams, to enable you to re-check later to verify that you entered the proper data for each student.

At this point, the program asks you for the answer key. If you are scoring an exam, provide the correct answers. The program displays "guide numbers" to help you keep track of which answers you are providing. If you are analyzing a questionnaire, you have no answer key, so just press the **RETURN** key.

Now the program asks you to begin providing the answers for each entry. Again, guide numbers are displayed above the area where you are to enter the data so you can more easily provide the proper answer for the proper question number. If no answer was given for a particular question, leave a blank space. However, if either the first or the last question was left blank, you will have to enclose the entire string of answers within quotation marks. This will cause a small problem in keeping your alignment straight with the guide numbers, but you'll get used to it. See below for an alternate way to do this.

If you make a mistake when entering the data, the program will tell you and ask you to re-enter it. This is most commonly caused by either failing to enter the correct number of answers or entering an invalid character instead of an acceptable answer number. Remember that each answer must be either a blank or a number from one to the number of choices you allowed per question.

By the way, you can avoid entering blanks for unanswered questions. Suppose you have a maximum of 5 possible answers per question. Simply tell the program there are 6 choices per question. Then, when a question is unanswered, you can enter a 6 instead of leaving it blank.

If you specified that you wanted names for each entry, the program asks you for the name after you have entered the person's answers. Do not use commas in the name unless you enclose the entire name in quotation marks.

If you provided an answer key, the program displays the number and percentage correct after each entry before going on to ask for the next one. When you have no more entries, press the **RETURN** key instead of entering a string of answers.

At this point, the program displays five options from which you choose your next action. Here are brief explanations. You can experiment to verify how they work.

Option one lets you analyze each question, to see how many people responded with each answer. The percentage of people who responded with each answer is also shown. In the case of an exam, the right answer is indicated with the word "RIGHT."

Option two allows you to go back and provide more entries. This allows you to pause after entering part of the data, do some analysis of what you have entered so far, and then go back and continue entering data.

Option three lets you review what you have entered, including the answer key. This permits you to check for duplicate, omitted, or erroneous entries.

Option four starts the program over at the beginning again, and option five ends the program.

SAMPLE RUN

```
QUESTIONNAIRE/EXAM ANALYZER
NUMBER OF QUESTIONS? 20
CHOICES PER QUESTION? 4
MAXIMUM NUMBER OF ENTRIES? 30
WANT NAMES FOR EACH ENTRY? YES

ENTER ANSWER KEY. IF NONE, PRESS RETURN.
          1         2
 12345678901234567890
?33124321443422121341

ENTRY NUMBER 1
          1         2
 12345678901234567890
?
```

The operator provides the required information about the examination being scored. The program waits for the data from the first examination paper.

```
NUMBER OF QUESTIONS? 20
CHOICES PER QUESTION? 4
MAXIMUM NUMBER OF ENTRIES? 30
WANT NAMES FOR EACH ENTRY? YES

ENTER ANSWER KEY. IF NONE, PRESS RETURN.
          1         2
 12345678901234567890
?33124321443422121341

ENTRY NUMBER 1
          1         2
 12345678901234567890
?33223321443421121341
NAME FOR ENTRY NUMBER 1
?H RANSONS
17 CORRECT,    85 PERCENT

ENTRY NUMBER 2
         1         2
 12345678901234567890
?
```

The answers are entered for the first student, followed by the student's name. The program responds with the number and percentage correct.

```
16 CORRECT,    80 PERCENT

ENTRY NUMBER 8
          1         2
 12345678901234567890
?33124321343424122341
NAME FOR ENTRY NUMBER 8
?S HAGGERTY
17 CORRECT,    85 PERCENT

ENTRY NUMBER 9
          1         2
 12345678901234567890
?

AVERAGE = 82.5 PERCENT

NEXT ACTION:
    1 - ANALYZE EACH QUESTION
    2 - ADD MORE ENTRIES
    3 - REVIEW DATA ENTERED
    4 - START OVER
    5 - END PROGRAM
?1
```

Later, instead of providing data for a ninth student, the operator presses the **RETURN** key, indicating no more entries. The program displays the overall percentage correct, and displays a "menu" of choices of actions. The operator picks number one.

```
       12345678901234567890
      ?

      AVERAGE = 82.5 PERCENT

      NEXT ACTION:
        1 - ANALYZE EACH QUESTION
        2 - ADD MORE ENTRIES
        3 - REVIEW DATA ENTERED
        4 - START OVER
        5 - END PROGRAM
      ?1


      ANALYSIS FOR QUESTION NO. 1
      RESPONSE   COUNT   PERCENT
      1            1      12.5
      2            0       0
      3            7      87.5            RIGHT
      4            0       0
      BLANK        0       0

      PRESS A KEY TO CONTINUE
```

The program provides an analysis of the responses for question number one, then waits for a key to be pressed. Note that seven students answered with number 3, the correct answer.

```
      PRESS A KEY TO CONTINUE

      NEXT ACTION:
        1 - ANALYZE EACH QUESTION
        2 - ADD MORE ENTRIES
        3 - REVIEW DATA ENTERED
        4 - START OVER
        5 - END PROGRAM
      ?3
                1          2
      12345678901234567890

      33124321443422121341-ANSWERS
      33223321443421121341-NO.1 H RANSONS
      33224321443422121341-NO.2 J LOPEZ
      33214422343422122331-NO.3 M MILLER
      33214311343421123231-NO.4 G LEE
      33124321443422121341-NO.5 J AMROMIN
      33124322443422321341-NO.6 H LEHMAN
      13124221433422121341-NO.7 R EDELMAN
      33124321343424122341-NO.8 S HAGGERTY
      PRESS A KEY TO CONTINUE
```

Later, the operator asks for option number 3, which lists the data entered for each of the students.

PROGRAM LISTING

```
100 REM: QUESTIONNAIRE/EXAM
110 REM: COPYRIGHT 1980 BY TOM RUGG AND PHIL FELDMAN
120 CLEAR:TEXT:HOME
130 PRINT"QUESTIONNAIRE/EXAM ANALYZER":PRINT
140 E$="** ERROR. RE-ENTER. **":P$=
    "PRESS A KEY TO CONTINUE"
150 INPUT"NUMBER OF QUESTIONS? ";Q
160 Q=INT(Q):IF Q<1 OR Q>35 THEN PRINT E$:GOTO 150
170 INPUT"CHOICES PER QUESTION? ";C
180 C=INT(C):IF C<2 OR C>9 THEN PRINT E$:GOTO 170
185 DIM C(C)
190 INPUT"MAXIMUM NUMBER OF ENTRIES? ";N
200 N=INT(N):IF N<1 THEN PRINT E$:GOTO 190
205 DIM Q$(N+1)
210 INPUT"WANT NAMES FOR EACH ENTRY? ";R$
220 R$=LEFT$(R$,1):IF R$="N" THEN 250
230 IF R$<>"Y" THEN PRINT E$:GOTO 210
240 DIM N$(N)
250 PRINT:PRINT
    "ENTER ANSWER KEY. IF NONE, PRESS RETURN."
260 GOSUB 900:C$=STR$(C):PRINT TAB(1);
310 INPUT A$:IF LEN(A$)=0 THEN 340
320 IF LEN(A$)<>Q THEN PRINT E$:GOTO 250
330 T$=A$:GOSUB 850:IF T$="B" THEN PRINT E$:GOTO 250
340 K=1
350 R=0:PRINT:PRINT"ENTRY NUMBER ";K
360 GOSUB 900:PRINT TAB(1);
370 INPUT Q$(K):W=LEN(Q$(K))
380 IF W=0 THEN 500
390 IF W<>Q THEN PRINT E$:GOTO 350
400 T$=Q$(K):GOSUB 850:IF T$="B" THEN PRINT E$:GOTO 350
410 IF R$="N" THEN 430
415 PRINT"NAME FOR ENTRY NUMBER ";K
420 INPUT N$(K)
430 IF LEN(A$)=0 THEN 480
440 FOR J=1 TO Q
450 IF MID$(A$,J,1)=MID$(Q$(K),J,1) THEN R=R+1
460 NEXT
470 TR=TR+R:PRINT R;" CORRECT,";TAB(15);R*100/Q;
    " PERCENT"
480 K=K+1:IF K<=N THEN 350
500 K=K-1:IF LEN(A$)=0 THEN 520
```

```
505 IF K=0 THEN 960
510 PRINT:PRINT"AVERAGE = ";TR*100/(Q*K);" PERCENT"
520 GOTO 960
530 PRINT:FOR J=1 TO Q
540 R=0:PRINT:PRINT"ANALYSIS FOR QUESTION NO. ";J
545 PRINT"RESPONSE  COUNT  PERCENT"
550 FOR L=0 TO C:C(L)=0:NEXT
560 FOR L=1 TO K:T$=MID$(Q$(L),J,1)
570 W=VAL(T$)
580 C(W)=C(W)+1
600 NEXT L
610 IF K=0 THEN 960
620 FOR L=1 TO C:PRINT L;TAB(11);C(L);TAB(17);C(L)*100/
    K;
630 IF LEN(A$)=0 THEN PRINT:GOTO 660
640 T$=STR$(L)
650 IF T$=MID$(A$,J,1) THEN PRINT TAB(29);"RIGHT":GOTO
    660
655 PRINT
660 NEXT:PRINT"BLANK";TAB(11);C(0);TAB(17);C(0)*100/K
670 PRINT:PRINT P$
680 GET T$
690 NEXT J:GOTO 960
700 L=0:GOSUB 900:PRINT:IF LEN(A$)=0 THEN 720
710 PRINT TAB(2);A$;"-ANSWERS"
720 FOR J=1 TO K
730 PRINT TAB(2);Q$(J);"-NO.";J;
740 IF R$="N" THEN PRINT:GOTO 750
745 PRINT" ";N$(J)
750 L=L+1:IF L<10 THEN 780
760 L=0:PRINT P$
770 GET T$
780 NEXT:PRINT P$
790 GET T$:GOTO 960
850 FOR J=1 TO LEN(T$):IF MID$(T$,J,1)=" " THEN 870
860 IF MID$(T$,J,1)<"1" OR MID$(T$,J,1)>C$ THEN 880
870 NEXT:RETURN
880 T$="B":RETURN
900 W=Q/10:W=INT(W):IF W<1 THEN 920
910 FOR J=1 TO W:X=J*10+1:PRINT TAB(X);J;:NEXT:PRINT
920 PRINT TAB(2);
930 FOR J=1 TO Q:PRINT RIGHT$(STR$(J),1);
940 NEXT:PRINT:RETURN
960 PRINT:PRINT"NEXT ACTION:"
```

```
970 PRINT" 1 - ANALYZE EACH QUESTION"
980 PRINT" 2 - ADD MORE ENTRIES"
990 PRINT" 3 - REVIEW DATA ENTERED"
1000 PRINT" 4 - START OVER"
1010 PRINT" 5 - END PROGRAM"
1050 INPUT T$:IF T$<"1" OR T$>"5" THEN 1070
1060 ON VAL(T$) GOTO 530,480,700,120,1100
1070 PRINT E$:GOTO 960
1100 END
```

EASY CHANGES

1. This program will run on an Apple with 4000 bytes free (see
   Appendix 1) if a limited amount of data is entered. The limit
   is about 25 questions, five choices per question, 30 entries,
   and no names for each entry. If you have 10,000 bytes free,
   there's easily room for 35 questions, nine choices per question,
   100 entries, with names for each entry.

MAIN ROUTINES

120 - 140	Initializes variables.
150 - 240	Performs initialization dialog. Selects options. Allocates arrays.
250 - 320	Gets answer key (if any) from operator.
330	Checks legality of answer key.
350 - 400	Gets exam data for Kth entry.
410 - 420	Gets name for Kth entry, if applicable.
430 - 470	Scores Kth exam, if applicable.
500 - 510	Displays average score, if an exam.
530 - 690	Analyzes responses to each question.
700 - 790	Displays data entered.
850 - 880	Subroutine to check legality of input data.
900 - 940	Subroutine to display guide numbers over input data area.
960 - 1100	Displays choices for next action. Gets response and goes to appropriate routine.

MAIN VARIABLES

E$	Error message.
P$	Message about pressing a key to continue.

Q	Number of questions (1 - 35).
C	Number of choices per question (2 - 9).
C	Array for tallying number of people responding with each choice.
N	Maximum number of entries.
Q$	Array of N strings of entries.
R$	Set to N if no names for each entry, or Y otherwise.
N$	Array of Q names (if R$ is Y).
A$	Answer key string (null if not an exam).
C$	String value of highest legal answer choice.
K	Counter of number of exams scored.
R	Number of questions answered right (if exam).
W	Work variable.
J, L, M	Loop variables.
TR	Total right for all entries.
T$	Temporary work string variable.

SUGGESTED PROJECTS

1. Add an option to change the answer key after the data for the exams is entered. This would be useful in case a mistake was found when reviewing the data.
2. Add an option to allow the operator to re-score each of the exams after all are entered, in case some were overlooked at the time of entry.
3. Combine some of the capabilities of the STATS program with this one.

Section 2

Educational Programs

INTRODUCTION TO EDUCATIONAL PROGRAMS

Education is one area where computers are certain to have more and more impact. Though a computer cannot completely replace a human teacher, the machine does have certain advantages. It is ready anytime you are, allows you to go at your own pace, handles rote drill effortlessly, and is devoid of any personality conflicts.

With a good software library, the Apple can be a valuable learning center in the school or at home. Here are six programs to get you started.

Mathematics is certainly a "natural" subject for computers. NUMBERS is designed for pre-school children. While familiarizing youngsters with computers, it provides an entertaining way for them to learn numbers and elementary counting. ARITHMETIC is aimed at older, grade school students. It provides drill in various kinds of math problems. The child can adjust the difficulty factors, allowing the program to be useful for several years.

The Apple is by no means restricted to mathematical disciplines. We include two programs designed to improve your word skills. VOCAB will help you expand your vocabulary. TACHIST turns the Apple into a reading clinic, helping you to improve your reading speed.

Do you have trouble familiarizing yourself with the increasingly prevalent metric system? METRIC is the answer.

Need help learning a certain subject? FLASHCARD allows you to create your own "computer flashcards." Then you can drill yourself until you get it right.

ARITHMETIC

PURPOSE

ARITHMETIC provides mathematics drills for grade school children. The student can request problems in addition, subtraction, or multiplication from the program. Also, he or she may ask that the problems be easy, medium, or hard. The program should be useful to a child over an extended period of time. He can progress naturally to a harder category of problems when he begins to regularly perform well at one level. The difficulty and types of problems encompass those normally encountered by school children between the ages of six and ten.

The problems are constructed randomly within the constraints imposed by the degree of difficulty selected. This gives the student fresh practice each time the program is used. After entering answers, he is told whether he was right or wrong. The correct answers are also displayed.

HOW TO USE IT

To begin, the student must indicate what type of problem he wishes to do. The program requests an input of 1, 2, or 3 to indicate addition, subtraction, or multiplication, respectively. It then asks whether easy, medium, or hard problems are desired. Again an input of 1, 2, or 3 is required.

Now the screen will clear and five problems of the desired type will be displayed. The user now begins to enter his answers to each problem.

A question mark is used to prompt the user for each digit of the answer, one digit at a time. This is done moving right to left, the way arithmetic problems are naturally solved.

To start each problem, the question mark will appear in the spot for the rightmost (or units column) digit of the answer. When the key for a digit from 0 - 9 is pressed, that digit will replace the question mark on the screen. The question mark moves to the immediate left waiting for a digit for the "tens" column.

Digits are entered in this right-to-left manner until the complete answer has been input. Then the **RETURN** key must be pressed. This will end the answer to the current problem and move the question mark to begin the answer for the next question.

If the **RETURN** key is pressed to begin a problem, an answer of zero is assumed intended. No problems created by this program have answers of more than three digits. If a four-digit answer is given, the program will accept the answer, but then go immediately to the next problem. Answers to the problems are never negative.

The program will display the correct answers to the five problems on the screen after the student has entered his five answers. The message "RIGHT!" or "WRONG!" will also be displayed below each problem.

Then the message "HIT ANY KEY TO CONTINUE" will be displayed. After the key is pressed, a new set of five problems of the same type will be presented.

This continues until twenty problems have been worked. Before ending, the program shows what the student's performance has been. This is expressed as the number of problems solved correctly and also as the percentage of problems solved correctly.

SAMPLE RUN

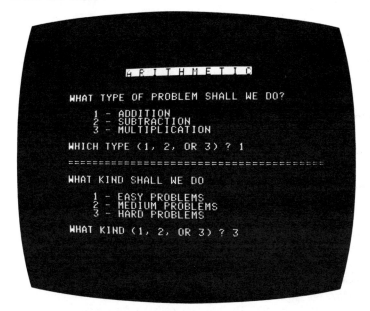

The operator chooses to do hard addition problems.

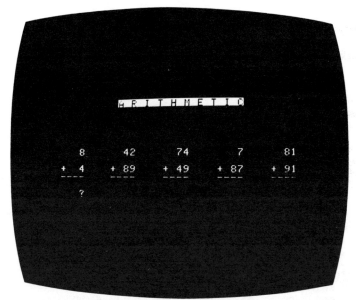

The initial set of five problems is presented. With a question mark, the program prompts the operator for the answer to the first problem.

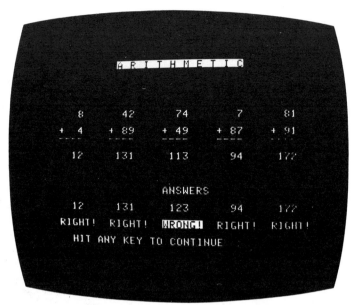

The operator has entered his or her five answers. The program displays the correct answers and indicates whether or not each problem was solved correctly. The program waits for the operator to hit any key in order to continue with the next set of five problems.

PROGRAM LISTING

```
100 REM: ARITHMETIC
110 REM: COPYRIGHT 1980 BY PHIL FELDMAN AND TOM RUGG
130 TEXT:K=PEEK(78)+256*PEEK(79):K=RND(-K)
150 ND=0
160 DIM A(5),B(5),C(5),G(5)
170 NP=20
180 GOSUB 910
200 PRINT:PRINT:PRINT"WHAT TYPE OF PROBLEM SHALL WE DO?"
    :PRINT
210 PRINT TAB(5);"1 - ADDITION"
220 PRINT TAB(5);"2 - SUBTRACTION"
230 PRINT TAB(5);"3 - MULTIPLICATION"
240 PRINT:INPUT"WHICH TYPE (1, 2, OR 3) ? ";R$
250 T=INT(VAL(R$)):IF T<1 OR T>3 THEN 240
260 PRINT:FOR J=1 TO 39:PRINT"=";:NEXT
270 PRINT:PRINT:PRINT"WHAT KIND SHALL WE DO"
280 PRINT:PRINT TAB(5);"1 - EASY PROBLEMS"
```

```
290 PRINT TAB(5);"2 - MEDIUM PROBLEMS"
300 PRINT TAB(5);"3 - HARD PROBLEMS"
310 PRINT:INPUT"WHAT KIND (1, 2, OR 3) ? ";R$
320 D=INT(VAL(R$))
330 IF D<1 OR D>3 THEN 310
350 ON D GOTO 360,370,390
360 GOSUB 940:GOSUB 920:GOSUB 930:GOTO 400
370 GOSUB 940:GOSUB 930:IF T=3 THEN GOSUB 960:GOSUB 920:
    GOTO 400
380 IF T<>3 THEN GOSUB 950:GOSUB 920:GOTO 400
390 GOSUB 950:GOSUB 920:GOSUB 930:IF T=3 THEN GOSUB 940:
    GOSUB 930
400 IF T<>2 THEN 450
410 FOR J=1 TO 5
420 IF B(J)>C(J) THEN R=C(J):C(J)=B(J):B(J)=R
430 NEXT
450 GOSUB 1000:GOSUB 910
600 Y=12:FOR J=1 TO 5:X=-4+J*8:GOSUB 1100:NEXT
610 FOR K=1 TO 5:X=-4+K*8:GOSUB 800:G(K)=N:NEXT
620 X=17:Y=16:GOSUB 1200:PRINT"ANSWERS"
630 Y=18:FOR J=1 TO 5:X=-4+J*8:GOSUB 1400:NEXT
640 Y=20:FOR J=1 TO 5:X=-7+J*8:GOSUB 1200
650 IF A(J)<>G(J) THEN INVERSE:PRINT"WRONG!":NORMAL:
    GOTO 670
660 PRINT"RIGHT!":NR=NR+1
670 NEXT
680 PRINT:FLASH:PRINT" HIT ANY KEY TO CONTINUE ";
690 GET R$:NORMAL
700 ND=ND+5
710 IF ND<NP THEN GOSUB 910:GOTO 350
720 GOSUB 1500
730 END
800 N=0:M=1
810 FLASH:P$="?":GOSUB 900
820 GET R$
830 A=ASC(R$):IF A=13 AND M=1 THEN P$="0":NORMAL:GOSUB
    900:RETURN
840 IF A=13 THEN P$=CHR$(32):NORMAL:GOSUB 900:RETURN
850 IF A<48 OR A>57 THEN 820
860 V=A-48:P$=CHR$(A):NORMAL:GOSUB 900:N=N+M*V:M=M*10
870 IF M>1000 THEN RETURN
880 X=X-1:GOTO 810
900 HTAB X:VTAB Y:PRINT P$;:HTAB X:VTAB Y:RETURN
910 HOME:PRINT TAB(10);:INVERSE:PRINT
```

```
        "A R I T H M E T I C":NORMAL:RETURN
 920 FOR K=1 TO 5:C(K)=INT(RND(1)*(H-L+1))+L:NEXT:RETURN
 930 FOR K=1 TO 5:B(K)=INT(RND(1)*(H-L+1))+L:NEXT:RETURN
 940 H=9:L=0:RETURN
 950 H=99:L=0:RETURN
 960 H=25:L=1:RETURN
1000 ON T GOTO 1010,1020,1030
1010 FOR J=1 TO 5:A(J)=B(J)+C(J):NEXT:RETURN
1020 FOR J=1 TO 5:A(J)=C(J)-B(J):NEXT:RETURN
1030 FOR J=1 TO 5:A(J)=C(J)*B(J):NEXT:RETURN
1100 GOSUB 1200:CU=5:CL=1:GOSUB 1300
1110 IF C(J)<10 THEN PRINT CHR$(32);
1120 PRINT C(J):GOSUB 1200:CU=3:CL=3:GOSUB 1300:IF T=1
     THEN PRINT CHR$(43);
1130 IF T=2 THEN PRINT CHR$(45);
1140 IF T=3 THEN PRINT CHR$(88);
1150 PRINT CHR$(32);:IF B(J)<10 THEN PRINT CHR$(32);
1160 PRINT B(J):GOSUB 1200:CU=2:CL=3:GOSUB 1300:FOR K=1
     TO 4:PRINT CHR$(45);
1170 NEXT:RETURN
1200 HTAB X:VTAB Y
1210 RETURN
1300 HTAB (PEEK(36)-CL+1)
1310 VTAB (PEEK(37)-CU+1):RETURN
1400 GOSUB 1200:CL=0:IF A(J)>9 THEN CL=1
1410 IF A(J)>99 THEN CL=2
1420 IF A(J)>999 THEN CL=3
1430 HTAB (PEEK(36)-CL+1)
1440 PRINT A(J):RETURN
1500 GOSUB 910:PRINT:PRINT
1510 PRINT"YOU GOT ";NR;" RIGHT"
1520 PRINT"OUT OF ";NP;" PROBLEMS"
1530 P=NR/NP*100
1540 PRINT:PRINT"THAT'S ";P;" PERCENT CORRECT":RETURN
```

EASY CHANGES

1. The program currently does twenty problems per session.
   You can change this number by altering the variable NP in
   line 170. For example,

$$170 \ NP=10$$

will cause the program to do only ten problems per session.
The value of NP should be kept a positive multiple of five.
2. Zero is currently allowed as a possible problem operand. If
you do not wish to allow this, change lines 940 and 950 to
read as follows:

                940 H=9:L=1:RETURN
                950 H=99:L=1:RETURN

MAIN ROUTINES

130 - 180	Initializes constants, displays header.
200 - 330	Asks operator for type of problems desired.
350 - 450	Sets A, B, C arrays, clears screen.
600 - 730	Mainline routine – displays problems, gets operator's answers, displays correct answers and user's performance.
800 - 880	Subroutine to get and display user's answers.
900	Character-printing subroutine.
910	Subroutine to clear screen and display title.
920 - 930	Subroutine to set B, C arrays.
940 - 960	Subroutine to set L, H.
1000 - 1030	Subroutine to calculate A array from B, C arrays.
1100 - 1170	Subroutine to display problems.
1200 - 1210	Subroutine to move cursor to screen position X, Y.
1300 - 1310	Subroutine to move cursor CU lines down and CL spaces left.
1400 - 1440	Subroutine to display the correct answers.
1500 - 1540	Subroutine to display operator's performance.

MAIN VARIABLES

NP	Number of problems to do in the session.
ND	Number of problems done.
NR	Number of correct answers given.
C,B,A	Arrays of top operand, bottom operand, and correct answer to each problem.
N	Operator's answer to current problem.
G	Array of operator's answers.

T	Type of problems requested (1=addition, 2=subtraction, 3=multiplication).
D	Kind of problem requested (1=easy, 2=medium, 3=hard).
H,L	Highest, lowest integers to allow as problem operands.
M	Answer column being worked on.
R$	Operator's input character.
V	Value of R$.
A	ASCII value of R$.
X,Y	Horizontal, vertical screen position of cursor.
J,K	Loop indices and work variables.
CU,CL	Number of positions to move cursor up, left.
P	Percentage of correct answers.
P$	Character to be printed.

SUGGESTED PROJECTS

1. Keep track of problems missed and repeat them quickly for additional practice.
2. No negative operands or answers are currently allowed. Rewrite the problem generation routines and the operator's answer routines to allow the possibility of negative answers.
3. The answers are now restricted to three-digit numbers. However, the program would work fine for four-digit numbers if the operands of the problems were allowed to be large enough. Dig into the routines at lines 350 - 450 and 940 - 960. See how they work and then modify them to allow possible four-digit answers.
4. The operator cannot currently correct any mistakes he makes while typing in his answers. Modify the program to allow him to do so.
5. Modify the program to allow problems in division.

FLASHCARD

PURPOSE

There are certain things that the human mind is capable of learning only through repetition. Not many people can remember the multiplication tables after their first exposure, for example. The same applies to learning the vocabulary of a foreign language, the capital cities of the fifty states, or famous dates in history. The best way to learn them is to simply review them over and over until you have them memorized.

A common technique for doing this involves the use of flashcards. You write one half of the two related pieces of information on one side of a card, and the other half on the other side. After creating a set of these cards, you can drill yourself on them over and over until you always remember what's on the other side of each card.

But why waste precious natural resources by using cards? Use your computer instead. This program lets you create flashcards, drill using them, and save them on cassette tape for later review.

HOW TO USE IT

As currently written, the program immediately begins drilling you on Spanish vocabulary words. After explaining how to use the program with these words, we'll show you how to enter your own flashcards (see Easy Changes).

The program flashes one side of one card on the screen for you. Both are chosen at random — the side and the card. Your job is to respond with the other side. If you enter it correctly, the program says "RIGHT!". If not, it tells you the correct answer. In either event, the program continues by picking another side and card at random. This goes on until you finally respond by simply pressing the **RETURN** key, which tells the program that you do not want to drill any more. It then tells you how many you got right out of the number attempted, as well as the percentage, and gives you the option of drilling more or ending the program.

During the drill, the program will not repeat a card that was used in the previous four questions.

SAMPLE RUN

FLASHCARD PROGRAM

30 FLASHCARDS

TELL ME WHAT'S ON THE OTHER
SIDE OF EACH CARD AS I SHOW IT.

EL SUELO

?THE FLOOR

RIGHT!

AZUL

?YELLOW

NO, THE CORRECT RESPONSE IS
BLUE

ENOUGH

?BASTANTE

RIGHT!

TO EAT

? (RETURN key pressed)

2 RIGHT OUT OF 3

66.6666667 PER CENT

NEXT ACTION:
  1 - DRILL MORE
  2 - END PROGRAM

?<u>2</u>

]

PROGRAM LISTING

```
100 REM: FLASHCARD
110 REM: COPYRIGHT 1980 BY TOM RUGG AND PHIL FELDMAN
120 TEXT:HOME:GOSUB 580
130 L=50:M=5
140 DIM F$(L),B$(L),P(M-1)
150 PRINT"FLASHCARD PROGRAM"
160 PRINT:PRINT
170 K=1:C=0:W=0
180 IF K>L THEN 240
190 READ R$:IF R$="XXX" THEN 250
200 F$(K)=R$
210 READ R$:B$(K)=R$
220 K=K+1
230 GOTO 180
240 PRINT"FLASHCARD ARRAY FULL.":PRINT
250 K=K-1
260 IF K<M THEN PRINT"NOT ENOUGH FLASHCARDS":END
270 PRINT K;" FLASHCARDS"
280 PRINT:PRINT
300 PRINT"TELL ME WHAT'S ON THE OTHER"
310 PRINT"SIDE OF EACH CARD AS I SHOW IT."
320 PRINT:PRINT
340 R=INT(K*RND(1))+1
350 FOR J=0 TO M-2
360 IF P(J)=R THEN 340
370 NEXT
390 J=RND(1):IF J>.5 THEN 420
400 PRINT F$(R):C$=B$(R)
410 GOTO 430
```

```
420 PRINT B$(R);C$=F$(R)
430 PRINT:INPUT R$
440 IF LEN(R$)=0 THEN 600
450 PRINT
460 IF R$=C$ THEN 500
470 PRINT"NO, THE CORRECT RESPONSE IS"
480 PRINT C$
490 W=W+1:GOTO 520
500 PRINT"RIGHT!"
510 C=C+1
520 FOR J=1 TO M-2
530 P(J-1)=P(J):NEXT
540 P(M-2)=R
550 PRINT
560 GOTO 340
580 J=256*PEEK(79)+PEEK(78)
590 J=RND(-J):RETURN
600 PRINT
610 IF C+W=0 THEN 700
620 PRINT C;" RIGHT OUT OF ";C+W
630 PRINT
640 PRINT C*100/(C+W);" PER CENT"
650 PRINT
700 PRINT"NEXT ACTION:"
710 PRINT" 1 - DRILL MORE"
720 PRINT" 2 - END PROGRAM"
730 PRINT
740 INPUT R$
750 IF R$="2" THEN END
760 IF R$="1" THEN 280
770 PRINT"ENTER 1 OR 2 PLEASE."
780 PRINT:GOTO 700
800 REM:FLASHCARD DATA FOLLOWS
810 DATA THE PEN,LA PLUMA
820 DATA THE DOOR,LA PUERTA
830 DATA THE SCHOOL,LA ESCUELA
840 DATA THE FLOOR,EL SUELO
850 DATA THE STORE,LA TIENDRA
860 DATA THE HAND,LA MANO
870 DATA THE HOUSE,LA CASA
880 DATA THE FRIEND,EL AMIGO
890 DATA THE DINNER,LA COMIDA
900 DATA THE CHAIR,LA SILLA
910 DATA TO ARRIVE,LLEGAR
920 DATA TO ASK,PREGUNTAR
```

```
930 DATA TO BUY,COMPRAR
940 DATA TO BRING,LLEVAR
950 DATA TO COME,VENIR
960 DATA TO EAT,COMER
970 DATA TO FIND,HALLAR
980 DATA TO GO,ANDAR
990 DATA TO HAVE,TENER
1000 DATA TO KNOW,SABER
1010 DATA BLUE,AZUL
1020 DATA GREEN,VERDE
1030 DATA RED,ROJO
1040 DATA WHITE,BLANCO
1050 DATA YELLOW,AMARILLO
1060 DATA ENOUGH,BASTANTE
1070 DATA FAR,LEJOS
1080 DATA FEW,POCOS
1090 DATA MANY,MUCHOS
1100 DATA NEAR,CERCA
9999 DATA XXX
```

EASY CHANGES

1. Replace the DATA statements with your own flashcards. A comma is used to separate the two sides of each card. Don't use commas, colons, or quotation marks as part of your cards. Leave line 9999 as it is to signal the end of the cards.
2. Change the limits of the number of flashcards that can be entered by altering line 130. L is the upper limit and M is the minimum. The current upper limit of 50 will fit in an Apple with 4000 bytes free (see Appendix 1) if each side of each flashcard averages no more than about twelve to fifteen characters in length. If you have 16,000 bytes free, you can make L as large as about four hundred for flashcards this size. Do not make M much larger than about ten or so, or you will slow down the program and use more memory than you might want. But, it increases the number of cards drilled upon before repeating.
3. To cause the program to always display side one of the flashcards (and ask you to respond with side two), change this line:

390 REM

To cause it to always display side two, change it this way:

390 GOTO 420

MAIN ROUTINES

130 - 170	Initializes variables. Creates arrays. Displays title.
180 - 270	Reads flashcards from DATA statements.
280 - 650	Drills operator on flashcards in memory.
700 - 780	Displays options and analyzes response. Branches to appropriate routine.

MAIN VARIABLES

L	Upper limit of number of flashcards that can be entered.
M	Minimum number of flashcards that can be entered.
R	Subscript of random flashcard chosen during drill.
K	Number of flashcards entered.
W	Number of wrong responses.
C	Number of correct responses.
F$	Array containing front side of flashcards (side 1).
B$	Array containing back side of flashcards (side 2).
P	Array containing subscripts of M − 1 previous flashcards during drill.
J	Loop and subscript variable.
C$	The correct response during drill.
R$	Response from operator. Also temporary string variable.

SUGGESTED PROJECTS

1. Modify the program for use in a classroom environment. Require the operator to drill a fixed number of times (maybe 20 or 50). Don't allow a null response to end the drill. For example, you could make these changes:

    440 REM
    515 IF C = 20 THEN 600
    660 END

This will cause the program to continue until 20 correct answers are given, and then end.

METRIC

PURPOSE

In case you don't realize it, we live in a metric world. The United States is one of the last holdouts, but that is changing rapidly. So if you're still inching along or watching those pounds, it's time to convert.

METRIC is an instructional program designed to familiarize you with the metric system. It operates in a quiz format; the program randomly forms questions from its data resources. You are then asked to compare two quantities — one in our old English units and one in the corresponding metric units. When you are wrong, the exact conversion and the rule governing it are given.

The two quantities to compare are usually within 50% of each other. Thus, you are constantly comparing an "English" quantity and a metric one which are in the same ball park. This has the effect of providing you with some insight by sheer familiarity with the questions.

HOW TO USE IT

The first thing the program does is ask you how many questions you would like to do for the session. Any value of one or higher is acceptable.

The sample run shows how each question is formulated. A quantity in English units is compared with one in metric units. Either one may appear first in the question. Each quantity will have an integral value. The relating word ("longer," "hotter," "heavier," etc.) indicates what type of quantities are being compared.

There are three possible replies to each question. Pressing **Y** or **N** means that you think the answer is yes or no, respectively. Pressing any other key indicates that you have no idea as to the correct answer.

If you answer the question correctly, you will be duly congratulated and the program will proceed to the next question. A wrong answer or a response of "no idea," however, will generate some diagnostic information. The first value used in the question will be shown converted to its exact equivalent in the corresponding units. Also, the rule governing the situation will be displayed. At the end of any question, the program will request that you hit any key to proceed to the next question.

The program will continue generating the requested number of questions. Before ending, it will show you how many correct answers you gave and your percentage correct.

SAMPLE RUN

```
        A METRIC QUIZ


HOW MANY QUESTIONS SHALL WE DO? 3

QUESTION 1 OF 3

IS 48 MILES LONGER THAN
   92 KILOMETERS ? ("N" key pressed)

YOU SAY 'NO'
   AND YOU'RE RIGHT - VERY GOOD!

*** HIT ANY KEY TO CONTINUE ***

QUESTION 2 OF 3

IS 73 DEGREES FAHRENHEIT HOTTER THAN
   22 DEGREES CENTIGRADE ? ("Y" key pressed)
```

YOU SAY 'YES'
    AND YOU'RE RIGHT - VERY GOOD!

*** HIT ANY KEY TO CONTINUE ***

QUESTION 3 OF 3

IS 79 KILOGRAMS HEAVIER THAN
    152 POUNDS ? ("N" key pressed)

YOU SAY 'NO' BUT YOU'RE WRONG

----

    79 KILOGRAMS EQUALS
    174.166097 POUNDS

---- THE RULE IS ----

    1 KILOGRAM EQUALS
    2.20463 POUNDS

*** HIT ANY KEY TO CONTINUE ***

YOU GOT 2 RIGHT OUT OF 3 QUESTIONS

PERCENTAGE CORRECT = 66.6666667

PROGRAM LISTING

```
100 REM: METRIC
110 REM: COPYRIGHT 1980 BY PHIL FELDMAN AND TOM RUGG
130 TEXT:Q=PEEK(78)+256*PEEK(79):Q=RND(-Q)
150 DIM ES$(30),MS$(30),R$(30),C(30),EP$(30),MP$(30)
160 B$=CHR$(32)
200 GOSUB 400:GOSUB 450
210 INPUT"HOW MANY QUESTIONS SHALL WE DO? ";NQ:NQ=INT(
    NQ):IF NQ<1 THEN 210
220 FOR J=1 TO NQ:GOSUB 600:GOSUB 900:NEXT
```

```
230 GOSUB 450:PRINT"YOU GOT ";NR;" RIGHT OUT OF ";NQ;
    " QUESTIONS":PRINT
240 P=100*NR/NQ:PRINT"PERCENTAGE CORRECT = ";P
250 END
400 RESTORE:ND=0
410 ND=ND+1:READ ES$(ND),MS$(ND),R$(ND),C(ND),EP$(ND),
    MP$(ND)
420 IF ES$(ND)<>"XXX" THEN 410
430 ND=ND-1:RETURN
450 HOME:PRINT TAB(11);"A METRIC QUIZ":PRINT:PRINT:
    RETURN
600 N=INT(ND*RND(1))+1
610 F=0:IF RND(1)>0.5 THEN F=1
620 V1=INT(RND(1)*99)+2:V3=V1*C(N):IF F=1 THEN V3=V1/C(
    N)
630 IF N=1 THEN V3=(V1-32)/1.8:IF F=1 THEN V3=(V1*1.8)+
    32
640 V2=V3*(0.5+RND(1)):V2=INT(V2+0.5):T=0:IF V2<V3 THEN
    T=1
650 GOSUB 450:PRINT"QUESTION ";J;" OF ";NQ:PRINT
660 IF F=0 THEN PRINT"IS ";V1;B$;EP$(N);B$;R$(N);" THAN"
    :PRINT B$;B$;V2;B$;MP$(N);B$;"?"
670 IF F=1 THEN PRINT"IS ";V1;B$;MP$(N);B$;R$(N);" THAN"
    :PRINT B$;B$;V2;B$;EP$(N);B$;"?"
680 GET Q$
700 IF Q$="Y" THEN PRINT:PRINT"YOU SAY 'YES' ";:R=1:
    GOTO 730
710 IF Q$="N" THEN PRINT:PRINT"YOU SAY 'NO' ";:R=0:GOTO
    730
720 PRINT:PRINT"YOU HAVE NO IDEA":R=2
730 X=T-R:IF R=2 THEN GOSUB 800:GOTO 760
740 IF X=0 THEN PRINT:PRINT
    "    AND YOU'RE RIGHT - VERY GOOD!":NR=NR+1:GOTO 760
750 PRINT"BUT YOU'RE WRONG":GOSUB 800
760 RETURN
800 PRINT:PRINT"----------------------":PRINT
810 IF F=0 THEN PRINT V1;B$;EP$(N);" EQUALS":PRINT V3;B$
    ;MP$(N)
820 IF F=1 THEN PRINT V1;B$;MP$(N);" EQUALS":PRINT V3;B$
    ;EP$(N)
830 PRINT:PRINT"---- THE RULE IS ----":PRINT
840 IF N=1 AND F=0 THEN PRINT" DEG.C = (DEG.F - 32)/1.8"
    :RETURN
850 IF N=1 AND F=1 THEN PRINT
```

```
    " DEG.F = (DEG.C * 1.8) + 32":RETURN
860 IF F=0 THEN PRINT" 1 ";ES$(N);" EQUALS":PRINT C(N);
    B$;MP$(N):RETURN
870 Q=INT(1.E5/C(N))/1.E5:PRINT" 1 ";MS$(N);" EQUALS":
    PRINT Q;B$;EP$(N):RETURN
900 PRINT:PRINT:PRINT"*** HIT ANY KEY TO CONTINUE ***"
910 GET Q$
920 RETURN
1000 DATA  DEGREE FAHRENHEIT,DEGREE CENTIGRADE,HOTTER,0.
     5
1010 DATA  DEGREES FAHRENHEIT,DEGREES CENTIGRADE
1020 DATA  MILE PER HOUR,KILOMETER PER HOUR,FASTER,1.
     60935
1030 DATA  MILES PER HOUR,KILOMETERS PER HOUR
1040 DATA  FOOT,METER,LONGER,0.3048
1050 DATA  FEET,METERS
1060 DATA  MILE,KILOMETER,LONGER,1.60935
1070 DATA  MILES,KILOMETERS
1080 DATA  INCH,CENTIMETER,LONGER,2.54
1090 DATA  INCHES,CENTIMETERS
1100 DATA  GALLON,LITRE,MORE,3.78533
1110 DATA  GALLONS,LITRES
1120 DATA  POUND,KILOGRAM,HEAVIER,0.45359
1130 DATA  POUNDS,KILOGRAMS
1999 DATA  XXX,XXX,XXX,0,XXX,XXX
```

EASY CHANGES

1. To have the program always ask a fixed number of questions,
   change line 210 to set NQ to the desired value. For example:

$$210 \text{ NQ}= 10$$

   will cause the program to do 10 questions.
2. There are currently seven conversions built into the program:

N	Type	English Unit	Metric Unit
1	temperature	degrees F.	degrees C.
2	speed	miles/hour	kilometers/hour
3	length	feet	meters
4	length	miles	kilometers
5	length	inches	centimeters
6	volume	gallons	litres
7	weight	pounds	kilograms

If you wish to be quizzed on only one type of question, set N to this value in line 600. Thus,

$$600 \text{ N}=4$$

will cause the program to only produce questions comparing miles and kilometers. To add additional data to the program, see the first "Suggested Project."

3. You can easily have the questions posed in one "direction" only. To go only from English to metric units use

$$610 \text{ F}=0$$

while to go from metric to English use

$$610 \text{ F}=1$$

4. You might want the converted value and governing rule to be displayed even when the correct answer is given. This is accomplished by changing line 740 and adding line 745 as follows:

```
740 IF X=0 THEN PRINT:PRINT" AND YOU'RE RIGHT –
                                 VERY GOOD"
745 IF X=0 THEN NR=NR+1:GOSUB 800:GOTO 760
```

MAIN ROUTINES

130 - 160	Dimensions and initializes variables.
200 - 250	Mainline routine, drives other routines.
400 - 430	Reads and initializes data.
450	Displays header.
600 - 760	Forms and asks questions. Processes user's reply.
800 - 870	Displays exact conversion and governing rule.
900 - 920	Waits for user to hit any key.
1000 - 1999	Data statements.

MAIN VARIABLES

ND	Number of conversions in the data.
ES$,EP$	String arrays of English units' names (singular, plural).
MS$,MP$	String arrays of metric units' names (singular, plural).
R$	String array of the relation descriptors.
C	Array of the conversion factors.

Q	Work variable.
B\$	String constant of one blank character.
J	Current question number.
NR	Number of questions answered right.
P	Percentage answered right.
NQ	Number of questions in session.
N	Index number of current question in the data list.
F	Flag on question "direction" (0= English to metric; 1=metric to English).
V1,V2	Numeric values on left, right sides of the question.
V3	The correct value of the right-hand side.
T	Flag on the question's correct answer (1=true; 0=false).
Q\$	User reply string.
R	User reply flag (0=no; 1=yes; 2=no idea).
X	User's result (0 if correct answer was given).

SUGGESTED PROJECTS

1. Each built-in conversion requires six elements of data in this order:

   Element   Data Description

1	English unit (singular)
2	Metric unit (singular)
3	Relation descriptor (e.g. "hotter," "faster," etc.)
4	Conversion factor (from English to metric)
5	English unit (plural)
6	Metric unit (plural)

   Each of these elements, except the fourth, is a string. The data statements in the listing should make clear how the information is to be provided. You can add new data to the program with appropriate data statements in this format. New data should be added after the current data; i.e., just before line 1999. Line 1999 is a special data statement to trigger the end of all data to the program. The program is dimensioned up to thirty entries while only seven are currently used. (Note: this format allows only conversions where one unit is a direct multiple of the other. Temperature, which does not fit this rule, is handled as a special case throughout the program.)

2. Convert the program to handle units conversion questions of any type.
3. Keep track of the questions asked and which ones were missed. Then, do not ask the same questions too soon if they have been answered correctly. However, do re-ask those questions missed for additional practice.

NUMBERS

PURPOSE

This is an educational program for preschool children. After a few weeks of watching Sesame Street on television, most three and four-year-old children will learn how to count from one to ten. The NUMBERS program allows these children to practice their numbers and have fun at the same time.

HOW TO USE IT

We know a child who learned how to type LOAD and RUN to get this program started before she turned three, but you'll probably have to help your child with this for a while. The program asks the question, "WHAT NUMBER COMES AFTER n?", where n is a number from one to nine. Even if the child can't read yet, he or she will soon learn to look for the number at the end of the line. The child should respond with the appropriate number, and then press the **RETURN** key.

If the answer is correct, the program displays the message "THAT'S RIGHT!", pauses for a couple of seconds, and then displays three geometric shapes. In the upper left of the screen a rectangle is drawn. In the lower center, a triangle is drawn. Then an asterisk (or a snowflake, perhaps?) is drawn in the lower right portion of the screen. After about a five-second delay, the program clears the screen and asks another question. The same number is never asked twice in a row. The size of the three figures is chosen at random each time.

If the child provides the wrong answer, a message indicates the error and the same question is asked again.

The program keeps on going until you enter "E" instead of a number. Remember that most children have a pretty short attention span, so please do not force your child to continue after his or her interest diminishes. Keep each session short and fun. This way, it will always be a treat to "play" with the computer.

SAMPLE RUN

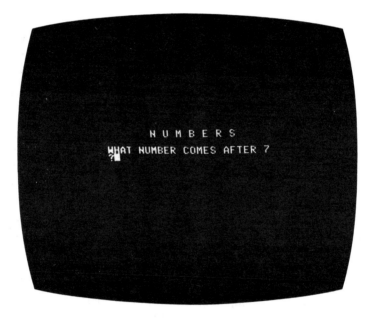

The program asks what number comes after 7, and waits for a response.

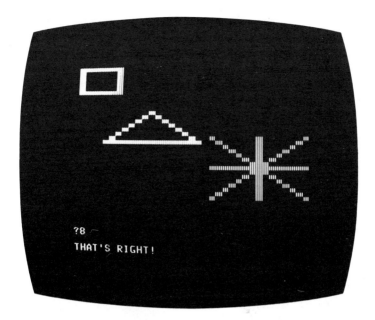

Because of the correct response, the program draws three geometric figures. See color section.

PROGRAM LISTING

```
100 REM: NUMBERS
110 REM: COPYRIGHT 1980 BY TOM RUGG AND PHIL FELDMAN
120 GR
130 M=9:E=10:TS=11
140 HOME
150 PRINT
160 PRINT TAB(8);"N U M B E R S"
170 R=INT(M*RND(1))+1:IF R=P THEN 170
180 PRINT
190 PRINT"WHAT NUMBER COMES AFTER ";R
200 INPUT R$
210 PRINT:IF R$="E" THEN TEXT:HOME:END
220 IF VAL(R$)=R+1 THEN 300
230 PRINT"NO, THAT'S NOT IT.  TRY AGAIN."
240 GOTO 180
300 PRINT"THAT'S RIGHT!"
310 FOR X=1 TO 1000:NEXT X
320 P=R
330 E=INT(8*RND(1))+4
340 C=INT(13*RND(1))+2
```

```
400 COLOR=C:HLIN 1,E AT 1
410 HLIN 1,E AT E
420 VLIN 1,E AT 1
430 VLIN 1,E AT E
450 COLOR=C+1:FOR J=1 TO E
460 Y=TS+J:X=TS+J:PLOT X,Y:NEXT
470 FOR J=1 TO E
480 Y=TS+J:X=TS-J+2:PLOT X,Y:NEXT
490 Y=TS+E+1:FOR X=TS-E+1 TO TS+E+1
500 PLOT X,Y:NEXT
520 COLOR=INT((C+1)/2):A=28:B=25
530 FOR J=1 TO E
540 X=A+J:Y=B+J:PLOT X,Y
550 Y=B-J:PLOT X,Y
560 Y=B:PLOT X,Y
570 X=A:PLOT X,Y
580 Y=B+J:PLOT X,Y
590 Y=B-J:PLOT X,Y
600 X=A-J:PLOT X,Y
610 Y=B:PLOT X,Y
620 Y=B+J:PLOT X,Y
630 NEXT
800 FOR J=1 TO 4000:NEXT
810 GR:PRINT
820 GOTO 170
```

EASY CHANGES

1. Change the range of numbers that the program asks by altering the value of M in line 130. For a beginner, use a value of 3 for M instead of 9. Later, increase the value of M to 5, and then 8.
2. Alter the delay after "THAT'S RIGHT!" is displayed by altering the value of 1000 in statement 310. Double it to double the time delay, etc. The same can be done with the 4000 in line 800 to alter the delay after the figures are drawn.
3. To avoid randomness in the size of the figures that are drawn, replace line 330 with

$$330 \ E=11$$

Instead of 11, you can use any integer from 3 to 11.
4. To slowly increase the size of the figures from small to large

as correct answers are given (and the reverse for incorrect answers), do the following:

a. Replace the 10 in line 130 with a 3.

b. Insert this line

$$225 \ E=E-3:IF \ E<3 \ THEN \ E=3$$

c. Replace line 330 with the following:

$$330 \ E=E+3:IF \ E>11 \ THEN \ E=11$$

MAIN ROUTINES

120 - 160	Initializes variables. Clears screen.
170	Picks random integer from 1 to M.
180 - 240	Asks question. Gets answer. Determines if right or wrong.
310	Delays about 1½ seconds.
320 - 430	Draws a rectangle.
450 - 500	Draws a triangle.
520 - 630	Draws an asterisk.
800	Delays about 5 seconds.
810 - 820	Clears screen. Goes back to ask next question.

MAIN VARIABLES

M	Maximum number that will be asked.
E	Edge length of geometric figures.
R	Random integer in range from 1 to M.
P	Previous number that was asked.
R$	Reply given by operator.
X,Y	Coordinates in CRT display.
TS	Triangle's starting location (top).
A,B	X,Y coordinate values.
J	Subscript variable.

SUGGESTED PROJECTS

1. Modify the program to ask the next letter of the alphabet. Use the ASC and CHR$ functions in picking a random letter from A to Y, and to check whether the response is correct or not.

2. Ask each number from 1 to M once (in a random sequence). At the end of the sequence, repeat those that were missed.
3. Add different shapes to the graphics display that is done after a correct answer. Try an octagon, a diamond, and a square. Or, combine this program with one of the graphics display programs.

TACHIST

PURPOSE

This program turns your computer into a tachistoscope (tah-KISS-tah-scope). A tachistoscope is used in reading classes to improve reading habits and, as a result, improve reading speed. The program displays a word or phrase on the screen for a fraction of a second, then asks you what it was. With a little practice, you will find that you can read phrases that are displayed for shorter and shorter time periods.

HOW TO USE IT

The program starts off by displaying a brief introduction and waiting for you to press any key (except the **RESET** key or shift keys, of course). If you press the **ESCAPE** key, the program ends. After you press a key, the screen is blanked out except for two horizontal dash lines in the upper left-hand corner. After two seconds, a phrase is flashed on the screen between the two lines. Then the screen is blanked again, and you are asked what the phrase was.

If you respond correctly, the next phrase is displayed for a shorter time period (half as long). If you respond incorrectly, the program shows you the correct phrase, and the next phrase is displayed for a longer period of time (twice as long).

The fastest the computer can display a phrase and erase it is about .02 seconds (one-fiftieth). See if you can reach the top speed and still continue to read the phrases correctly.

A great deal of research has been done to determine how people read and what they should do to read both faster and with better comprehension. We will not try to explain it all (see the bibliography), but a couple of things are worth mentioning.

To read fast, you should not read one word at a time. Instead, you should learn to quickly read an entire phrase at once. By looking at a point in the center of the phrase (and slightly above it), your eyes can see the whole phrase *without* the necessity of scanning it from left to right, word by word. Because the tachistoscope flashes an entire phrase on the screen at once, it forces you to look at a single point and absorb the whole phrase, rather than scanning left to right, word by word.

If you can incorporate this technique into your reading and increase the width of the phrases you absorb, your reading speed can increase dramatically.

SAMPLE RUN

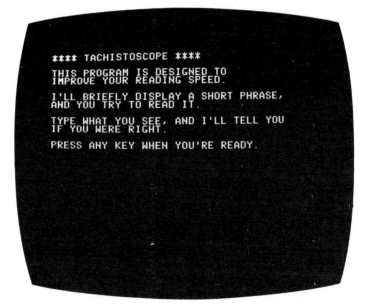

```
**** TACHISTOSCOPE ****

THIS PROGRAM IS DESIGNED TO
IMPROVE YOUR READING SPEED.

I'LL BRIEFLY DISPLAY A SHORT PHRASE,
AND YOU TRY TO READ IT.

TYPE WHAT YOU SEE, AND I'LL TELL YOU
IF YOU WERE RIGHT.

PRESS ANY KEY WHEN YOU'RE READY.
```

The program displays an introduction, then waits.

The program clears the screen and displays two parallel lines in the
upper left corner of the screen for a couple of seconds.

The program flashes a short phrase (chosen at random) between the
two lines for a fraction of a second, then clears the screen.

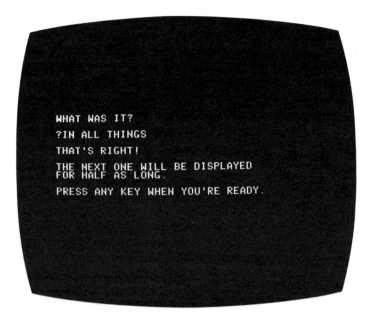

The program asks what the phrase was. The operator responds correctly. The program acknowledges the correct response, and indicates that the next phrase will be shown for half as long.

PROGRAM LISTING

```
100 REM: TACHISTOSCOPE
110 REM: COPYRIGHT 1980 BY TOM RUGG AND PHIL FELDMAN
130 T=256
140 L=50
150 DIM T$(L)
160 C=0
170 READ R$
180 IF R$="XXX" THEN 250
190 C=C+1
200 IF C>L THEN PRINT"TOO MANY DATA STATEMENTS":END
210 T$(C)=R$
220 GOTO 170
250 TEXT:HOME:GOSUB 800
270 PRINT"**** TACHISTOSCOPE ****"
280 PRINT
290 PRINT"THIS PROGRAM IS DESIGNED TO"
300 PRINT"IMPROVE YOUR READING SPEED."
310 PRINT
320 PRINT"I'LL BRIEFLY DISPLAY A SHORT PHRASE,"
```

```
330 PRINT"AND YOU TRY TO READ IT."
340 PRINT
350 PRINT"TYPE WHAT YOU SEE, AND I'LL TELL YOU"
360 PRINT"IF YOU WERE RIGHT."
370 PRINT
410 PRINT"PRESS ANY KEY WHEN YOU'RE READY."
420 GET R$:IF ASC(R$)=27 THEN END
430 R=INT(C*RND(1))+1
440 IF R=P1 OR R=P2 OR R=P3 THEN 430
450 IF R=P4 OR R=P5 THEN 430
460 GOSUB 840:FOR K=1 TO 1500:NEXT
470 VTAB 2:PRINT T$(R)
480 FOR J=1 TO T:NEXT
500 HOME:FOR K=1 TO 500:NEXT
510 PRINT:PRINT:PRINT:PRINT
520 PRINT"WHAT WAS IT?"
530 PRINT:INPUT R$
550 IF R$<>T$(R) THEN 700
560 PRINT:PRINT"THAT'S RIGHT!"
570 T=T/2
590 R$="FOR HALF AS LONG."
600 P1=P2:P2=P3:P3=P4:P4=P5:P5=R
610 PRINT
620 IF T<=16 THEN T=16:R$="AT MAXIMUM SPEED."
630 PRINT"THE NEXT ONE WILL BE DISPLAYED":PRINT R$
640 PRINT:GOTO 410
700 PRINT"NO, THAT'S NOT IT.  IT WAS"
710 PRINT:PRINT"'";T$(R);"'"
720 T=T*2
730 IF T>2048 THEN T=2048:R$="AT THE SAME SPEED.":GOTO
    600
740 R$="FOR TWICE AS LONG.":GOTO 600
800 J=256*PEEK(79)+PEEK(78)
810 J=RND(-J):RETURN
840 HOME:PRINT"------------"
850 PRINT
860 PRINT"------------"
870 RETURN
910 DATA"AT THE TIME"
920 DATA"THE BROWN COW"
930 DATA"LOOK AT THAT"
940 DATA"IN THE HOUSE"
950 DATA"THIS IS MINE"
960 DATA"SHE SAID SO"
970 DATA"THE BABY CRIED"
```

```
980 DATA"TO THE STORE"
990 DATA"READING IS FUN"
1000 DATA"HE GOES FAST"
1010 DATA"IN ALL THINGS"
1020 DATA"GREEN GRASS"
1030 DATA"TWO BIRDS FLY"
1040 DATA"LATE LAST NIGHT"
1050 DATA"THEY ARE HOME"
1060 DATA"ON THE PHONE"
1070 DATA"THROUGH A DOOR"
1080 DATA"WE CAN TRY"
1090 DATA"MY FOOT HURTS"
1100 DATA"HAPPY NEW YEAR"
9999 DATA   XXX
```

EASY CHANGES

1. Change the phrases that are displayed by changing the DATA
   statements that start at line 910. Add more and/or replace
   those shown with your own phrases or words. Line 140 must
   specify a number that is at least as large as the number of
   DATA statements. So, to allow for up to 100 DATA statements, change line 140 to say

                    140 L=100

   Be sure to enter your DATA statements in the same form as
   shown in the program listing. To begin with, you may want
   to start off with shorter phrases or single words. Later, try
   longer phrases. Do not alter line 9999, which has to be the
   last DATA statement. If you have 4000 bytes free (see
   Appendix 1), you have room for about 80 phrases of the
   approximate size shown in the program listing.

2. To change the length of time the first phrase is displayed,
   change the value of T in line 130. Double it to double the
   length of time, etc. Don't make it less than 16.

3. To cause all phrases to be displayed for the same length of
   time, remove lines 570 and 720, and insert these lines:

            595 R$="AT THE SAME SPEED"
            725 R$="AT THE SAME SPEED":GOTO 600

4. If you want to change the waiting period before the phrase is
   flashed on the screen, change the 1500 in line 460. To make

the delay five seconds, change it to 4000. To make it one second, change it to 800.

5. To put the program into a sort of flashcard mode, in which the phrases are flashed, but no replies are necessary, insert these three lines:

```
515 GOTO 710
595 R$= "AT THE SAME SPEED"
715 GOTO 590
```

This will cause each phrase to be flashed (all for the same length of time), and then to be displayed again so you can verify what it was.

MAIN ROUTINES

130 - 150	Initializes variables.
160 - 220	Reads DATA statements into T$ array.
250 - 370	Displays introduction.
410 - 420	Waits for operator to press a key.
430 - 450	Picks random phrase from T$ array. Ensures no duplication from previous five phrases.
460	Clears screen and displays horizontal lines.
470 - 500	Displays phrase for appropriate length of time.
510 - 530	Asks what phrase was.
550	Determines if typed phrase matches the phrase displayed.
560 - 640	Shortens time for next phrase if reply was correct. Saves subscript to avoid repetition. Goes back to wait for key to be pressed.
700 - 740	Shows what phrase was. Lengthens time for next phrase. Ensures that time period does not exceed maximum.
800 - 810	Subroutine to initialize RND function.
840 - 870	Subroutine to display horizontal dash lines.
910 - 9999	DATA statements with phrases to be displayed.

MAIN VARIABLES

T	Time that phrase will be displayed.
J	Loop variable.
L	Limit of number of phrases.

T$ Array of phrases (read into from DATA statements).

C   Count of number of phrases actually read.

R$ Temporary string variable. Also, reply of operator.

R   Work variable. Also, subscript of phrase to be displayed.

P1,P2,   Subscripts of the five previous phrases.
P3,P4,P5

K   Temporary work variable.

SUGGESTED PROJECTS

1. Instead of picking phrases at random, go through the list once sequentially. Change line 250 to set R to zero, and line 430 to add one to R, then check if R is greater than C.
2. Instead of only verifying that the current phrase does not duplicate any of the previous five phrases, modify the program to avoid duplication of the previous ten or more. Changes will be needed to lines 440, 450, and 600.
3. Keep score of the number of correct and incorrect replies, and display the percentage each time. Alternatively, come up with a rating based on the percentage correct and the speed attained, possibly in conjunction with a difficulty factor for the phrases used.
4. Add the capability to the program to also have a mode in which it can display a two to seven digit number, chosen at random. Have the operator try several of the numbers first (maybe five digit ones) before trying the phrases. The phrases will seem easy after doing the numbers.

VOCAB

PURPOSE

Did you ever find yourself at a loss for words? Well, this vocabulary quiz can be used in a self-teaching environment or as reinforcement for classroom instruction to improve your ability to remember the jargon of any subject. It allows you to drill at your own pace, without the worry of ridicule from other students or judgment by an instructor. When you make mistakes, only the computer knows, and it's not telling anyone except you. Modifying the program to substitute a different vocabulary list is very simple, so you can accumulate many different versions of this program, each with a different set of words.

HOW TO USE IT

This program is pretty much self-explanatory from the sample run. After you enter "RUN," it asks you how many questions you would like. If you respond with a number less than five, you will still do five. Otherwise, you will do the number you enter.

Next, you get a series of multiple-choice questions. Each question is formatted in one of two ways — either you are given a word and asked to select from a list of definitions, or you are given a definition and asked to select from a list of words. The format is chosen at random. You respond with the number of the choice you think is correct. If you are right, you are told so. If not, you are shown the correct answer. From the second answer on, you are shown a status report of the number correct out of the number attempted so far.

Finally, after the last question, you are shown the percentage you got correct, along with a comment on your performance. Then you have the option of going back for another round of questions or stopping.

SAMPLE RUN

RUN

**** VOCABULARY QUIZ ****

THIS PROGRAM WILL TEST YOUR KNOWLEDGE
OF SOME USEFUL VOCABULARY WORDS.

HOW MANY QUESTIONS SHALL WE DO? 5

    1 -- WHAT WORD MEANS ALL-KNOWING?
         1 -- LACONIC
         2 -- HEDONISTIC
         3 -- OMINOUS
         4 -- CONGENITAL
         5 -- OMNISCIENT

? 5
RIGHT!

    2 -- WHAT DOES PARSIMONIOUS MEAN?
         1 -- INDIFFERENT OR UNINTERESTED
         2 -- KEEN IN JUDGMENT
         3 -- STINGY OR FRUGAL
         4 -- WEAK OR EXHAUSTED
         5 -- OF UNKNOWN OR HIDDEN ORIGIN

? 4
NO, THE ANSWER IS NUMBER 3

(. . . later)

YOU HAVE 3 RIGHT OUT OF 5 QUESTIONS.

THAT'S 60 PERCENT.
NOT BAD, BUT ROOM FOR IMPROVEMENT.

WANT TO TRY AGAIN?<u>NO</u>

CHECK YOU LATER.

PROGRAM LISTING

```
100 REM: VOCABULARY QUIZ
110 REM: COPYRIGHT 1980 BY TOM RUGG AND PHIL FELDMAN
300 GOSUB 1000
400 GOSUB 2000
500 GOSUB 3000
600 GOSUB 4000
700 GOSUB 5000
800 GOSUB 6000
900 IF E=0 THEN 500
910 GOTO 300
990 REM
1000 IF E<>0 THEN 1060
1010 TEXT:HOME
1020 PRINT"**** VOCABULARY QUIZ ****"
1030 PRINT
1040 PRINT"THIS PROGRAM WILL TEST YOUR KNOWLEDGE"
1050 PRINT"OF SOME USEFUL VOCABULARY WORDS."
1060 PRINT
1110 INPUT"HOW MANY QUESTIONS SHALL WE DO? ";L
1120 IF L>4 THEN 1140
1130 PRINT"THAT'S NOT ENOUGH.  LET'S DO 5.":L=5
1140 IF E<>0 THEN 1200
1150 PRINT
1170 J=256*PEEK(79)+PEEK(78)
1180 J=RND(-J)
1200 RETURN
2000 IF E<>0 THEN 2200
2010 C=5
2020 D=26
2030 DIM D$(D),E$(D)
2040 DIM P(C)
2050 J=1
2060 READ D$(J)
2070 IF D$(J)="XXX" THEN 2140
```

```
2090 READ E$(J)
2100 J=J+1
2110 IF J<=D THEN 2060
2120 PRINT"TOO MANY DATA STATEMENTS."
2130 PRINT"ONLY FIRST ";D;" ARE USED."
2140 D=J-1
2200 Q=1
2210 E=0
2220 Q1=0
2300 RETURN
3000 FOR J=1 TO C
3010 P(J)=0
3020 NEXT
3030 FOR J=1 TO C
3040 P=INT(D*RND(1))+1
3045 IF P=P1 OR P=P2 OR P=P3 THEN 3040
3050 FOR K=1 TO J
3060 IF P(K)=P THEN 3040
3070 NEXT K
3080 P(J)=P
3090 NEXT J
3110 A=INT(C*RND(1))+1
3200 RETURN
4000 PRINT
4010 M=RND(1)
4020 IF M>.5 THEN 4100
4030 PRINT Q;" -- WHAT WORD MEANS ";E$(P(A));"?"
4040 FOR J=1 TO C
4050 PRINT TAB(5);J;" -- ";D$(P(J))
4060 NEXT
4070 GOTO 4210
4100 PRINT Q;" -- WHAT DOES ";D$(P(A));" MEAN?"
4110 FOR J=1 TO C
4120 PRINT TAB(5);J;" -- ";E$(P(J))
4130 NEXT
4210 RETURN
5000 INPUT R
5010 IF R>=1 AND R<=C THEN 5050
5020 PRINT"I NEED A NUMBER FROM 1 TO ";C
5030 GOTO 5000
5050 IF (R=A) THEN 5100
5060 PRINT"NO, THE ANSWER IS NUMBER ";A
5070 GOTO 5210
5100 PRINT"RIGHT!"
5110 Q1=Q1+1
```

```
5210 IF Q=1 THEN 5300
5220 PRINT"YOU HAVE ";Q1;" RIGHT OUT OF ";Q;
     " QUESTIONS."
5300 P3=P2
5310 P2=P1
5320 P1=P(A)
5330 RETURN
6000 Q=Q+1
6010 IF Q<=L THEN RETURN
6020 E=1
6030 Q=Q1*100/(Q-1)
6040 IF Q>0 THEN 6070
6050 PRINT"WELL, THAT'S A 'PERFECT' SCORE..."
6060 GOTO 6200
6070 PRINT"THAT'S ";Q;" PERCENT."
6080 IF Q>25 THEN 6110
6090 PRINT"CONGRATULATIONS ON AVOIDING A SHUTOUT."
6100 GOTO 6200
6110 IF Q>50 THEN 6140
6120 PRINT"YOU CAN USE SOME MORE PRACTICE."
6130 GOTO 6200
6140 IF Q>75 THEN 6170
6150 PRINT"NOT BAD, BUT ROOM FOR IMPROVEMENT."
6160 GOTO 6200
6170 PRINT"VERY GOOD!"
6180 IF Q>95 THEN PRINT"YOU'RE ALMOST AS SMART AS I AM!"
6200 PRINT
6210 INPUT"WANT TO TRY AGAIN? ";R$
6220 IF LEFT$(R$,1)<>"N" THEN 6240
6230 PRINT:PRINT"CHECK YOU LATER.":PRINT:END
6240 IF LEFT$(R$,1)<>"Y" THEN 6200
6250 RETURN
7000 REM: ON LINE 2020, D MUST BE AT LEAST ONE GREATER
7005 REM: THAN THE NUMBER OF DIFFERENT WORDS.
7010 DATA ANONYMOUS,"OF UNKNOWN OR HIDDEN ORIGIN"
7020 DATA OMINOUS,"THREATENING OF MENACING"
7030 DATA AFFLUENT,"WEALTHY"
7040 DATA APATHETIC,"INDIFFERENT OR UNINTERESTED"
7050 DATA LACONIC,"TERSE"
7060 DATA INTREPID,"FEARLESS OR COURAGEOUS"
7070 DATA GREGARIOUS,"SOCIAL OR COMPANY-LOVING"
7080 DATA ENERVATED,"WEAK OR EXHAUSTED"
7090 DATA VENERABLE,"WORTHY OF RESPECT OR REVERENCE"
7100 DATA DISPARATE,"DIFFERENT AND DISTINCT"
7110 DATA VIVACIOUS,"LIVELY OR SPIRITED"
```

```
7120 DATA  ASTUTE,"KEEN IN JUDGMENT"
7130 DATA  URSINE,"BEARLIKE"
7140 DATA  PARSIMONIOUS,"STINGY OR FRUGAL"
7150 DATA  OMNISCIENT,"ALL-KNOWING"
7999 DATA  XXX
```

EASY CHANGES

1. Add more DATA statements between lines 7000 and 7999, or replace them all with your own. Be careful not to use two or more words with very similar definitions; the program might select more than one of them as possible answers to the same question. Note that each DATA statement first has the vocabulary word, then a comma, and then the definition or synonym. Be sure there are no commas or colons in the definition (unless you enclose the definition in quotes). If you add more DATA statements, you have to increase the value of D in line 2020 to be at least one greater than the number of words. The number of DATA statements you can have depends on how long each one is and how much user memory your computer has. Using DATA statements that average the same length as these, you can probably have about 40 of them if you have 4000 bytes free (see Appendix 1), or over 200 with 10,000 bytes free. Be sure to leave statement 7999 as it is—it signals that there are no more DATA statements.

2. To get something other than five choices for each question, change the value of C in line 2010. You might want only three or four choices per question.

3. If you do not want to be given a choice of how many questions are going to be asked, remove lines 1110 through 1140 and insert the following lines:

   > 1110 PRINT"WE'LL DO TEN QUESTIONS."
   > 1120 L=10

   This will always cause ten questions to be asked. Of course, you can use some number other than ten if you want.

MAIN ROUTINES

300 - 910	Mainline routine. Calls major subroutines.
1000 - 1200	Displays introduction. Determines number of questions to be asked.

2000 - 2300   Reads vocabulary words and definitions into arrays. Performs housekeeping.

3000 - 3200   Selects choices for answers and determines which will be the correct one.

4000 - 4210   Determines in which format the question will be asked. Asks it.

5000 - 5330   Accepts answer from operator. Determines if right or wrong. Keeps score. Saves subscripts of last three correct answers.

6000 - 6250   Gives final score. Asks about doing it again.

7000 - 7999   DATA statements with vocabulary words and definitions.

MAIN VARIABLES

E	Set to 1 to avoid repeating introduction after the first round.
L	Limit of number of questions to ask.
R	Operator's reply to each question.
C	Number of choices of answers given for each question.
D	At least one greater than number of DATA statements. Used to DIM arrays.
D$	Array of vocabulary words.
E$	Array of definitions.
P	Array for numbers of possible answers to each question.
J	Work variable (subscript for FOR-NEXT loops).
Q	Number of questions asked so far (later used to calculate percent correct).
Q1	Number of questions correct so far.
P	Work variable.
P1,P2, P3	Last three correct answers.
A	Subscript of correct answer in P array.
M	Work variable to decide which way to ask question.
R$	Yes or no reply about doing another round.

SUGGESTED PROJECTS

1. Modify lines 6030 through 6200 to display the final evaluation messages based on a finer breakdown of the percent correct.

For example, show one message if 100 percent, another if 95 to 99, another if 90 to 94, etc.

2. Ask the operator's name in the introduction routine, and personalize some of the messages with his/her name.

3. Instead of just checking about the last three questions, be sure that the next question has not been asked in the last eight or ten questions. (Check lines 3045 and 5300 through 5320.)

4. Keep track of which questions the operator misses. Then, after going through the number of questions he/she requested, repeat those that were missed.

Section 3

Game Programs

INTRODUCTION TO GAME PROGRAMS

Almost everyone likes to play games. Computer games are a fun and entertaining use of your Apple. Besides providing relaxation and recreation, they have some built-in practical bonuses. They often force you to think strategically, plan ahead, or at least be orderly in your thought processes. They are also a good way to help some friends over their possible "computer phobia." We present a collection of games to fit any game-playing mood.

Maybe you desire a challenging all-skill game? Like chess or checkers, WARI involves no luck and considerable thinking. The computer will be your opponent, and a formidable one indeed.

Perhaps you're in the mood for a game with quick action and mounting excitement. GROAN is a fast-paced dice game involving mostly luck with a dash of skill (or intuition) thrown in. The computer is ready for your challenge any time.

JOT is a word game. You and the Apple each take secret words and then try to home in on each other's selection.

Do you like solving puzzles? If so, try DECODE. The computer will choose a secret code and then challenge you to break it.

Graphic electronic arcade games have been a prevalent landmark of the past few years. We include two such games. ROADRACE puts you behind the wheel of a high-speed race car. You must steer accurately to stay on course. OBSTACLE lets you and a friend compete in a game of cut and thrust. Each of you must avoid crossing the path laid by the other, and by yourself!

DECODE

PURPOSE

Decode is really more of a puzzle than a game, although you can still compete with your friends to see who can solve the puzzles the fastest. Each time you play, you are presented with a new puzzle to solve.

The object is to figure out the computer's secret code in as few guesses as possible. The program gives you information about the accuracy of each of your guesses. By carefully selecting your guesses to make use of the information you have, you can determine what the secret code must be in a surprisingly small number of guesses. Five or six is usually enough.

The first few times you try, you will probably require quite a few more guesses than that, but with practice, you'll discover that you can learn a lot more from each guess than you originally thought.

HOW TO USE IT

The program starts off by displaying a brief introduction. Here are some more details.

The program selects a secret code for you to figure out. The code is a four-digit number that uses only the digits 1 through 6. For example, your Apple might pick 6153 or 2242 as a secret code.

You object is to guess the code in the fewest possible guesses. After each of your guesses, the program tells you a "black" and a "white" number. The black number indicates the number of digits in your guess that were correct – the digit was correct *and* in the correct position. So, if the secret code is 6153 and your guess is 4143, you will be told that black is 2 (because the 1 and the 3 are correct). Of course, you aren't told *which* digits are correct. That is for you to figure out by making use of the information that you get from other guesses.

Each of the white numbers indicates a digit in your guess that is correct, but which is in the wrong position. For example, if the secret code is 6153 and your guess is 1434, you will told that white is 2. The 1 and 3 are correct, but in wrong positions.

The white number is determined by ignoring any digits that accounted for a black number. Also, a single position in the secret code or guess can only account for one black or white number. These facts become significant when the secret code and/or your guess have duplicate digits. For example, if the code is 1234 and your guess is 4444, there is only one black, and no whites. If the code is 2244 and your guess is 4122, there are no blacks and three whites.

This may sound a little tricky, but you will quickly get the hang of it.

At any time during the game, you can ask for a "SUMMARY" by entering an S instead of a guess. This causes the program to clear the screen and display each guess (with the corresponding result) that has occurred so far.

Also, if you get tired of trying and want to give up, you can enter a Q (for "quit") to end your misery and find out the answer. Otherwise, you continue guessing until you get the code right (four black, zero white), or until you have used up the maximum of 12 guesses.

SAMPLE RUN

```
**** DECODE ****

FIGURE OUT A 4 POSITION CODE
USING THE DIGITS 1 THRU 6

'BLACK' INDICATES A CORRECT DIGIT
IN THE RIGHT POSITION.
'WHITE' INDICATES SOME OTHER CORRECT
DIGIT, BUT IN THE WRONG POSITION.

I'VE CHOSEN MY SECRET CODE.
GUESS NUMBER 1 ?6413
GUESS NO.1 -- BLACK = 2   WHITE = 0
GUESS NUMBER 2 ?
```

The program displays an introduction, chooses its secret code, and
asks for the operator's first guess. After the operator makes a guess,
the program responds with a "black" and a "white" number, and
asks for the second guess.

```
NO.   GUESS   BLACK   WHITE
1     6413      2       0
2     6414      1       1
3     6452      1       0
4     6611      0       0
5     4433      3       0

GUESS NUMBER 6 ?4443
GUESS NO.6 -- BLACK = 4   WHITE = 0

YOU GOT IT IN 6 GUESSES.
...THAT'S PRETTY GOOD
WANT TO TRY AGAIN? I
```

Later in the same game, the operator asks for a summary, then
makes the guess that turns out to be correct. The program acknowledges that the guess is correct and asks about trying another game.

PROGRAM LISTING

```
100 REM: DECODE
110 REM: COPYRIGHT 1980 BY TOM RUGG AND PHIL FELDMAN
120 D=6:P=4:L=12
130 DIM G$(L),G(P),C(P),B(L),W(L)
150 GOSUB 1200
170 GOSUB 300:GOSUB 370
180 PRINT"GUESS NUMBER ";G;" ";
190 INPUT A$
200 IF LEFT$(A$,1)="S" THEN 500
210 IF LEFT$(A$,1)="Q" THEN 600
220 GOSUB 700:IF K=1 THEN 180
230 GOSUB 800
240 GOSUB 1000
250 IF B(G)=P THEN 2000
260 G$(G)=A$
270 G=G+1:IF G>L THEN 2200
280 GOTO 180
300 G=1:C$=""
310 RETURN
370 FOR J=1 TO P
380 R=INT(D*RND(1))+1
390 C$=C$+STR$(R)
400 NEXT J
410 PRINT"I'VE CHOSEN MY SECRET CODE."
420 PRINT
430 RETURN
500 IF G=1 THEN PRINT"NO GUESSES YET.":GOTO 180
510 HOME:PRINT"SUMMARY":PRINT
520 PRINT"NO.    GUESS    BLACK    WHITE"
530 PRINT:FOR J=1 TO G-1
540 PRINT J;TAB(7);G$(J);TAB(17);B(J);TAB(25);W(J)
550 IF G<10 THEN PRINT
560 NEXT:PRINT
570 GOTO 180
600 PRINT
610 PRINT"CAN'T TAKE IT, HUH?"
620 PRINT:PRINT"WELL, MY CODE WAS ";
630 FOR J=1 TO 4
640 PRINT" .";
650 FOR K=1 TO 900:NEXT
660 NEXT J
670 PRINT C$:PRINT
680 GOTO 2090
```

Color Section

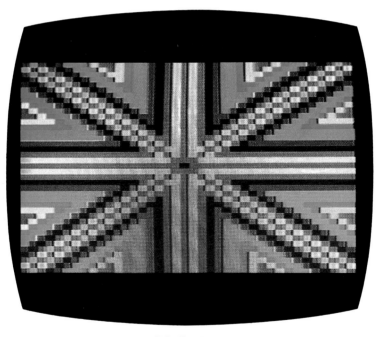

KALEIDO

GROAN

GROAN

GROAN

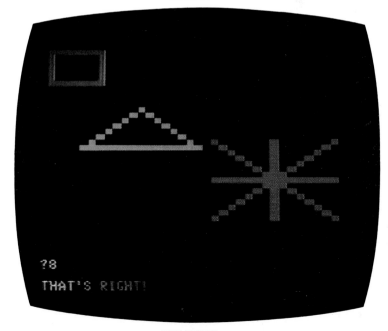

NUMBERS

SQUARES

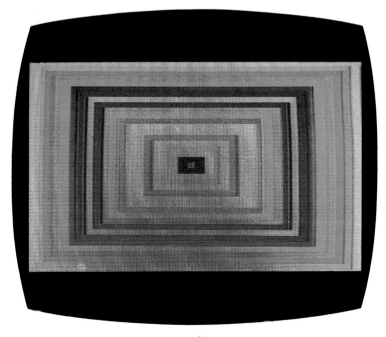

SQUARES

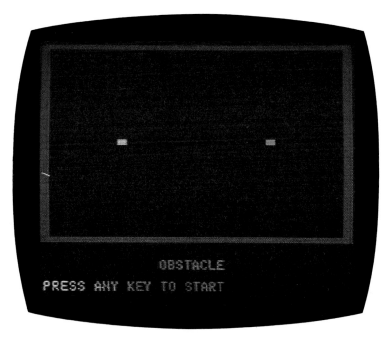

OBSTACLE

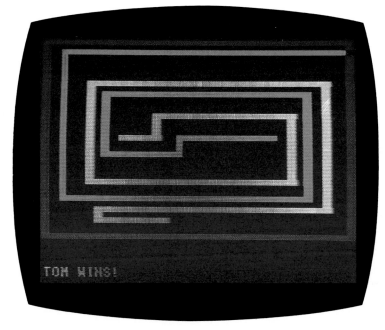

OBSTACLE

ROADRACE

ROADRACE

ROADRACE

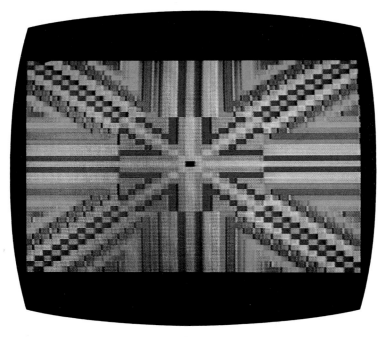

KALEIDO

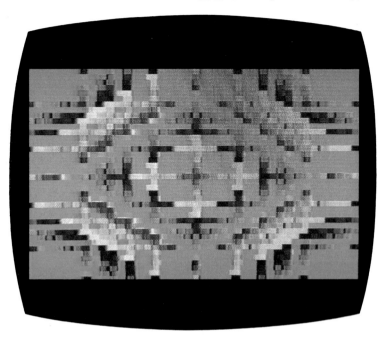

SPARKLE

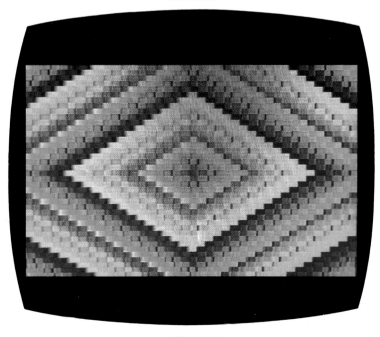

SPARKLE

```
700 K=0:IF LEN(A$)<>P THEN 780
710 FOR J=1 TO P
720 R=VAL(MID$(A$,J,1))
730 IF R<1 OR R>D THEN 780
740 NEXT
750 RETURN
780 PRINT"ILLEGAL.  TRY AGAIN."
790 K=1:RETURN
800 B=0:W=0
810 FOR J=1 TO P
820 G(J)=VAL(MID$(A$,J,1))
830 C(J)=VAL(MID$(C$,J,1))
840 IF G(J)=C(J) THEN B=B+1:G(J)=0:C(J)=0
850 NEXT
860 FOR J=1 TO P:IF C(J)=0 THEN 920
870 H=0:FOR K=1 TO P
880 IF C(J)=0 THEN 910
890 IF C(J)<>G(K) THEN 910
900 H=1:G(K)=0:C(J)=0
910 NEXT K:W=W+H
920 NEXT J
930 RETURN
1000 B(G)=B:W(G)=W:PRINT
1010 PRINT"GUESS NO.";G;" -- BLACK = ";B;"  WHITE = ";W
1020 PRINT:RETURN
1200 TEXT:HOME
1210 PRINT"**** DECODE ****"
1220 PRINT:PRINT
1230 PRINT"FIGURE OUT A ";P;" POSITION CODE"
1240 PRINT
1250 PRINT"USING THE DIGITS 1 THRU ";D
1260 PRINT:PRINT
1270 PRINT"´BLACK´ INDICATES A CORRECT DIGIT"
1280 PRINT:PRINT"IN THE RIGHT POSITION."
1290 PRINT
1300 PRINT"´WHITE´ INDICATES SOME OTHER CORRECT"
1310 PRINT
1320 PRINT"DIGIT, BUT IN THE WRONG POSITION."
1330 PRINT:PRINT
1340 J=256*PEEK(79)+PEEK(78)
1350 J=RND(-J):RETURN
2000 PRINT
2010 PRINT"YOU GOT IT IN ";G;" GUESSES."
2020 IF G<5 THEN B$="OUTSTANDING!"
2030 IF G=5 OR G=6 THEN B$="PRETTY GOOD"
```

```
2040 IF G=7 THEN B$="NOT BAD"
2050 IF G=8 THEN B$="NOT TOO GREAT"
2060 IF G>8 THEN B$="PRETTY BAD"
2070 PRINT:PRINT"...THAT'S ";B$
2080 PRINT
2090 INPUT"WANT TO TRY AGAIN? ";A$
2100 IF LEFT$(A$,1)="Y" THEN 150
2110 IF LEFT$(A$,1)<>"N" THEN 2090
2120 PRINT:PRINT"COWARD.":PRINT
2130 END
2200 PRINT
2210 PRINT"THAT'S YOUR LIMIT OF ";L;" GUESSES."
2220 PRINT
2230 PRINT"MY CODE WAS ";C$
2240 GOTO 2080
```

EASY CHANGES

1. Modify line 120 to change the complexity of the code and/or the number of guesses you are allowed. For example, the following line would allow fifteen guesses at a five-position code using the digits 1 through 8:

$$120\ D=8:P=5:L=15$$

The introduction will automatically reflect the new values for D and P. Be sure that neither D nor P is set greater than 9.

2. To change the program so that it will always display the "Summary" information after each guess automatically, replace line 280 with:

$$280\ GOTO\ 500$$

MAIN ROUTINES

120 - 170	Initializes variables. Displays introduction. Chooses secret code.
180 - 240	Gets a guess from operator. Analyzes reply. Displays result.
250	Determines if operator guessed correctly.
260 - 280	Saves guess. Adds one to guess-counter. Determines if limit on number of guesses was exceeded.
300 - 310	Subroutine to initialize variables.
370 - 430	Subroutine to choose secret code and inform operator.

500 - 570	Subroutine to display summary of guesses so far.
600 - 680	Subroutine to slowly display secret code when operator quits.
700 - 790	Subroutine to determine if operator's guess was legal.
800 - 930	Subroutine to determine number of black and white responses for the guess.
1000 - 1020	Subroutine to display number of black and white responses for the guess.
1200 - 1340	Subroutine to display title and introduction.
2000 - 2130	Subroutine to analyze operator's performance after correct answer is guessed and ask about playing again.
2200 - 2240	Subroutine to display secret code after operator exceeds limit of number of guesses.

MAIN VARIABLES

D	Number of possible digits in each position of the code (i.e., a digit from 1 to D).
P	Number of positions in the code.
L	Limit of number of guesses that can be made.
G$	Array in which guesses are saved.
G, C	Work arrays in which each guess is analyzed.
B, W	Arrays in which the number of black and white responses is saved for each guess.
R, H	Work variables.
G	Counter of the number of guesses made.
A$	Reply by the operator.
C$	Secret code chosen by the program.
J, K	Loop variables.
B, W	Number of black and white responses for this guess.
B$	String with message about operator's performance.

SUGGESTED PROJECTS

1. Change the analysis at the end of the game to take into account the difficulty of the code as well as the number of guesses it took to figure the code out. A four-position code using the digits 1 through 6 has 1296 possibilities, but a five-position code using 1 through 8 has 32,768 possibilities. Change lines 2020 through 2060 to determine the message to

be displayed based on the number of possibilities in the code as well as G.

2. At the beginning of the game, give the operator the option of deciding the complexity of the code. Ask for the number of positions and the number of digits. Make sure only "reasonable" numbers are used—do not try to create a code with zero positions, for example. Another approach is to ask the operator if he/she wants to play the easy, intermediate, or advanced version. Then set the values of D and P accordingly. Suggestions are:

Easy:	D=3 and P=3
Intermediate:	D=6 and P=4
Advanced:	D=8 and P=5

3. In addition to using the number of guesses to determine how well the operator did, keep track of the amount of time. This will require some logic to replace the INPUT in line 190. You'll have to build the A$ string one character at a time by doing PEEK (–16384) to see if a key has been pressed. By counting the number of times through the loop when no key was pressed, you can "time" the operator.

GROAN

PURPOSE

Do you like the thrills of fast-paced dice games? If so, GROAN is right up your alley. It is a two-person game with the computer playing directly against you. There is a considerable amount of luck involved. However, the skill of deciding when to pass the dice to your opponent also figures prominently.

The Apple will roll the dice for both players, but don't worry — it will not cheat. (We wouldn't think of stooping to such depths.)

Why is the game called GROAN? You will know soon after playing it.

HOW TO USE IT

The game uses two dice. They are just like regular six-sided dice except for one thing. The die face where the "1" would normally be has a picture of a frowning face instead. The other five faces of each die have the usual numbers two through six on them.

The object is to be the first player to achieve a score agreed upon before the start of the game. Players alternate taking turns. A turn consists of a series of dice rolls (at least one roll, possibly several) subject to the following rules.

As long as no frown appears on either die, the roller builds a running score for this current series of rolls. After each roll with no frown, he has the choice of rolling again or passing the dice to his opponent. If he passes the dice, his score achieved on the current series is added to any previous total he may have had.

But if he rolls and a frown appears, he will be groaning. A frown on only one die cancels any score achieved for the current series of rolls. Any previous score is retained in this case. However, if he rolls a double frown, his entire previous total is wiped out as well as his current total. Thus, he reverts back to a total score of zero — true despair.

The program begins by asking what the winning score should be. Values between 50 and 100 tend to produce the best games, but any positive value is acceptable. Next, a simulated coin toss randomly decides who will get the first roll.

Each dice roll is portrayed with a short graphics display. The dice are shown rolling and then the outcome is displayed pictorially. During each roll, the Apple indicates who is rolling.

Each roll is followed by a display of the scoreboard. This scoreboard gives all relevant information: score needed to win, both players' scores before the current series of rolls, and the total score for the current series.

If a frown should appear on a die, the scoreboard will indicate the current running total as zero. In addition, the previous total will become zero in the case of the dreaded double frown. In either case, the dice will be passed automatically to the next player.

If a scoring roll results, the roller must decide whether to roll again or to pass the dice. The program has a built-in strategy to decide this for the Apple. For you, the question will be asked after the scoreboard is displayed. The two legal replies are P and R. The R means that you wish to roll again. The P means that you choose to pass the dice to the computer. If you should score enough to win, you must still pass the dice to add the current series to your previous total.

The first player to pass the dice with a score greater than or equal to the winning score is the victor. This will surely cause his opponent to GROAN. The computer will acknowledge the winner before signing off.

SAMPLE RUN

The operator has decided to challenge the Apple to a 75-point game of GROAN. See color section.

The computer wins the coin toss and gets the first dice roll. See color section.

The computer's roll, however, results in a three and a "groan." This scores no points and the dice pass to the operator. See color section.

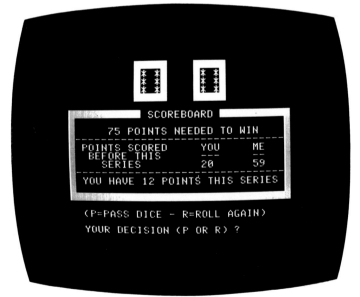

Much later in the same game, the operator rolls a 12 to start a series of rolls. The score was Apple-59, operator-20 before the roll. The operator must now decide whether to pass the dice or risk rolling again.

PROGRAM LISTING

```
100 REM: GROAN
110 REM: COPYRIGHT 1980 BY PHIL FELDMAN AND TOM RUGG
150 A=0:H=0:T=0:B$=CHR$(32)
160 C$="*":BZ=-16336:Q=PEEK(78)+256*PEEK(79):Q=RND(-Q)
200 GR:HOME:GOSUB 2080:COLOR=C
210 XS=6:YS=2
220 GOSUB 2100:GOSUB 2200:DL=250:GOSUB 2050:GOSUB 2150
230 HOME:PRINT"HOW MUCH NEEDED TO WIN":PRINT
240 INPUT"(BETWEEN 50-100 IS BEST) ? ";W
250 W=INT(W):IF W<=0 THEN 230
260 GOSUB 2080:GOSUB 2500
270 IF Q>0.5 THEN 500
300 T=0
310 GOSUB 2700:T=T+R1+R2:IF F>0 THEN T=0
320 IF F=2 THEN H=0
330 GR:HOME:PRINT:PRINT TAB(13);"YOU'RE ROLLING"
340 P$="YOU":GOSUB 3200
350 IF F>0 THEN P$="ME":GOSUB 1560:DL=4000:GOSUB 2050:
    GOTO 500
360 GOSUB 1300:IF Q$="R" THEN 310
370 H=H+T:IF H>=W THEN 900
500 T=0
510 GR:HOME:GOSUB 2700
520 T=T+R1+R2:IF F>0 THEN T=0
530 IF F=2 THEN A=0
540 PRINT:PRINT TAB(15);"I'M ROLLING"
550 P$="I":GOSUB 3200
560 IF F>0 THEN P$="YOU":GOSUB 1560:DL=4000:GOSUB 2050:
    GOTO 300
570 HTAB XS:VTAB YS:GOSUB 5000
580 IF AD=1 THEN PRINT"I'LL ROLL AGAIN":DL=3500:GOSUB
    2050:GOTO 510
590 PRINT"I'LL STOP WITH THIS":A=A+T
600 IF A>=W THEN DL=3500:GOSUB 2050:GOTO 900
610 YS=YS+2:P$="YOU":GOSUB 1560:DL=3500:GOSUB 2050:GOTO
    300
900 XS=4:YS=2:HOME:P$="WE":T=0:GOSUB 1010
910 VTAB 16:HTAB 6:IF A>=W THEN PRINT
    "I WIN -- SKILL TRIUMPHS AGAIN"
920 IF H>=W THEN PRINT"YOU WIN -- IT WAS SHEER LUCK"
930 IF A>=W THEN GOSUB 2110
940 IF H>=W THEN BL=250:GOSUB 2000
950 VTAB 22:END
```

```
1000 TEXT:HOME:XS=4:YS=9
1010 VTAB YS:HTAB XS:INVERSE
1020 FOR J=1 TO 11:PRINT B$;:NEXT
1030 NORMAL:PRINT" SCOREBOARD ";:INVERSE
1040 FOR J=1 TO 11:PRINT B$;:NEXT
1050 FOR Y=YS TO YS+10:HTAB XS:VTAB Y:PRINT B$;
1060 HTAB XS+33:PRINT B$;:NEXT
1070 HTAB XS:FOR J=1 TO 34:PRINT B$;:NEXT
1080 NORMAL:HTAB XS+6:VTAB YS+2
1090 PRINT W;" POINTS NEEDED TO WIN";
1100 HTAB XS+1:VTAB YS+3:FOR J=1 TO 32
1110 PRINT"-";:NEXT
1120 HTAB XS+2:VTAB YS+4
1130 PRINT"POINTS SCORED     YOU     ME";
1140 HTAB XS+3:VTAB YS+5
1150 PRINT"BEFORE THIS       ---     --";
1160 HTAB XS+5:VTAB YS+6
1170 PRINT"SERIES";:HTAB XS+20:PRINT H;
1180 HTAB XS+28:PRINT A;
1190 HTAB XS+1:VTAB YS+7:FOR J=1 TO 32
1200 PRINT"-";:NEXT:HTAB XS+2:VTAB YS+8
1210 PRINT P$;" HAVE ";T;" POINTS THIS SERIES";
1220 NORMAL:RETURN
1300 HTAB XS:VTAB YS
1310 PRINT"(P=PASS DICE - R=ROLL AGAIN)"
1320 PRINT:HTAB XS
1330 PRINT"YOUR DECISION (P OR R) ?";:Q=POS(0)
1340 HTAB Q:GET Q$
1350 IF Q$="P" THEN RETURN
1360 IF Q$="R" THEN RETURN
1370 GOTO 1340
1400 INVERSE:FOR Y=YS-2 TO YS+2 STEP 4
1410 FOR X=XS-2 TO XS+2:GOSUB 1500:NEXT
1420 FOR X=XS+7 TO XS+11:GOSUB 1500:NEXT:NEXT
1430 FOR X=XS-2 TO XS+2 STEP 4
1440 FOR Y=YS-2 TO YS+2:GOSUB 1500:NEXT:NEXT
1450 FOR X=XS+19 TO XS+23 STEP 4:FOR Y=YS-6 TO YS-2
1460 FOR X=XS+7 TO XS+11 STEP 4:FOR Y=YS-2 TO YS+2
1470 GOSUB 1500:NEXT:NEXT:NORMAL:RETURN
1500 HTAB X:VTAB Y:PRINT B$;:RETURN
1520 HTAB X:VTAB Y:PRINT"G R O A N";:RETURN
1540 HTAB X:VTAB Y:PRINT"D E S P A I R !";:RETURN
1560 HTAB XS:VTAB YS:PRINT"DICE PASS TO ";P$:RETURN
1600 HTAB XS:VTAB YS:PRINT C$;:RETURN
1610 HTAB XS-1:VTAB YS-1:PRINT C$;
```

```
1620 HTAB XS+1:VTAB YS+1:PRINT C$;:RETURN
1630 GOSUB 1600:GOSUB 1610:RETURN
1640 HTAB XS+1:VTAB YS-1:PRINT C$;
1650 HTAB XS-1:VTAB YS+1:PRINT C$;:GOSUB 1610:RETURN
1660 GOSUB 1600:GOSUB 1640:RETURN
1670 HTAB XS-1:VTAB YS:PRINT C$;:HTAB XS+1
1680 PRINT C$;:GOSUB 1640:RETURN
1700 HTAB XS-1:VTAB YS-1:PRINT"@ @";
1710 HTAB XS:VTAB YS:PRINT"↑";
1720 HTAB XS-1:VTAB YS+1
1730 PRINT"∠∠";:RETURN
1800 LX=XS-L:RX=XS+L:UY=YS-L:LY=YS+L
1810 HLIN LX,RX AT UY:HLIN LX,RX AT LY
1820 VLIN UY,LY AT LX:VLIN UY,LY AT RX:RETURN
1900 PLOT XS,YS:RETURN
1910 PLOT XS-4,YS-5:PLOT XS+4,YS+5:RETURN
1920 GOSUB 1900:GOSUB 1910:RETURN
1930 PLOT XS-4,YS+5:PLOT XS+4,YS-5:GOSUB 1910:RETURN
1940 GOSUB 1900:GOSUB 1930:RETURN
1950 PLOT XS-4,YS:PLOT XS+4,YS:GOSUB 1930:RETURN
1960 GOSUB 1940:FOR J=1 TO 3
1970 PLOT XS-J-1,YS+J+2:PLOT XS+J+1,YS+J+2
1980 NEXT:PLOT XS-1,YS+3:PLOT XS,YS+3:PLOT XS+1,YS+3
1990 RETURN
2000 FOR J=1 TO BL:Q=PEEK(BZ):NEXT:RETURN
2050 FOR J=1 TO DL:NEXT:RETURN
2080 C=RND(1)*14+2:RETURN
2100 BL=120:GOSUB 2000:DL=100:GOSUB 2050
2110 BL=40:DL=40
2120 FOR K=1 TO 2:GOSUB 2050:GOSUB 2000
2130 NEXT:DL=60:BL=70:GOSUB 2050:GOSUB 2000
2140 RETURN
2150 BL=200:GOSUB 2000:RETURN
2200 HLIN XS,XS+3 AT YS:VLIN YS,YS+4 AT XS
2210 HLIN XS,XS+3 AT YS+4:VLIN YS+2,YS+4 AT XS+3
2220 PLOT XS+2,YS+2:VLIN YS,YS+4 AT XS+6
2230 HLIN XS+6,XS+9 AT YS:HLIN XS+6,XS+9 AT YS+2
2240 PLOT XS+9,YS+1:PLOT XS+8,YS+3
2250 PLOT XS+9,YS+4:HLIN XS+12,XS+15 AT YS
2260 HLIN XS+12,XS+15 AT YS+4:VLIN YS,YS+4 AT XS+12
2270 VLIN YS,YS+4 AT XS+15:VLIN YS,YS+4 AT XS+18
2280 VLIN YS,YS+4 AT XS+21:HLIN XS+18,XS+21 AT YS
2290 HLIN XS+18,XS+21 AT YS+2:VLIN YS,YS+4 AT XS+24
2300 VLIN YS,YS+4 AT XS+27:VLIN YS,YS+2 AT XS+25
2310 VLIN YS+2,YS+4 AT XS+26:RETURN
```

```
2500 DL=25:X=20:Y=33
2510 HOME:PRINT"AND NOW A COIN TOSS FOR FIRST ROLL"
2520 PRINT:PRINT"THE COIN IS IN THE AIR AND . . . ."
2530 Y=Y-1:COLOR=C:GOSUB 2650:GOSUB 2050
2540 COLOR=0:GOSUB 2650:COLOR=C:GOSUB 2660:GOSUB 2050
2550 COLOR=0:GOSUB 2660:IF Y>9 THEN 2530
2560 Y=Y+1:COLOR=C:GOSUB 2650:GOSUB 2050
2570 COLOR=0:GOSUB 2650:COLOR=C:GOSUB 2660:GOSUB 2050
2580 COLOR=0:GOSUB 2660:IF Y<33 THEN 2560
2590 COLOR=C:Y=33:GOSUB 2650:BL=50:GOSUB 2000
2600 Q=RND(1):Q$="YOU":IF Q>.5 THEN Q$="I"
2610 HOME:PRINT
2620 PRINT B$;B$;Q$;B$;"GET FIRST ROLL"
2630 DL=3000:GOSUB 2050:RETURN
2650 HLIN X-2,X+2 AT Y:RETURN
2660 VLIN Y-2,Y+2 AT X:RETURN
2700 R1=INT(RND(1)*6+1):R2=INT(RND(1)*6+1)
2710 F=0:IF R1=1 THEN F=1
2720 IF R2=1 THEN F=F+1
2730 RETURN
2800 FOR J=0 TO 14:L=J/2
2810 XS=9:YS=8+J:COLOR=C:GOSUB 1800
2820 XS=30:GOSUB 1800:COLOR=0:XS=9:GOSUB 1800
2830 XS=30:GOSUB 1800:NEXT
2840 COLOR=C:XS=9:GOSUB 1800
2850 XS=30:GOSUB 1800:RETURN
3000 XS=16:YS=5:GOSUB 1400:Q=R1:GOSUB 3100
3010 XS=25:Q=R2:GOSUB 3100
3020 IF R1=1 THEN X=4:Y=YS:GOSUB 1520
3030 IF R2=1 THEN X=29:Y=YS:GOSUB 1520
3040 IF F>0 THEN GOSUB 2150
3050 IF F<2 THEN RETURN
3060 DL=400:GOSUB 2050:GOSUB 2100:DL=800:GOSUB 2050
3070 X=14:Y=1:GOSUB 1540:GOSUB 2150:RETURN
3100 ON Q GOSUB 1700,1610,1630,1640,1660,1670:RETURN
3200 GOSUB 2080:GOSUB 2800:XS=9:YS=22:Q=R1:GOSUB 3250
3210 XS=30:Q=R2:GOSUB 3250:GOSUB 2080:COLOR=C:XS=6
3220 YS=2:IF F>0 THEN GOSUB 2200:GOSUB 2150:GOTO 3240
3230 DL=1000:GOSUB 2050
3240 GOSUB 1000:GOSUB 3000:XS=6:YS=21:RETURN
3250 ON Q GOSUB 1960,1910,1920,1930,1940,1950:RETURN
5000 V=A+T:IF V>=W THEN 5100
5010 IF (W-H)<10 THEN 5110
5020 IF A>=H THEN CT=T/25:GOTO 5050
5030 IF V<H THEN CT=T/35:GOTO 5050
```

```
5040 CT=T/30
5050 IF RND(1)>CT THEN 5110
5100 AD=0:RETURN
5110 AD=1:RETURN
```

EASY CHANGES

1. If you wish to set the program for a fixed value of the winning score, it can be done by changing line 230 and deleting line 240. Simply set W to the winning score desired. For example:

   230 W= 100: HOME

   would make the winning score 100. Don't forget to delete line 240.
2. The rolling dice graphics display before each roll can be eliminated by deleting lines 2810, 2820, 2830, 2840 and changing lines 2800 and 2850 as follows:

   2800 YS=22:L=7:COLOR=C
   2850 XS=9:GOSUB 1800:XS=30:GOSUB 1800:RETURN

   This has the effect of speeding up the game by showing each dice roll immediately.
3. After you play the game a few times, you may wish to change the "pacing" of the game; i.e. the time delays between various messages, etc. To speed up the game try:

   2050 DL=DL/2:FOR J=1 TO DL:NEXT
   2055 DL=2*DL:RETURN

   To slow down the pacing, try:

   2050 DL=2*DL:FOR J=1 TO DL:NEXT
   2055 DL=DL/2:RETURN

4. Colors are selected randomly throughout the program. If you wish a particular color, say orange, for your dice and another color, say pink, for the Apple's dice, make these changes:

   2080 C=RND(1)*14+2
   2082 IF P$="YOU" THEN C=9
   2084 IF P$="I" THEN C=11
   2086 RETURN

   You can, of course, select any of the fifteen available colors as described in your Applesoft manual under the COLOR=

command. Your color is selected in statement 2082 and the
computer's in statement 2084.
5. As currently written, the program will not quite fit in a 16K
   Apple using cassette Applesoft (see Appendix 1). However,
   it can be made to squeeze into this system configuration by:
   implementing Easy Change #2 above; deleting lines 2210
   through 2310; deleting lines 2540 through 2590; and adding

> 2200 RETURN
> 2500 REM
> 2530 DL=4000:GOSUB 2050

These changes remove some of the program's fancy effects
but do not materially change the performance of the game.

MAIN ROUTINES

150 - 160	Initializes constants.
200 - 270	Initial displays. Gets winning score.
300 - 370	Human rolls.
500 - 610	Apple rolls.
900 - 950	Ending messages.
1000 - 1220	Displays scoreboard.
1300 - 1370	Asks user for re-roll decision.
1400 - 1470	Draws scoreboard dice outline.
1500 - 1560	Subroutines to print various messages.
1600 - 1730	Draws scoreboard dice faces.
1800 - 1820	Draws graphics dice outline.
1900 - 1990	Draws graphics dice faces.
2000 - 2150	Delay loops and buzzer tone control loops.
2200 - 2310	Draws graphics "groan."
2500 - 2660	Performs coin toss.
2700 - 2730	Determines dice roll.
2800 - 2850	Controls graphics dice rolling.
3000 - 3100	Controls scoreboard display.
3200 - 3250	Subroutine to control scoreboard and dice faces.
5000 - 5110	Apple's strategy. Sets AD=0 to stop rolling or AD=1 to continue rolling.

MAIN VARIABLES

A	Previous score of Apple.
H	Previous score of human.
T	Score of current series of rolls.

B$	String of one blank character.
C$	String of one asterisk.
BZ	Peek argument for tone generation.
C	Graphics color.
XS,YS	Horizontal, vertical reference print position.
W	Amount needed to win.
Q	Work variable.
R1,R2	Outcome of roll for die 1, die 2.
F	Result of roll (0=no frown, 1=one frown, 2=double frown).
DL	Delay length.
BL	Buzzer length (length of tone generation).
P$	String name of current roller.
Q$	Work string variable.
AD	Apple strategy flag (0=stop rolling, 1=roll again).
J,K	Loop indices.
X,Y	Horizontal, vertical print position.
L	Half length of a die side.
LX,RX	Left, right position of a die face.
UY,LY	Upper, lower position of a die face.
V	Score Apple would have if it passed the dice.
CT	Cutoff threshold used in Apple's built-in strategy.

SUGGESTED PROJECTS

1. The computer's built-in strategy is contained from line 5000 on. Remember, after a no-frown roll, the Apple must decide whether or not to continue rolling. See if you can improve on the current strategy. You may use, but not modify, the variables A, T, H, and W. The variable AD must be set before returning. Set AD=0 to mean the Apple passes the dice or AD=1 to mean the Apple will roll again.
2. Ask the operator for his/her name. Then personalize the messages and scoreboard more.
3. Dig into the workings of the graphics routines connected with the dice rolling. Then modify them to produce new, perhaps more realistic, effects.

JOT

PURPOSE

JOT is a two-player word game involving considerable mental deduction. The Apple will play against you. But be careful! You will find your computer quite a formidable opponent.

The rules of JOT are fairly simple. The game is played entirely with three-letter words. All letters of each word must be distinct—no repeats. (See the section on Easy Changes for further criteria used in defining legal words.)

To begin the game, each player chooses a secret word. The remainder of the game involves trying to be the first player to deduce the other's secret word.

The players take turns making guesses at their opponent's word. After each guess, the asker is told how many letters (or hits) his guess had in common with his opponent's secret word. The position of the letters in the word does not matter. For example, if the secret word was "own," a guess of "who" would have two hits. The winner is the first person to correctly guess his opponent's secret word.

HOW TO USE IT

The program begins with some introductory messages while asking you to think of your secret word. It then asks whether or not you wish to make the first guess. This is followed by you and the Apple alternating guesses at each other's secret word.

After the computer guesses, it will immediately ask you how it did. Possible replies are **0, 1, 2, 3,** or **R**. The response of **R** (for right) means the Apple has just guessed your word correctly—a truly humbling experience. The numerical replies indicate that the word guessed by the Apple had that number of hits in your secret word. A response of 3 means that all the letters were correct, but they need to be rearranged to form the actual secret word (e.g. a guess of "EAT" with the secret word being "TEA").

After learning how it did, the computer will take some time to process its new information. If this time is not trivial, the Apple will display the message: "I'M THINKING" so you do not suspect it of idle daydreaming. If it finds an inconsistency in its information, it will ask you for your secret word and then analyze what went wrong.

When it is your turn to guess, there are two special replies you can make. These are the single letters S and Q. The S, for summary, will display a table of all previous guesses and corresponding hits. This is useful as a concise look at all available information. It will then prompt you again for your next guess. The Q, for quit, will simply terminate the game.

When not making one of these special replies, you will input a guess at the computer's secret word. This will be, of course, a three-letter word. If the word used is not legal, the computer will so inform you. After a legal guess, you will be told how many hits your guess had. If you correctly guess the computer's word, you will be duly congratulated. The Apple will then ask you for your secret word and verify that all is on the "up and up."

SAMPLE RUN

                    JOT

    JUST A MOMENT PLEASE.....

    THANKS, NOW LET'S EACH THINK
    OF OUR SECRET WORD

    (THIS TAKES ME A WHILE...)

    I'VE ALMOST GOT IT...

```
OK, DO YOU WANT TO GO FIRST? NO

MY GUESS IS -- NIP
HOW DID I DO (0-3 OR R)? 1

I'M THINKING...

YOUR GUESS (OR S OR Q)? DOG
# OF HITS IS 1

MY GUESS IS -- NOR
HOW DID I DO (0-3 OR R)? O

I'M THINKING...
                    .
                    .
                    .
        (later in the same game)
                    .
                    .
                    .
YOUR GUESS (OR S OR Q)? S

-------------------------------------
YOUR  GUESSES    SUMMARY    MY GUESSES
WORD    HITS                WORD  HITS
 DOG     1          1       NIP    1
 CAT     0          2       NOR    0
 LIP     0          3       DIG    0
 SON     0          4       PUT    2
                    5       PUB    1

YOUR GUESS (OR S OR Q)? FED
# OF HITS IS 2

MY GUESS IS -- PET
HOW DID I DO (0-3 OR R)? R

IT SURE FEELS GOOD

MY WORD WAS - WED

HOW ABOUT ANOTHER GAME? NO
```

PROGRAM LISTING

```
100 REM: JOT
110 REM: COPYRIGHT 1980 BY PHIL FELDMAN AND TOM RUGG
150 M=25:N=406
160 DIM A$(N)
170 DIM G1$(M),G2$(M),H1(M),H2(M)
200 G1=0:G2=0
210 L=N:Q=PEEK(78)+256*PEEK(79):Q=RND(-Q)
250 TEXT:HOME:PRINT TAB(17);"J O T":PRINT
260 PRINT"JUST A MOMENT PLEASE .....":GOSUB 3000:Q=RND(
    1)*N+1:PRINT
270 PRINT"THANKS, NOW LET'S EACH THINK":PRINT
    "OF OUR SECRET WORD"
280 PRINT:PRINT"(THIS TAKES ME A WHILE ...)"
290 GOSUB 2200:M$=A$(Q):PRINT:PRINT"OK, ";
300 INPUT"DO YOU WANT TO GO FIRST? ";Q$
310 Q$=LEFT$(Q$,1):IF Q$="N" THEN 600
320 IF Q$="Y" THEN 500
330 PRINT:PRINT"YES OR NO PLEASE":PRINT:GOTO 300
500 PRINT:INPUT"YOUR GUESS (OR S OR Q)? ";P$:IF P$="S"
    THEN GOSUB 1000:GOTO 500
510 IF P$="Q" THEN 1200
520 IF P$=M$ THEN G1=G1+1:G1$(G1)=P$:H1(G1)=9:GOTO 3400
530 GOSUB 1800:IF F=0 THEN PRINT
    "THAT'S NOT A LEGAL WORD -- TRY AGAIN":GOTO 500
540 Q$=M$:GOSUB 2600:Q$=P$:GOSUB 1500
550 PRINT"# OF HITS IS ";Q
560 G1=G1+1:G1$(G1)=Q$:H1(G1)=Q
570 IF G1=M THEN 3600
600 Q$=A$(L):G2=G2+1:G2$(G2)=Q$
610 PRINT:PRINT"MY GUESS IS -- ";Q$
620 INPUT"HOW DID I DO (0-3 OR R)? ";P$
630 P$=LEFT$(P$,1)
640 IF P$="R" THEN H2(G2)=9:GOTO 3200
650 P=VAL(P$):IF P>3 OR (P=0 AND P$<>"0") THEN PRINT
    "BAD ANSWER":GOTO 610
660 IF L>100 THEN PRINT:PRINT"I'M THINKING ..."
670 H2(G2)=P:GOSUB 800
680 GOTO 500
800 Q$=G2$(G2):H=H2(G2):J=0:GOSUB 2600:L=L-1:IF L<1
    THEN 900
810 J=J+1:IF J>L THEN 870
820 Q$=A$(J):GOSUB 1500
830 IF Q=H THEN 810
```

```
840 A=J:B=L:GOSUB 2400:L=L-1
850 IF L<1 THEN 900
860 IF L>=J THEN 820
870 RETURN
900 PRINT:PRINT"SOMETHING'S WRONG !!"
910 PRINT:INPUT"WHAT'S YOUR SECRET WORD? ";P$:GOSUB
    1800
920 IF F=0 THEN PRINT:PRINT
    "ILLEGAL WORD -- I NEVER HAD A CHANCE":GOTO 1200
930 PRINT:PRINT"YOU GAVE A BAD ANSWER SOMEWHERE --"
940 PRINT"CHECK THE SUMMARY":GOSUB 1000
950 GOTO 1200
1000 PRINT:Q=G1:IF G2>G1 THEN Q=G2
1010 IF Q=0 THEN PRINT"NO GUESSES YET":RETURN
1020 PRINT TAB(1);:FOR J=1 TO 37:PRINT"-";:NEXT:PRINT"-"
1030 PRINT TAB(1);:INVERSE:PRINT"YOUR GUESSES";:NORMAL
1040 PRINT"     SUMMARY      ";:INVERSE
1050 PRINT"MY GUESSES":NORMAL:PRINT TAB(1);
1060 PRINT"WORD   HITS";TAB(29);"WORD   HITS"
1070 FOR J=1 TO Q:K=1:IF J>9 THEN K=0
1080 IF J>G1 THEN PRINT TAB(19+K);J;TAB(30);G2$(J);
     TAB(36);H2(J):GOTO 1110
1090 IF J>G2 THEN PRINT TAB(2);G1$(J);TAB(9);H1(J);
     TAB(19+K);J:GOTO 1110
1100 PRINT TAB(2);G1$(J);TAB(9);H1(J);TAB(19+K);J;
     TAB(30);G2$(J);TAB(36);H2(J)
1110 NEXT:RETURN
1200 PRINT:INPUT"HOW ABOUT ANOTHER GAME? ";Q$
1210 Q$=LEFT$(Q$,1):IF Q$="Y" THEN 200
1220 IF Q$="N" THEN END
1230 PRINT:PRINT"YES OR NO PLEASE":GOTO 1200
1500 P$=LEFT$(Q$,1):Q=0:GOSUB 1600
1510 P$=MID$(Q$,2,1):GOSUB 1600
1520 P$=RIGHT$(Q$,1):GOSUB 1600:RETURN
1600 IF P$=M1$ OR P$=M2$ OR P$=M3$ THEN Q=Q+1
1610 RETURN
1800 F=0
1810 FOR J=1 TO N
1820 IF A$(J)=P$ THEN F=1:RETURN
1830 NEXT:RETURN
2200 FOR A=N TO 100 STEP -1:B=INT(RND(1)*A)+1
2210 GOSUB 2400:NEXT
2220 PRINT:PRINT"I'VE ALMOST GOT IT ..."
2230 FOR A=99 TO 2 STEP -1:B=INT(RND(1)*A)+1
2240 GOSUB 2400:NEXT:RETURN
```

```
2400 Q$=A$(B):A$(B)=A$(A):A$(A)=Q$:RETURN
2600 M1$=LEFT$(Q$,1):M2$=MID$(Q$,2,1)
2610 M3$=RIGHT$(Q$,1):RETURN
3000 RESTORE:FOR P=1 TO N:READ A$(P):NEXT:RETURN
3200 PRINT:PRINT"IT SURE FEELS GOOD"
3210 PRINT:PRINT"MY WORD WAS -- ";M$
3220 GOTO 1200
3400 PRINT:PRINT"CONGRATULATIONS - THAT WAS IT":PRINT
3410 INPUT"WHAT WAS YOUR WORD? ";P$:GOSUB 1800:J=1
3420 IF F=0 THEN PRINT:PRINT
     "ILLEGAL WORD - I HAD NO CHANCE":GOTO 1200
3430 IF A$(J)=P$ THEN PRINT:PRINT"NICE WORD":GOTO 1200
3440 J=J+1:IF J<=L THEN 3430
3450 PRINT:PRINT"YOU MADE AN ERROR SOMEWHERE":PRINT
     "-- CHECK THE SUMMARY"
3460 GOSUB 1000:GOTO 1200
3600 PRINT:PRINT"SORRY, I'M OUT OF MEMORY":PRINT
3610 PRINT"MY WORD WAS - ";M$:GOTO 1200
5000 DATA  ACE,ACT,ADE,ADO,ADS,AFT,AGE
5010 DATA  AGO,AID,AIL,AIM,AIR,ALE,ALP
5020 DATA  AND,ANT,ANY,APE,APT,ARC,ARE
5030 DATA  ARK,ARM,ART,ASH,ASK,ASP,ATE
5040 DATA  AWE,AWL,AXE,AYE,BAD,BAG,BAN
5050 DATA  BAR,BAT,BAY,BED,BEG,BET,BID
5060 DATA  BIG,BIN,BIT,BOA,BOG,BOW,BOX
5070 DATA  BOY,BUD,BUG,BUM,BUN,BUS,BUT
5080 DATA  BUY,BYE,CAB,CAD,CAM,CAN,CAP
5090 DATA  CAR,CAT,COB,COD,COG,CON,COP
5100 DATA  COT,COW,COY,CRY,CUB,CUD,CUE
5110 DATA  CUP,CUR,CUT,DAB,DAM,DAY,DEN
5120 DATA  DEW,DIE,DIG,DIM,DIN,DIP,DOE
5130 DATA  DOG,DON,DOT,DRY,DUB,DUE,DUG
5140 DATA  DYE,DUO,EAR,EAT,EGO,ELK,ELM
5150 DATA  END,ELF,ERA,FAD,FAG,FAN,FAR
5160 DATA  FAT,FED,FEW,FIG,FIN,FIR,FIT
5170 DATA  FIX,FLY,FOE,FOG,FOR,FOX,FRY
5180 DATA  FUN,FUR,GAP,GAS,GAY,GEM,GET
5190 DATA  GIN,GNU,GOB,GOD,GOT,GUM,GUN
5200 DATA  GUT,GUY,GYP,HAD,HAG,HAM,HAS
5210 DATA  HAT,HAY,HEN,HEX,HID,HIM,HIP
5220 DATA  HIS,HIT,HER,HEM,HOE,HOG,HOP
5230 DATA  HOT,HOW,HUB,HUE,HUG,HUM,HUT
5240 DATA  ICE,ICY,ILK,INK,IMP,ION,IRE
5250 DATA  IRK,ITS,IVY,JAB,JAR,JAW,JAY
5260 DATA  JOB,JOG,JOT,JOY,JUG,JAG,JAM
```

```
5270 DATA  JET,JIB,JIG,JUT,KEG,KEY,KID
5280 DATA  KIN,KIT,LAB,LAD,LAG,LAP,LAW
5290 DATA  LAY,LAX,LED,LEG,LET,LID,LIE
5300 DATA  LIP,LIT,LOB,LOG,LOP,LOT,LOW
5310 DATA  LYE,MAD,MAN,MAP,MAR,MAT,MAY
5320 DATA  MEN,MET,MID,MOB,MOP,MOW,MUD
5330 DATA  MIX,MUG,NAB,NAG,NAP,NAY,NET
5340 DATA  NEW,NIL,NIP,NOD,NOT,NOR,NOW
5350 DATA  NUT,OAF,OAK,OAR,OAT,ODE,OIL
5360 DATA  OLD,ONE,OPT,ORE,OUR,OUT,OVA
5370 DATA  OWE,OWL,OWN,PAD,PAL,PAN,PAR
5380 DATA  PAT,PAW,PAY,PEA,PEG,PEN,PET
5390 DATA  PEW,PIE,PIG,PIT,PLY,POD,POT
5400 DATA  POX,PER,PIN,PRO,PRY,PUB,PUN
5410 DATA  PUS,PUT,RAG,RAM,RAN,RAP,RAT
5420 DATA  RAW,RAY,RED,RIB,RID,REV,RIG
5430 DATA  RIM,RIP,ROB,ROD,ROE,ROT,ROW
5440 DATA  RUB,RUE,RUG,RUM,RUN,RUT,RYE
5450 DATA  SAD,SAG,SAP,SAT,SAW,SAY,SET
5460 DATA  SEW,SEX,SHY,SEA,SIN,SHE,SIP
5470 DATA  SIR,SIT,SIX,SKI,SKY,SLY,SOB
5480 DATA  SOD,SON,SOW,SOY,SPA,SPY,STY
5490 DATA  SUE,SUM,SUN,TAB,TAD,TAG,TAN
5500 DATA  TAP,TAX,TAR,TEA,TEN,THE,THY
5510 DATA  TIC,TIE,TIN,TIP,TOE,TON,TOP
5520 DATA  TOW,TOY,TRY,TUB,TUG,TWO,URN
5530 DATA  USE,UPS,VAN,VAT,VEX,VIA,VIE
5540 DATA  VIM,VOW,YAK,YAM,YEN,YES,YET
5550 DATA  YOU,WAD,WAG,WAN,WAR,WAS,WAX
5560 DATA  WAY,WEB,WED,WET,WHO,WHY,WIG
5570 DATA  WIN,WIT,WOE,WON,WRY,ZIP,FIB
```

EASY CHANGES

1. It is fairly common for players to request a summary before most guesses that they make. If you want the program to automatically provide a summary before each guess, change line 500 to read:

> 500 GOSUB 1000:PRINT:INPUT
> "YOUR GUESS (OR Q)?";P$

2. The maximum number of guesses allowed, M, can be changed in line 150. You may wish to increase it in conjunction with

Suggested Project 2. You might decrease it to free some memory needed for other program additions. The current value of 25 is somewhat larger than necessary. An actual game almost never goes beyond 15 guesses. To set M to 15, change line 150 to read

150 M=15:N=406

3. Modifying the data list of legal words is fairly easy. Our criteria for legal words were as follows: they must have three distinct letters and *not* be

  – capitalized
  – abbreviations
  – interjections (like "ugh", "hey", etc.)
  – specialized words (like "ohm", "sac", "yaw", etc.)

In line 150, N is set to be the total number of words in the data list. The data list itself is from line 5000 on.

To add word(s), do the following. Enter them in data statements after the current data (use line numbers larger than 5570). Then redefine the value of N to be 406 plus the number of new words added. For example, to add the words "ohm" and "yaw" into the list, change line 150 to read

150 M=25:N=408

and add a new line

5580 DATA OHM,YAW

To delete word(s), the opposite must be done. Remove the words from the appropriate data statement(s) and decrease the value of N accordingly.

MAIN ROUTINES

150 - 170	Dimensions arrays.
200 - 330	Initializes new game.
500 - 570	Human guesses at the computer's word.
600 - 680	Apple guesses.
800 - 870	Evaluates human's possible secret words. Moves them to the front of A$ array.
900 - 950	Processes inconsistency in given information.
1000 - 1110	Displays the current summary table.
1200 - 1230	Inquires about another game.

1500 - 1610   Compares a guess with key word.
1800 - 1830   Checks if input word is legal.
2200 - 2240   Shuffles A$ array randomly.
2400   Swaps elements A and B in the A$ array.
2600 - 2610   Breaks word Q$ into separate letters.
3000   Fill A$ array from data.
3200 - 3220   Post-mortem after Apple wins.
3400 - 3460   Post-mortem after human wins.
3600 - 3610   Error routine – too many guesses.
5000 - 5570   Data.

MAIN VARIABLES

N	Total number of data words.
M	Maximum number of guesses allowed.
A$	String array holding data words.
G1$, G2$	String arrays of human's, computer's guesses.
H1,H2	Arrays of human's, computer's hits corresponding to G1$, G2$.
G1,G2	Current number of human's, computer's guesses.
M$	Computer's secret word.
M1$, M2$, M3$	First, second, and third letters of a word.
P$,Q$	String temporaries and work variables.
L	Current number of human's possible secret words.
F	Flag for input word legality.
H	Number of hits in last guess.
A,B	A$ array locations to be swapped.
J,P,Q	Temporaries; array and loop indices.
K	Formatting variable for the summary display.

SUGGESTED PROJECTS

1. Additional messages during the course of the game can personify the program even more. After the Apple finds out how its last guess did, you might try an occasional message like one of these:

   JUST AS I THOUGHT . . .
   HMM, I DIDN'T EXPECT THAT . . .
   JUST WHAT I WAS HOPING TO HEAR . . .

The value of L is the number of words to which the computer has narrowed down the human's secret word. You might check its value regularly and, when it gets low, come out with something like

BE CAREFUL, I'M CLOSING IN ON YOU.

2. Incorporate a feature to allow the loser to continue guessing at the other's word. The summary display routine will already work fine even if G1 and G2 are very different from each other. It will display a value of "9" for the number of hits corresponding to the correct guess of a secret word.

3. Incorporate the legalization of words with repeat letters; i.e., make such words legal as both possible secret words and possible guesses. This involves compiling such a word list, adding it to the data, and modifying the program to allow the new kind of words.

OBSTACLE

PURPOSE

This program allows you and a friend (or enemy) to play the game of OBSTACLE, an arcade-like game that's one of our favorites. A combination of physical skills (reflex speed, hand-to-eye coordination, etc.) and strategic skills are needed to beat your opponent. Each game generally takes only a minute or two, so you'll want to play a match of several games to determine the better player.

HOW TO USE IT

The object of the game is to keep moving longer than your opponent without bumping into an obstacle. When the program starts, it asks in turn for the name of the player on the left and on the right. Then it displays the playing field, shows the starting point for each player, and tells you to press any key to start. Pressing the **ESCAPE** key ends the game.

After a key is pressed, each player begins moving independently in one of four random directions—up, down, left, or right. As each player moves, he or she builds a "wall" inside the playing field. The computer determines the speed of the move; the player can only control his own direction. The player on the left can change direction to up, down, left, or right by pressing the key **W, Z, A,** or **S,** respectively. The player on the right does the same by using the keys for **P,** . (period), **L,** and ; (semicolon). Find these keys on the Apple keyboard and you will see the logic behind these choices.

The first time either player bumps into the wall surrounding the playing field or the obstacle wall built by either player, he loses. When this happens, the program indicates the point of impact for a few seconds and displays the name of the winner. Then the game starts over.

The strategic considerations for this game are interesting. Should you attack your opponent, trying to build a wall around him that he must crash into? Or should you stay away from him and try to make efficient moves in an open area until your opponent runs out of room on his own? Try both approaches and see which yields the most success.

When pressing a key to change direction, be sure to press it quickly and release it. *Do not* hold a key down—you might inhibit the computer from recognizing a move your opponent is trying to make. Once in a while, only one key will be recognized when two are hit at once.

SAMPLE RUN

```
                    OBSTACLE
        NAME OF PLAYER ON LEFT? TOM
        PLAYER ON RIGHT? PHIL
```

The program starts off by asking for the names of the two players.

The program draws the playing field and waits for a key to be pressed. See color section.

The program starts both players moving in random directions. Phil (on the right) doesn't change direction soon enough and crashes into the wall, making Tom the winner. See color section.

PROGRAM LISTING

```
100 REM: OBSTACLE
110 REM: COPYRIGHT 1980 BY TOM RUGG AND PHIL FELDMAN
120 GOSUB 600
125 GR
130 PRINT TAB(15);"OBSTACLE"
140 PRINT
150 PRINT"PRESS ANY KEY TO START"
155 Z=15:F=-16384:S=-16368:T=36
160 AX=INT(T/4):AY=INT(T/2):BX=3*AX:BY=AY:A=7:B=13
165 E=12:AD=INT(4*RND(1))+1:BD=INT(4*RND(1))+1
170 GOSUB 950:GOSUB 900
175 C=PEEK(F):POKE S,0
180 C=PEEK(F):IF C<128 THEN 180
190 POKE S,0:HOME
195 IF C=155 THEN END
200 GOSUB 950:GOSUB 900
205 FOR J=1 TO 5:C=PEEK(F):POKE S,0:NEXT J
210 X=AX:Y=AY:D=AD:GOSUB 1000
220 AR=R:AX=X:AY=Y
230 X=BX:Y=BY:D=BD:GOSUB 1000
240 BR=R:BX=X:BY=Y
245 IF AR=1 OR BR=1 THEN 400
250 GOSUB 900
260 FOR J=1 TO 6:C=PEEK(F):POKE S,0
270 IF C=215 THEN AD=1
280 IF C=218 THEN AD=2
290 IF C=193 THEN AD=3
300 IF C=211 THEN AD=4
310 IF C=208 THEN BD=1
320 IF C=174 THEN BD=2
330 IF C=204 THEN BD=3
340 IF C=187 THEN BD=4
350 NEXT J:GOTO 210
400 GOSUB 700:X=AX:Y=AY
410 IF AR=1 THEN 420
415 X=BX:Y=BY
420 FOR J=1 TO 15
430 COLOR=Z:PLOT X,Y
440 FOR K=1 TO 100:NEXT K
450 COLOR=0:PLOT X,Y
460 FOR K=1 TO 100:NEXT K
470 NEXT J
490 GOTO 125
```

```
600 TEXT:HOME:PRINT TAB(15);"OBSTACLE":PRINT
610 INPUT"NAME OF PLAYER ON LEFT? ";AN$
620 PRINT
630 INPUT"PLAYER ON RIGHT? ";BN$
640 J=256*PEEK(79)+PEEK(78)
650 J=RND(-J):RETURN
700 PRINT
705 FOR J=1 TO 30:C=PEEK(-16336):NEXT J
710 IF AR=0 OR BR=0 THEN 730
720 PRINT"YOU BOTH LOSE!":RETURN
730 R$=AN$:IF AR=1 THEN R$=BN$
740 PRINT R$;" WINS!"
750 RETURN
900 COLOR=A:PLOT AX,AY
910 COLOR=B:PLOT BX,BY
920 RETURN
950 COLOR=E:Y=0:FOR X=1 TO T
960 PLOT X,Y:PLOT X,Y+T:NEXT X
970 X=0:FOR Y=0 TO T
980 PLOT X,Y:PLOT X+T,Y:NEXT Y
990 RETURN
1000 IF D=1 THEN Y=Y-1
1010 IF D=2 THEN Y=Y+1
1020 IF D=3 THEN X=X-1
1030 IF D=4 THEN X=X+1
1040 R=0:IF SCRN(X,Y)<>0 THEN R=1
1050 RETURN
```

EASY CHANGES

1. To speed the game up, change the 6 in line 260 to a 4 or so.
   To slow it down, make it 12 or 15.
2. To make both players always start moving upward at the
   beginning of each game (instead of in a random direction),
   insert the following statement:

$$168 \text{ AD}=1:\text{BD}=1$$

To make the players always start off moving toward each
other, use this statement instead:

$$168 \text{ AD}=4:\text{BD}=3$$

3. To change the length of time that the final messages are displayed after each game, modify line 420. Change the 15 to 8
   (or so) to shorten it, or to 25 to lengthen it.

MAIN ROUTINES

120 - 170	Initializes variables. Gets players' names. Displays titles, playing field.
175 - 205	Waits for key to be pressed to start game. Re-displays playing field.
210 - 250	Makes move for player A (on left side) and B (on right). Saves results.
260 - 350	Accepts moves from keyboard and translates direction.
400 - 490	Displays winner's name at bottom of screen. Flashes a square where collision occurred. Goes back to start next game.
600 - 650	Subroutine that gets each player's name.
700 - 750	Subroutine that displays winner's name.
900 - 920	Subroutine that displays each graphics character of each player's obstacle on the screen.
950 - 990	Subroutine that displays playing field.
1000 - 1050	Subroutine that moves marker and determines if space moved to is empty.

MAIN VARIABLES

AX,AY	Coordinates of player A's current position.
BX,BY	Coordinates of player B's current position.
A	A's graphics color.
B	B's graphics color.
F	Peek address for reading keyboard.
S	Poke address for resetting keyboard.
T	Length of edge of playing field.
AD,BD	Current direction in which A and B are going (1=up, 2=down, 3=left, 4=right).
E	Graphics color for edge of playing field.
C	Character being read from keyboard.
X,Y	Temporary position on screen.
D	Temporary direction.
AR,BR	Result of A's and B's moves (0=okay, 1=loser).
AN$, BN$	Names of players A and B.
Z	Graphics color displayed when collision is made.
J,K	Loop variables.
R$	Name of winner.

SUGGESTED PROJECTS

1. Keep score over a seven-game (or so) match. Display the current score after each game. Don't forget to allow for ties.
2. Modify the program to let each player press only two keys — one to turn left from the current direction of travel, and one to turn right.
3. Instead of a game between two people, make it a game of a person against the computer. Develop a computer strategy to keep finding open areas to move to and/or to cut off open areas from the human opponent.

ROADRACE

PURPOSE

Imagine yourself at the wheel of a high-speed race car winding your way along a treacherous course. The road curves unpredictably. To stay on course, you must steer accurately or risk collision. How far can you go in one day? How many days will it take you to race cross-country? Thrills galore without leaving your living room.

The difficulty of the game is completely under your control. By adjusting the road width and visibility conditions, ROAD-RACE can be made as easy or as challenging as you wish.

HOW TO USE IT

The program begins with a short color graphics display. It then asks you for two inputs; road width and visibility. The road width (in characters) can be set anywhere between 3 and 12. The degree of difficulty changes appreciably with different widths. A very narrow setting will be quite difficult and a wide one relatively easy. Visibility can be set to any of four settings, ranging from "terrible" to "good." When visibility is good, the car appears high on the screen. This allows a good view of the twisting road ahead. When visibility is poor, the car appears low on the screen allowing only a brief look at the upcoming road.

Having set road width and visibility, the race is ready to start. The car appears on the road at the starting line. A five-step starting light counts down the start. When the bottom light goes on, the race begins. The road moves continually up the screen. Its twists and turns are controlled randomly. You must steer the car accurately to keep it on track.

The car is controlled with the use of two keys near the lower right corner of the keyboard. Pressing the left arrow (←) will cause the car to move to the left while pressing the right arrow (→) will cause the car to move to the right. Doing neither will cause the car to continue straight down.

The race proceeds until the car goes "off the road." Each such collision is considered to terminate one day of the race. After each day, you are shown the number of miles achieved that day along with the cumulative miles achieved for consecutive days of the race.

After each collision, you can proceed by pressing either **C, R,** or **Q**. Selecting **C** will continue the race for another day with the same road conditions. Cumulative totals will be retained. **R** will restart the race. This allows changing the road conditions and initializing back to day one. **Q** simply quits the race and returns the Apple back to direct BASIC. Either of the last two options will produce a display of the average miles traveled per day for the race.

There are several different ways to challenge yourself with the program. You can try to see how far you get in a given number of days. You might see how many days it takes you to go a given number of miles—say 3000 miles for a cross-country trip. As you become proficient at one set of road conditions, make the road narrower and/or the visibility poorer. This will increase the challenge. Different road conditions can also be used as a handicapping aid for two unequally-matched opponents.

SAMPLE RUN

The program displays its logo. See color section.

The operator selects fair visibility and a course-width of six characters. Now the race is ready to begin.

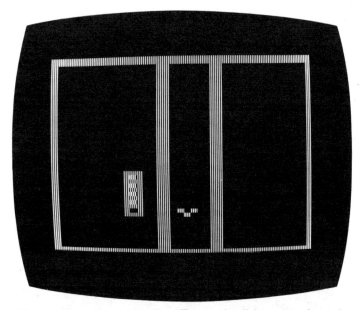

The car is on the starting line. The starting light counts down the beginning of the race. When the last light goes on, the race will be off and running.   See color section.

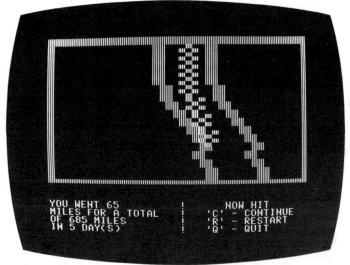

The operator, steering the car from the keyboard, finally crashes. A distance of 65 miles is obtained on this leg for a total of 685 miles in 5 days (legs). The options for continuing are displayed while the program waits for the operator's choice. See color section.

PROGRAM LISTING

```
100 REM: ROADRACE
110 REM: COPYRIGHT 1980 BY PHIL FELDMAN AND TOM RUGG
130 U=1:Z=0:SC=-912:T8=38:F7=47
140 CR=2:CC=9
150 X=0:Y=0:KP=-16384:RK=-16368:L=0:R=0
160 LC=0.4
170 ML=136:MR=149
180 EL=1:ER=37:F5=45:F6=46:RC=1-LC
190 Q=PEEK(78)+256*PEEK(79):Q=RND(-Q):GOTO 210
200 PLOT X,Y:PLOT X-U,Y-U:PLOT X+U,Y-U:RETURN
210 GOSUB 2000:TEXT:HOME:PRINT
220 PRINT TAB(11);"R O A D R A C E"
230 PRINT:T=0:N=0
240 INPUT"ROAD WIDTH (3-12)? ";W
250 W=INT(W):IF W<3 OR W>12 THEN 240
260 PRINT:PRINT"VISIBILITY CONDITIONS"
270 PRINT"  1 - TERRIBLE"
280 PRINT"  2 - BAD"
290 PRINT"  3 - FAIR"
300 PRINT"  4 - GOOD":PRINT
310 INPUT"VISIBILITY (1-4)? ";V:V=INT(V)
320 IF V<1 OR V>4 THEN 310
330 N=N+1:L=19-W/2:R=L+W+2
340 X=20:H=0:Y=47-V*V
350 GR:POKE -16302,Z:POKE 34,U
360 POKE 33,38:POKE 32,U
370 COLOR=Z:FOR Q=40 TO F7
380 HLIN Z,39 AT Q:NEXT
390 COLOR=CR:HLIN Z,39 AT Z:HLIN Z,39 AT U
400 VLIN Z,F7 AT Z:VLIN Z,F7 AT 39
410 HLIN Z,39 AT F7
420 FOR Q=Z TO F7:HLIN L,L+U AT Q
430 HLIN R,R+U AT Q:NEXT
440 COLOR=CC:GOSUB 200
450 GOSUB 3000
500 COLOR=Z:HLIN U,T8 AT F7:CALL SC:COLOR=CR
510 HLIN U,T8 AT F7:HLIN L,L+U AT F5:HLIN R,R+U AT F5
520 H=H+U:Q=RND(U):IF Q>RC AND R<ER THEN L=L+U:R=R+U
530 IF Q<LC AND L>EL THEN L=L-U:R=R-U
540 HLIN L,L+U AT F6:HLIN R,R+U AT F6
550 COLOR=CC
600 Q=PEEK(KP):POKE RK,Z
610 IF Q=ML THEN X=X-U
```

```
620 IF Q=NR THEN X=X+U
630 IF SCRN(X,Y)=Z THEN GOSUB 200:GOTO 500
640 GOTO 1000
1000 FOR Q=U TO 6:COLOR=CC:GOSUB 200
1010 FOR J=U TO 100:NEXT:COLOR=Z:GOSUB 200
1020 FOR J=U TO 30:K=PEEK(-16336):NEXT:NEXT
1030 COLOR=CC:GOSUB 200:POKE 32,Z:POKE 33,40:CALL SC
1040 COLOR=Z:FOR Q=U TO 5:HLIN Z,39 AT F7:CALL SC
1050 NEXT:POKE -16304,0:POKE 34,20:POKE -16301,0:HOME
1060 M=H*5:T=T+M
1070 PRINT"YOU WENT ";M;:GOSUB 1300
1080 PRINT TAB(28);"NOW HIT"
1090 PRINT"MILES FOR A TOTAL";:GOSUB 1300
1100 PRINT TAB(25);"'C' - CONTINUE"
1110 PRINT"OF ";T;" MILES";:GOSUB 1300
1120 PRINT TAB(25);"'R' - RESTART"
1130 PRINT"IN ";N;" DAY(S)";:GOSUB 1300
1140 PRINT TAB(25);"'Q' - QUIT ";
1150 GET Q$:IF Q$="C" THEN 330
1160 IF Q$<>"R" AND Q$<>"Q" THEN 1150
1170 TEXT:HOME:PRINT
1180 PRINT"AVERAGE MILES PER DAY=";T/N
1190 PRINT:PRINT:PRINT:IF Q$="R" THEN 220
1200 END
1300 PRINT TAB(21);:PRINT"!";:RETURN
1310 NORMAL:RETURN
2000 GR:HOME:COLOR=CR:RESTORE
2010 X=16:Y=0:PLOT X,Y:PLOT X+8,Y
2020 FOR Y=1 TO 39:READ Q:X=X+Q-U
2030 PLOT X,Y:PLOT X+8,Y:NEXT
2040 COLOR=CC:X=20:RESTORE
2050 FOR Y=1 TO 39:READ Q:X=X+Q-U
2060 GOSUB 200:FOR J=1 TO 30:NEXT
2070 COLOR=Z:GOSUB 200:COLOR=CC:NEXT:Y=39:GOSUB 200
2080 FOR J=1 TO 25:Q=PEEK(-16336):NEXT
2090 FOR J=1 TO 6:HOME:PRINT:PRINT TAB(7);
2100 PRINT"R  O  A  D  R  A  C  E"
2110 FOR Q=1 TO 500:NEXT:HOME:PRINT:PRINT
2120 FOR Q=1 TO 250:NEXT:NEXT:RETURN
2200 DATA  1,1,1,1,1,1,1,2,2,2,2,2,2,2,2
2210 DATA  0,0,0,0,0,0,0,0,0,0,0,0,0,0,0
2220 DATA  2,2,2,2,2,2,2,1,1,1,1
3000 COLOR=CR:VLIN Y-10,Y AT L-5
3010 VLIN Y-10,Y AT L-3:FOR Q=Y-10 TO Y STEP 2
```

```
3020 PLOT L-4,Q:NEXT:FOR Q=1 TO 1000:NEXT
3030 COLOR=CC:FOR Q=Y-9 TO Y-1 STEP 2
3040 FOR J=1 TO 500:NEXT:PLOT L-4,Q:NEXT:RETURN
```

EASY CHANGES

1. The amount of windiness in the road can be adjusted by changing the value of LC in line 160. Maximum windiness is achieved with a value of 0.5 for LC. To get a straighter road, make LC smaller. A value of 0 will produce a completely straight road. LC should lie between 0 and 0.5. To get a somewhat more winding road, you might change line 160 to read

160 LC=0.45

2. The colors used for the road and for the car are assigned to the variables CR and CC respectively. These are set in line 140. Currently, dark blue is used for the road and orange for the car. You may wish to use different colors for variety. (Don't use black, however, for that is the color of the background.) Consult your Applesoft manual for the numerical values corresponding to the different low-resolution graphics colors. For example, to get a green road and yellow car, change line 140 to read

140 CR=12:CC=13

3. The keys which cause the car to move left and right can be easily changed. You may wish to do this if you are left handed or find that two widely separated keys would be more convenient. The changes are to be made in line 170. The constants that are assigned to the variables ML and MR control which keys will cause the car to move left and right respectively. To find the correct constants, first type in this short program:

10 Q=PEEK(-16384):IF Q < 128 THEN 10
20 POKE -16368,0:PRINT Q

Run the program, then press the key you wish to use to make the car move left. A number will appear on the screen. This number will be assigned to the variable ML. Run the program again and hit the key you want to cause the car to move right. Assign the number that now appears to the variable

MR. If, for example, you want 1 to cause a left move and 9 to cause a right move, line 170 will become

170 ML=177:MR=185

4. Instead of the keyboard, a game paddle can be used to control the car's movements. We'll assume paddle 0 will be used. The first step is to "calibrate" it. Run this program with paddle 0 in hand.

10 PRINT PDL(0):GOTO 10

Adjust the paddle until the number 100 appears continually on your screen. Mark this position on the paddle itself; we will use any position to the left of it to cause the car to move left. Now give the paddle a comfortable twist to the right. Mark this position on the paddle also; we will use any position to the right of it to cause the car to move right. A number (larger than 100) should be repeating itself on the screen. It will be assigned to the variable MR shortly. For the remainder of this discussion, we'll assume it has a value of 160. Now make the following changes to the main program:

170 ML=100:MR=160
600 Q=PDL(0)
610 IF Q < ML THEN X=X-U
620 IF Q > MR THEN X=X+U

The paddle will now control the car. When the paddle lies between the two calibration marks, the car will continue straight down the road. If the paddle is turned to the left of the first mark, the car will *continue* to move left. If the paddle is turned to the right of the second mark, the car will *continue* to move right.

MAIN ROUTINES

130 - 190	Variable initialization.
200	Subroutine to draw the car.
210 - 230	Displays introduction.
240 - 320	Gets road conditions from user.
330 - 340	Initializes road.
350 - 450	Graphics to begin race.
500 - 550	Draws next road segment.
600 - 640	Updates the car position.

1000 - 1310   Processes end of race day.
2000 - 2220   Subroutine to do initial graphics display.
3000 - 3040   Subroutine to display traffic light.

MAIN VARIABLES

W	Road width.
V	Visibility.
M	Miles driven on current day.
N	Number of days of the race.
T	Total miles driven for whole race.
H	Elapsed time during race.
ML,MR	Peek constants to move car left, right.
L,R	Position of left, right side of road.
LC,RC	Random value cutoff to move road left, right.
EL,ER	Leftmost, rightmost allowable road position.
Q$	User replies.
X,Y	Horizontal, vertical position of car.
J,K,Q	Loop indices and work variables.
CR	Color of road.
CC	Color of car.
KP	Peek argument for last key pressed.
RK	Poke argument to reset key sensing.
SC	Call argument to scroll screen.
Z,U,T8, F5,F6, F7	Numeric constants.

SUGGESTED PROJECTS

1. Write a routine to evaluate a player's performance after each collision. Display a message rating him anywhere from "expert" to "back-seat driver." This should involve comparing his actual miles achieved against an expected (or average) number of miles for the given road width and visibility. For starters, you might use

$$\text{Expected miles} = 5W^3 + 50V - 100$$

This formula is crude, at best. The coding can be done between lines 1110 and 1120.
2. Incorporate provisions for two players racing one at a time.

Keep cumulative totals separately. After each collision, display the current leader and how far he is ahead.

3. Add physical obstacles or other hazards onto the road in order to increase the challenge. This can be done with appropriate plotting statements after line 540. The program will recognize a collision if the car moves into any non-blank square.

WARI

PURPOSE

Wari is an old game with roots that are much older. Its origins go back thousands of years to a variety of other similar games, all classified as being members of the Mancala family. Other variations are Awari, Oware, Pallanguli, Kalah, and countless other offshoots.

The program matches you against the computer. You are probably going to lose a few games before you win one – the computer plays a pretty good game. This may hurt your ego a little bit, since Wari is purely a skill game (like chess or checkers). There is no element of luck involved, as would be the case with backgammon, for example. When you lose, it's because you were outplayed.

HOW TO USE IT

When you start the program, the first thing it does is display the Wari board and ask you if you want to go first. The board is made up of twelve "squares" in two rows of six. Your side is the bottom side, numbered one through six from left to right. The computer's side is on the top, numbered seven through twelve from right to left.

At the start of the game, each square has four "stones" in it. There is no way to differentiate between your stones and the computer's. They all look alike and will move from one side to the other during the course of play.

The first player "picks up" all the stones in one of the squares on his side of the board and drops them, one to a square, starting with the next highest numbered square. The stones continue to be dropped consecutively in each square, continuing over onto the opponent's side if necessary (after square number 12 comes square number 1 again).

If the last stone is dropped onto the opponent's side *and* leaves a total of either two or three stones in that square, these stones are captured by the player who moved, and removed from the board. Also, if the next-to-last square in which a stone was dropped meets the same conditions (on the opponent's side and now with two or three stones), its stones are also captured. This continues backwards until the string of consecutive squares of two or three on the opponent's side is broken.

Regardless of whether any captures are made, play alternates back and forth between the two players.

The object of the game is to be the first player to capture 24 or more stones. That's half of the 48 stones that are on the board at the beginning of the game.

There are a few special rules to cover some situations that can come up in the game. It is not legal to capture all the stones on the opponent's side of the board, since this would leave the opponent with no moves on his next turn. By the same token, when your opponent has no stones on his side (because he had to move his last one to your side on his turn), you have to make a move that gives him at least one stone to move on his next turn, if possible. If you cannot make such a move, the game is over and counted as a draw.

During the course of the game, it's possible for a square to accumulate 12 or more stones in it. Moving from such a square causes stones to be distributed all the way around the board. When this happens, the square from which the move was made is skipped over. So, the square moved from is always left empty.

It takes the computer anywhere from five seconds to about thirty seconds to make a move, depending on the complexity of the board position. The word THINKING is displayed during this time, and a period is added to it as each possible move is evaluated in sequence (seven through twelve).

SAMPLE RUN

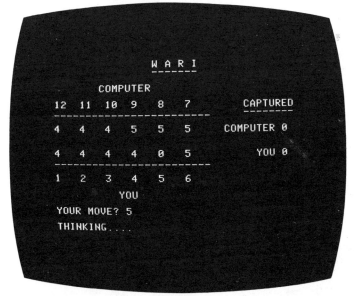

The program starts off by drawing the playing "board" and asking who should move first. The operator decides to go first.

The program asks for the operator's move. He or she decides to move square number 5. The program alters the board accordingly, and begins "thinking" about what move to make.

Later in the same game, the computer is about to move square number 10, which will capture four more stones and win the game.

PROGRAM LISTING

```
100 REM: WARI
110 REM: COPYRIGHT 1980 BY TOM RUGG AND PHIL FELDMAN
120 J=1:K=1:Q=14:P=13:F=50:D=12
130 DIM T(Q),Y(Q),W(Q),V(6),E(6),B(Q)
140 ZB=RND(1):ZB=ZB/Q:ZA=.25+ZB:ZB=.25-ZB:GOSUB 750
150 FOR J=1 TO D:B(J)=4:NEXT:B(P)=0:B(Q)=0:MN=0:GOSUB
    1200:GOSUB 900
160 GOSUB 990:INPUT"WANT TO GO FIRST? ";R$
170 GOSUB 990:PRINT D$:R$=LEFT$(R$,1):IF R$="Y" THEN
    250
180 IF R$<>"N" THEN 160
190 GOSUB 1050:PRINT D$;D$;D$;:GOSUB 1050:PRINT
    "THINKING";:GOSUB 510
195 IF M<1 THEN 2000
200 GOSUB 1050:PRINT D$;:GOSUB 1050:PRINT"MY MOVE IS ";
    M
210 FOR J=1 TO Q:T(J)=B(J):NEXT:GOSUB 350
220 FOR J=1 TO Q:B(J)=T(J):NEXT:GOSUB 900
230 IF B(Q)<24 THEN 250
240 GOSUB 1050:PRINT"I WIN!";D$:GOTO 810
```

```
250 GOSUB 990:PRINT D$;D$:GOSUB 990:INPUT"YOUR MOVE? ";
    R$
260 M=INT(VAL(R$)):IF M>6 OR M<1 THEN 330
270 FOR J=1 TO Q:T(J)=B(J):NEXT
280 GOSUB 350:IF M<0 THEN 330
290 FOR J=1 TO Q:B(J)=T(J):NEXT
300 MN=MN+1:GOSUB 900
310 IF B(P)<24 THEN 190
320 GOSUB 1050:PRINT"YOU WIN!";D$:GOTO 810
330 GOSUB 990:PRINT TAB(15);" ILLEGAL ";:FOR J=1 TO
    3000:NEXT:GOTO 250
350 IF T(M)=0 THEN M=-1:RETURN
360 R$="H":IF M>6 THEN R$="C":GOTO 380
370 FOR J=1 TO Q:Y(J)=T(J):NEXT:GOTO 400
380 FOR J=1 TO 6:Y(J)=T(J+6):Y(J+6)=T(J):NEXT
390 Y(P)=T(Q):Y(Q)=T(P):M=M-6
400 C=M:N=Y(C):FOR J=1 TO N:C=C+1
410 IF C=P THEN C=1
420 IF C=M THEN C=C+1:GOTO 410
430 Y(C)=Y(C)+1:NEXT:Y(M)=0:L=C
440 IF L<7 OR Y(L)>3 OR Y(L)<2 THEN 460
450 Y(P)=Y(P)+Y(L):Y(L)=0:L=L-1:GOTO 440
460 S=0:FOR J=7 TO D:S=S+Y(J):NEXT
470 IF S=0 THEN M=-2:RETURN
480 IF R$="H" THEN FOR J=1 TO Q:T(J)=Y(J):NEXT:RETURN
490 FOR J=1 TO 6:T(J)=Y(J+6):T(J+6)=Y(J):NEXT
500 T(Q)=Y(P):T(P)=Y(Q):RETURN
510 FOR A=1 TO 6:M=A+6:IF B(M)=0 THEN E(A)=-F:GOTO 690
530 FOR J=1 TO Q:T(J)=B(J):NEXT:GOSUB 350
540 IF M<0 THEN E(A)=-F:GOTO 690
550 IF T(Q)>23 THEN M=A+6:RETURN
560 FOR J=1 TO Q:W(J)=T(J):NEXT:FOR K=1 TO 6
570 IF T(K)=0 THEN V(K)=F:GOTO 670
580 FOR J=1 TO Q:T(J)=W(J):NEXT:M=K:GOSUB 350
590 IF M<0 THEN V(K)=F:GOTO 670
600 FA=0:FB=.05:FC=0:FD=0:FOR J=7 TO D
610 FB=FB+T(J):IF T(J)>0 THEN FA=FA+1
620 IF T(J)<3 THEN FC=FC+1
630 IF T(J)>FD THEN FD=T(J)
640 NEXT:FE=FB:FOR J=1 TO 6:FE=FE+T(J):NEXT
650 FA=FA/6:FD=1-FD/FB:FC=1-FC/6:FB=FB/FE
660 V(K)=ZA*(FA+FB)+ZB*(FC+FD)+T(Q)+B(P)-B(Q)-T(P)
670 NEXT:E(A)=F:FOR J=1 TO 6:IF V(J)<E(A) THEN E(A)=V(J)
680 NEXT
690 PRINT".";:NEXT:M=0:FA=-F:FOR J=1 TO 6
```

```
700 IF (E(J)>FA) THEN FA=E(J):M=J+6
710 NEXT:RETURN
750 A$="-":FOR J=1 TO 23:A$=A$+"-":NEXT
760 C$=CHR$(95):FOR J=1 TO 23:C$=C$+CHR$(95):NEXT
790 D$=" ":FOR J=1 TO 5:D$=D$+D$:NEXT
800 RETURN
810 PRINT"GOOD GAME!"
840 INPUT"WANT TO PLAY AGAIN? ";R$
850 R$=LEFT$(R$,1):IF R$="Y" THEN 140
860 IF R$<>"N" THEN 840
870 PRINT"SEE YOU LATER"
880 PRINT:END
900 VTAB 9
920 FOR J=0 TO 5:PRINT TAB(4*J+1);B(12-J);:IF B(12-J)=0
    THEN GOSUB 1100
930 NEXT:PRINT TAB(27);"COMPUTER ";B(Q)
940 VTAB 12:FOR J=0 TO 5
950 PRINT TAB(4*J+1);B(J+1);:IF B(J+1)=0 THEN GOSUB
    1100
960 NEXT:PRINT TAB(32);"YOU ";B(P)
970 RETURN
990 VTAB 19:HTAB 1:RETURN
1050 VTAB 21:HTAB 1:RETURN
1100 PRINT" ";:RETURN
1200 TEXT:HOME:PRINT TAB(16);"W A R I"
1210 PRINT TAB(16);"-------"
1220 PRINT:PRINT TAB(8);"COMPUTER":PRINT
1230 FOR J=0 TO 5:PRINT TAB(4*J+1);12-J;:NEXT
1240 PRINT TAB(30);"CAPTURED":PRINT C$;TAB(30);LEFT$(A$,
    8)
1250 PRINT:PRINT:PRINT:PRINT:PRINT:PRINT C$:PRINT
1260 FOR J=0 TO 5:PRINT TAB(4*J+1);J+1;:NEXT
1270 PRINT:PRINT:PRINT TAB(11);"YOU"
1280 PRINT:RETURN
2000 PRINT"NO LEGAL MOVES."
2010 PRINT"GAME IS A DRAW."
2020 GOTO 840
```

EASY CHANGES

1. Want a faster-moving game against an opponent who isn't quite such a good player? Insert the following two lines:

```
555 GOTO 600
665 E(A)=V(K):GOTO 690
```

In the standard version of the game, the computer looks at each of its possible moves and each of your possible replies when evaluating which move to make. This change causes the computer to only look at each of its moves, without bothering to look at any of your possible replies. As a result, the computer does not play as well, but it takes only a few seconds to make each move.

2. If you are curious about what the computer thinks are the relative merits of each of its possible moves, you can make this change to find out. Change line 690 so it looks like this:

690 PRINT E(A);"/";:NEXT:M=0:FA=-F:FOR J=1 TO 6

This will cause the program to display its evaluation number for each of its moves in turn (starting with square seven). It will select the largest number of the six. A negative value means that it will lose stones if that move is made, assuming that you make the best reply you can. A value of negative 50 indicates an illegal move. A positive value greater than one means that a capture can be made by the computer, and it will come out ahead after your best reply.

MAIN ROUTINES

120 - 150	Initializes variables. Displays board.
160 - 180	Asks who goes first. Evaluates answer.
190 - 220	Determines computer's move. Displays new board position.
230 - 240	Determines if computer's move resulted in a win. Displays a message if so.
250 - 300	Gets operator's move. Checks for legality. Displays new board position.
310 - 320	Determines if operator's move resulted in a win.
330	Displays message if illegal move attempted.
350 - 500	Subroutine to make move M in T array.
360 - 390	Copies T array into Y array (inverts if computer is making the move).
400 - 430	Makes move in Y array.
440 - 450	Checks for captures. Removes stones. Checks previous square.
460 - 470	Sees if opponent is left with a legal move.
480 - 500	Copies Y array back into T array.
510 - 710	Subroutine to determine computer's move.

750 - 800	Subroutine to create graphics strings for board display.
810 - 880	Displays ending message. Asks about playing again.
900 - 970	Subroutine to display stones on board and captured.
990	Subroutine to move cursor to "YOUR MOVE" position on screen.
1050	Subroutine to move cursor to "MY MOVE" position on screen.
1100	Subroutine to display one blank character.
1200 - 1280	Subroutine to display Wari board (without stones).
2000 - 2020	Displays message when computer has no legal move.

MAIN VARIABLES

Q,P,F,D	Constant values of 14, 13, 50 and 12, respectively.
T,Y,W	Arrays with temporary copies of the Wari board.
V	Array with evaluation values of operator's six possible replies to computer's move being considered.
E	Array with evaluation values of computer's six possible moves.
B	Array containing Wari board. Thirteenth element has stones captured by operator. Fourteenth has computer's.
ZA,ZB	Weighting factors for evaluation function.
MN	Move number.
R$	Operator's reply. Also used as switch to indicate whose move it is (C for computer, H for human).
M	Move being made (1-6 for operator, 7-12 for computer). Set negative if illegal.
C	Subscript used in dropping stones around board.
L	Last square in which a stone was dropped.
S	Stones on opponent's side of the board after a move.
A	Subscript used to indicate which of the six possible computer moves is currently being evaluated.
FA	First evaluation factor used in determining favorability of board position after a move (indicates computer's number of occupied squares).
FB	Second evaluation factor (total stones on computer's side of the board).
FC	Third evaluation factor (number of squares with two or less stones).

FD   Fourth evaluation factor (number of stones in most
          populous square on computer's side).
FE   Total stones on board.
A$,C$ Strings of graphics characters used to display the
          Wari board.
D$ String of 32 blanks.

SUGGESTED PROJECTS

1. Modify the program to declare the game a draw if neither
   player has made a capture in the past 30 moves. Line 300
   adds one to the counter of the number of moves made. To
   make the change, keep track of the move number of the last
   capture, and compare the difference between it and the
   current move number with 30.
2. Modify the evaluation function used by the computer strategy
   to see if you can improve the quality of its play. Lines 600
   through 660 examine the position of the board after the
   move that is being considered. Experiment with the factors
   and/or the weighting values, or add a new factor of your own.
3. Change the program so it can allow two people to play against
   each other, instead of just a person against the computer.

Section 4

Graphics Display Programs

INTRODUCTION TO GRAPHICS DISPLAY PROGRAMS

The Apple is an amazing machine. It has very useful graphics capabilities in addition to its other capacities. Programs in the other sections of this book take advantage of these graphics to facilitate and "spice up" their various output. Here we explore the use of the Apple's graphic capabilities for sheer fun, amusement, and diversion.

Ever look through a kaleidoscope and enjoy the symmetric changing patterns produced? KALEIDO will create such effects with full eight-point symmetry.

Two other programs produce ever-changing patterns but with much different effects. SPARKLE will fascinate you with a changing shimmering collage. SQUARES uses geometric shapes to obtain its pleasing displays.

WALLOONS demonstrates a totally different aspect of the Apple. This program will keep you entertained with an example of computer animation.

KALEIDO

PURPOSE

If you have ever played with a kaleidoscope, you were probably fascinated by the endless symmetrical patterns you saw displayed. This program creates a series of kaleidoscope-like designs, with each one overlaying the previous one. Some of the designs are symmetrical about eight axes (others about four) — can you find them?

HOW TO USE IT

There is not much to say about how to use this one. Just type RUN, then sit back and watch. Turning down the lights and playing a little music is a good way to add to the effect.

By the way, it is a little misleading to say that the designs you see are symmetrical. It is more accurate to say that the positions occupied by the individual graphics characters are located symmetrically. The overall design is really not completely symmetrical, since each individual graphics character is not completely symmetrical.

Have a few friends bring their Apples over (all your friends *do* have Apples, don't they?), and get them all going with KALEIDO at once. Let us know if you think you have set a new world's record. Please note that we will not be responsible for any hypnotic trances induced this way.

SAMPLE RUN

One of the patterns generated by the KALEIDO program.

See color section.

PROGRAM LISTING

```
100 REM: KALEIDO
110 REM: COPYRIGHT 1980 BY TOM RUGG AND PHIL FELDMAN
120 HOME:GR
125 P=19
130 A=P:B=P:D=-1
135 M=15
140 DIM R(10)
150 FOR J=0 TO 10
160 R(J)=INT(M*RND(1))
170 NEXT J
180 D=-D:K=1:L=P:IF D>0 THEN 200
190 K=P:L=1
200 FOR J=K TO L STEP D
210 X=A+J:Y=B:GOSUB 900
220 X=A-J:GOSUB 900
230 X=A:Y=B+J:GOSUB 900
240 Y=B-J:GOSUB 900
250 X=A+J:Y=B+J:GOSUB 900
260 X=A-J:Y=B-J:GOSUB 900
270 Y=B+J:GOSUB 900
```

```
280 X=A+J:Y=B-J:GOSUB 900
700 NEXT J
750 FOR J=1 TO 2000:NEXT J
800 GOTO 150
900 COLOR=R(0):PLOT X,Y
910 IF J=1 THEN RETURN
920 W=INT(J/2):T=J-W-1
930 FOR N=1 TO W
940 IF X<>(A) THEN 950
945 Y2=Y:X2=X+N:GOSUB 2000:X2=X-N:GOSUB 2000:NEXT N:
    RETURN
950 IF Y<>B THEN 970
960 X2=X:Y2=Y+N:GOSUB 2000:Y2=Y-N:GOSUB 2000:NEXT N:
    RETURN
970 Y2=Y:IF X>=(A) THEN 980
975 X2=X+N:GOSUB 2000:GOTO 990
980 X2=X-N:GOSUB 2000
990 X2=X:IF Y>=B THEN 1000
995 Y2=Y+N:GOSUB 2000:GOTO 1010
1000 Y2=Y-N:GOSUB 2000
1010 NEXT N:RETURN
2000 COLOR=R(N):PLOT X2,Y2:RETURN
```

EASY CHANGES

1. To clear the screen before the next pattern about 20% of the time (chosen at random), insert this:

   175 IF RND(1) <= .2 THEN GR

   For 50%, use .5 instead of .2, etc.

2. To randomly change the size of the patterns, insert:

   177 P=INT(15*RND(1))+5

3. To cause only the outward patterns to be displayed, insert line 178 to say

   178 D=-1

   To cause only inward patterns, change it to say

   178 D=1

4. To alter the number of graphics colors used in the patterns, alter the value of M in line 135. Be sure it is an integer from 2 to 16.

5. To lengthen the delay after each pattern is drawn, change this
   line:

750 FOR J= 1 TO 5000:NEXT J

Or, eliminate line 750 to eliminate the delay.

Note: These changes add a lot to the appeal of the designs.
Experiment! Each change can be done by itself or in combination with other changes.

MAIN ROUTINES

120 - 140	Housekeeping. Initializes variables.
150 - 170	Picks 11 random graphics colors.
180	Reverses direction of display (inward-outward).
190 - 700	Displays a full screen of the pattern.
800	Goes back to create next pattern.
900 - 1010	Plots points on axes of design.
2000	Subroutine to plot points between axes.

MAIN VARIABLES

P	Distance from center to edge of design.
A,B	Pointer to center of design.
D	Direction in which design is drawn (1=outward, −1=inward).
M	Multiplier used to determine the range of random graphics colors.
R	Array for the 11 random graphics colors.
J,K,L	Subscript variables.
X,Y	Coordinates of point to be plotted on axes.
X2,Y2	Coordinates of point to be plotted between axes.
N,W	Work variables.

SPARKLE

PURPOSE

This graphics display program provides a continuous series of hypnotic patterns, some of which seem to sparkle at you while they are created. Two types of patterns are used. The first is a set of concentric diamond shapes in the center of the screen. Although the pattern is regular, the sequence in which it is created is random, which results in the "sparkle" effect.

The second type of pattern starts about two seconds after the first has finished. It is a series of "sweeps" across the screen — left to right and top to bottom. Each sweep uses a random graphics color that is spaced equally across the screen. The spacing distance is chosen at random for each sweep. Also, the number of sweeps to be made is chosen at random each time in the range from 10 to 30.

After the second type of pattern is complete, the program goes back to the first type, which begins to overlay the center of the second type.

HOW TO USE IT

Confused by what you just read? Never mind. You have to see it to appreciate it. Just enter the program into your Apple, then sit back and watch the results of your labor.

SAMPLE RUN

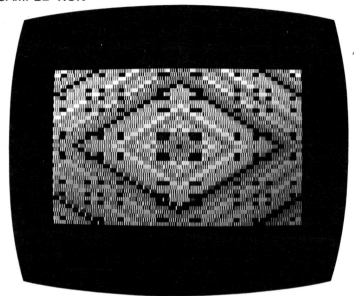

One of the patterns generated by the SPARKLE program.

See color section.

PROGRAM LISTING

```
100 REM: SPARKLE
110 REM: COPYRIGHT 1980 BY TOM RUGG AND PHIL FELDMAN
120 HOME:GR
125 S=19
130 DIM A(S),B(S):X=19:Y=19
140 T=INT(16*RND(1))
150 FOR J=0 TO S:A(J)=J:B(J)=J:NEXT J
160 FOR J=0 TO S:R=INT((S+1)*RND(1))
170 W=A(J):A(J)=A(R):A(R)=W:NEXT J
180 FOR J=0 TO S:R=INT((S+1)*RND(1))
190 W=B(J):B(J)=B(R):B(R)=W:NEXT J
200 FOR J=0 TO S:FOR K=0 TO S
210 R=A(J):W=B(K):C=R+W+T
220 COLOR=C
240 PLOT X+R,Y+W
250 PLOT X+R,Y-W
260 PLOT X-R,Y-W
270 PLOT X-R,Y+W
280 PLOT X+W,Y+R
```

```
290 PLOT X+W,Y-R
300 PLOT X-W,Y-R
310 PLOT X-W,Y+R
320 NEXT K:NEXT J
350 FOR J=1 TO 2000:NEXT J
400 M=15
405 N=INT(21*RND(1))+10
410 FOR J=1 TO N
420 R=INT(22*RND(1))+1:W=INT(M*RND(1))
430 COLOR=W
450 FOR L=Y-S TO Y+S STEP INT(R/4)+1
460 FOR K=X-S TO X+S STEP R
470 PLOT K,L
480 NEXT K:NEXT L:NEXT J
490 GOTO 140
```

EASY CHANGES

1. Make the second type of pattern appear first by inserting this line:

   135 GOTO 400

   Or, eliminate the first type of pattern by inserting:

   145 GOTO 400

   Or, eliminate the second type of pattern by inserting:

   360 GOTO 140

2. Increase the delay after the first type of pattern by increasing the 2000 in line 350 to, say, 5000. Remove line 350 to eliminate the delay.

3. Increase the numbers of sweeps across the screen of the second type of pattern by changing the 10 at the right end of line 405 into a 30 or a 50, for example. Decrease the number of sweeps by changing the 10 to a 1, and also changing the 21 in line 405 to 5 or 10.

4. Watch the effect on the second type of pattern if you change the 22 in line 420 into various integer values between 2 and 39.

5. Change the value of M in line 400 to alter the graphics color used in the second type of pattern. For example, try

   400 M=4

   Be sure that M is an integer from 2 to 16.

MAIN ROUTINES

120 - 130	Initializes variables. Clears screen.
140 - 320	Displays diamond pattern in center of screen.
150 - 190	Shuffles the numbers 0 through 19 in the A and B arrays.
200 - 320	Displays graphics colors on the screen.
350	Delays for about two seconds.
400 - 480	Overlays the entire screen with a random graphics color spaced at a fixed interval chosen at random.

MAIN VARIABLES

S	Size of first type of pattern.
R	Random integer. Also, work variable.
A,B	Arrays in which shuffled integers from 0 to S are stored for use in making first type of pattern.
X,Y	Coordinates of center for screen (19 across, 19 down).
T	Integer from 0 to 15, used in creating random graphics colors.
J,K,L	Work and loop variables.
W	Work variable.
C	Graphics color to be displayed on screen in first pattern.
N	Number of repetitions of second type of pattern.
M	Multiplier used in getting a random color for second type of pattern.

SUGGESTED PROJECTS

Make the second type of pattern alternate between "falling from the top" (as it does now) and rising from the bottom of the screen.

SQUARES

PURPOSE

This is another graphics-display program. It draws a series of concentric squares with the graphics color used for each one chosen at random. After a full set of concentric squares is drawn, the next set starts again at the center and overlays the previous one. They are actually rectangles, not squares, but let's not be nit-pickers.

HOW TO USE IT

As with most of the other graphics display programs, you just sit back and enjoy watching this one once you get it started.

SAMPLE RUN

One of the patterns generated by the SQUARES program.
See color section.

PROGRAM LISTING

```
100 REM: SQUARES
110 REM: COPYRIGHT 1980 BY TOM RUGG AND PHIL FELDMAN
120 HOME:GR
130 X=20:Y=20:N=1
135 COLOR=INT(16*RND(1)):PLOT X,Y-1
140 C=INT(16*RND(1))
170 COLOR=C:FOR J=0 TO N:PLOT X+J,Y:NEXT J
180 X=X+N:N=N+1
190 FOR J=0 TO N:PLOT X,Y-J:NEXT J
200 Y=Y-N:FOR J=0 TO N:PLOT X-J,Y:NEXT J
210 X=X-N
220 FOR J=0 TO N:PLOT X,Y+J:NEXT J
230 N=N+1:Y=Y+N
240 IF N<38 THEN 140
250 FOR J=1 TO 1000:NEXT J
260 GOTO 130
```

EASY CHANGES

1. Change the delay after each set of patterns by changing the 1000 in line 250. A bigger number causes a longer delay.
2. To occasionally blank out the screen (about 20% of the time), insert this:

$$255 \text{ IF RND}(1) < .2 \text{ THEN GR}$$

MAIN ROUTINES

120	Housekeeping. Clears screen.
130	Initializes counters for each pattern. Points to the center of the screen.
135	Plots random color at center.
140	Picks a graphics color.
170	Draws the bottom side of the square.
190	Draws the right side.
200	Draws the top side.
220	Draws the left side.
240	Tests if the outermost square has been drawn.
250	Delays about one second.
260	Goes back to start at the center again.

MAIN VARIABLES

X,Y	Coordinates of points being plotted.
N	Length of the side currently being drawn.
C	Numeric equivalent of the random graphics color chosen.
J	Loop variable.

WALLOONS

PURPOSE

The Apple is quite a versatile machine. This program takes advantage of its powerful graphics capability to produce computer animation. That's right, animation! WALLOONS will entertain you with a presentation from the Apple Arena.

The Apple Arena searches the world over to bring you the best in circus acts and other performing artists. Today, direct from their performance before the uncrowned heads of Europe, the Arena brings you the Flying Walloons.

HOW TO USE IT

Just sit back, relax, and get ready to enjoy the show. Type RUN and the Flying Walloons will be ready to perform. You have a front-row-center seat and the curtain is about to go up.

Applause might be appropriate if you enjoy their performance. Please note that the Walloons have been working on a big new finish to their act which they haven't yet quite perfected.

SAMPLE RUN

The billboard announces a new presentation of the (in)famous Apple Arena.

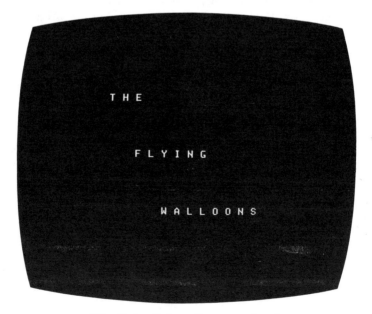

"The Flying Walloons" are to perform!

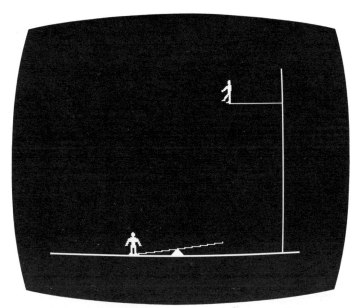

The Walloons attempt a dangerous trick from their repertoire.

PROGRAM LISTING

```
100 REM: WALLOONS
110 REM: COPYRIGHT 1980 BY PHIL FELDMAN AND TOM RUGG
120 GOTO 800
200 HCOLOR=Z:HPLOT 90,177 TO 190,189:HCOLOR=3
210 HPLOT 90,189 TO 190,177:DRAW 6 AT 140,183:RETURN
220 HCOLOR=Z:HPLOT 90,189 TO 190,177:HCOLOR=3
230 HPLOT 90,177 TO 190,189:DRAW 6 AT 140,183:RETURN
240 HPLOT 198,40 TO 258,40:HPLOT 259,5 TO 259,190:RETURN
250 XDRAW F AT X,Y:DRAW G AT X1,Y1:RETURN
260 XDRAW F AT X1,Y1:ROT=RV:DRAW G AT X,Y
270 X1=X:Y1=Y:GOSUB 500:RETURN
280 XDRAW G AT X1,Y1:DRAW F AT X,Y2:RETURN
290 XDRAW G AT X1,Y1:DRAW F AT X2,Y:RETURN
300 IF X<219 THEN FOR J=1 TO 80*(219-X):NEXT
310 RETURN
320 XDRAW F AT X,Y:DRAW G AT X,Y:RETURN
330 XDRAW G AT X,Y:DRAW F AT X,Y:RETURN
340 X=X3:Y=Y4:F=1:G=2:GOSUB 320:GOSUB 600
350 GOSUB 330:GOSUB 600:RETURN
360 DRAW F AT X3,Y3:DRAW G AT X4,Y4:RETURN
370 DRAW F AT X3,Y4:DRAW G AT X4,Y3:RETURN
```

```
400 FOR Y1=150 TO 30 STEP -5:Y=Y1+5:GOSUB 250:GOSUB 520
410 HPLOT 90,Y6 TO 190,Y7:NEXT:G=2:Y=30:Y1=35:GOSUB 250:
    F=2
420 FOR Y1=40 TO 155 STEP 5:Y=Y1-5:GOSUB 250:GOSUB 520:
    NEXT:XDRAW 2 AT X,Y3:RETURN
450 ROT=32:XDRAW F AT X4,187:DRAW G AT X4,187:ROT=Z:
    RETURN
470 FOR Y2=155 TO 55 STEP -20:Y1=Y2:Y=Y1+6:X=X6-11:RV=
    48:X1=X6
480 GOSUB 260:X=X6+1:Y=Y2+12:RV=32:GOSUB 260:X=X6+11
490 Y=Y2-4:RV=16:GOSUB 260:X=X6:Y=Y2-20:RV=Z:GOSUB 260:
    NEXT:RETURN
500 FOR J=1 TO 50:NEXT:RETURN
520 FOR J=1 TO 10:NEXT:RETURN
530 FOR J=1 TO 25:NEXT:RETURN
540 FOR J=1 TO 100:NEXT:RETURN
600 FOR J=1 TO 500:NEXT:RETURN
620 FOR J=1 TO 1000:NEXT:RETURN
700 FOR J=1 TO 25:PRINT C$;:NEXT:RETURN
720 GOSUB 530:CALL -958:RETURN
740 FOR Y=1 TO 18:HTAB X:VTAB Y:PRINT B$;:HTAB X
750 VTAB Y+1:PRINT"O";:GOSUB 500:NEXT:RETURN
800 Z=0:X=Z:Y=Z:X1=Z:Y1=Z:X2=Z:Y2=Z
810 F=Z:G=Z:X3=92:X4=188:Y3=155:Y4=167
830 B$=CHR$(32):C$="*":BL$=CHR$(7)
900 HGR2:TEXT:HOME:GOSUB 1000
910 GOSUB 5000:GOSUB 1100:HGR2
920 HCOLOR=3:ROT=Z:SCALE=1:GOSUB 1500
990 TEXT:HOME:GOSUB 4000:END
1000 X=9:Y=7:HTAB X+2:VTAB Y+2
1010 PRINT"A P P L E    A R E N A"
1020 HTAB X+6:VTAB Y+5:PRINT"P R O U D L Y"
1030 HTAB X+5:VTAB Y+8:PRINT"P R E S E N T S"
1040 HTAB X:VTAB Y:GOSUB 700:FOR J=1 TO 9:VTAB Y+J
1050 HTAB X:PRINT C$;:HTAB X+24:PRINT C$;:NEXT
1060 HTAB X:VTAB Y+10:GOSUB 700:RETURN
1100 X=9:VTAB 12:FOR K=6 TO 18 STEP 2:HTAB X+K:GOSUB
     600
1110 PRINT"-";:NEXT:FOR K=1 TO 3:GOSUB 620:NEXT:HOME:
     VTAB 5
1120 FOR X=34 TO 9 STEP -1:HTAB X:PRINT"T H E";
1130 GOSUB 720:NEXT:VTAB 12:FOR X=28 TO 13 STEP -1:HTAB
     X
1140 PRINT"F L Y I N G";:GOSUB 720:NEXT:VTAB 19
```

```
1150 FOR X=24 TO 17 STEP -1:HTAB X:PRINT
     "W A L L    N S";
1160 GOSUB 720:NEXT:GOSUB 620:GOSUB 620:X=25:GOSUB 740
1170 X=27:GOSUB 740:GOSUB 620:GOSUB 620:RETURN
1500 HPLOT Z,190 TO 279,190:HPLOT Z,191 TO 279,191
1510 GOSUB 200:GOSUB 240:X=12:Y=Y4:X1=X:Y1=Y
1520 DRAW 1 AT X,Y:DRAW 1 AT 269,Y:GOSUB 620:GOSUB 620
1530 F=1:G=3:GOSUB 250:GOSUB 620:GOSUB 620:X1=X:Y1=Y:F=
     3
1540 RV=16:X=X+32:Y=Y+11:GOSUB 260:RV=32:X=X+10:Y=Y+11
1550 GOSUB 260:RV=48:X=X+8:Y=Y-11:GOSUB 260:RV=Z:G=1:X=
     X+30
1560 Y=Y-11:GOSUB 260:PRINT BL$;BL$:GOSUB 340:X=269:Y=
     167:X1=264:Y1=Y:F=1:G=4
1570 GOSUB 620:GOSUB 620:GOSUB 250:GOSUB 600
1600 FOR Y=Y4 TO 21 STEP -6:Y1=Y-3:Y2=Y-6:X=X1:F=4:G=5
1610 GOSUB 250:GOSUB 500:GOSUB 280:GOSUB 240:GOSUB 500
1620 NEXT:Y=Y2:X=264:X1=X:Y1=Y:GOSUB 250:GOSUB 540
1630 FOR X=264 TO 201 STEP -6:X1=X-3:X2=X-6:F=5:G=4
1640 GOSUB 250:GOSUB 240:GOSUB 540:GOSUB 300
1650 GOSUB 290:GOSUB 540:GOSUB 300:NEXT
1800 GOSUB 620:GOSUB 340:FOR X=198 TO 216 STEP 6:X1=X+3
1810 X2=X+6:Y=Y2:Y1=Y:F=5:G=4:GOSUB 250:GOSUB 530:GOSUB
     290
1820 GOSUB 530:NEXT:GOSUB 620:X=X2:GOSUB 250:GOSUB 620
1830 F=4:G=4:RV=48:X=X4:Y=37:GOSUB 260:GOSUB 620
1840 ROT=Z:GOSUB 340:GOSUB 340
2000 GOSUB 600:GOSUB 620:ROT=48:RV=32:X1=X4:Y1=37
2010 X=191:Y=50:F=4:G=4:GOSUB 260:GOSUB 240:RV=16:X=190:
     Y=55:GOSUB 260
2020 RV=Z:X=189:Y=60:GOSUB 260:X1=X4:Y1=65:GOSUB 250
2030 X=X3:Y=Y4:F=1:G=2:GOSUB 320:X=X4:GOSUB 500:X1=X:F=
     4:G=4
2040 FOR Y1=70 TO Y3 STEP 5:Y=Y1-5:GOSUB 250:GOSUB 530:
     NEXT
2050 Y=Y3:X1=X3:Y1=Y4:F=4:G=2:XDRAW 4 AT X4,Y3:XDRAW 2
     AT X3,Y4
2100 FOR K=1 TO 2
2110 GOSUB 220:F=1:G=2:GOSUB 360:X=X3:X1=X:G=1:Y6=177:
     Y7=189
2120 GOSUB 400:XDRAW 2 AT X4,Y4:GOSUB 200:F=2:G=1:GOSUB
     370
2130 X=X4:X1=X:F=1:Y6=189:Y7=177:GOSUB 400:XDRAW 2 AT
     X3,Y4:NEXT
```

```
2300 GOSUB 220:F=3:G=2:GOSUB 360:G=3
2310 X6=X3:GOSUB 470:FOR Y2=35 TO 135 STEP 20:Y1=Y2:Y=
     Y2+16
2320 X1=X3:X=X1-11:RV=48:GOSUB 260:RV=32:X=X3+1:Y=Y2+32:
     GOSUB 260
2330 RV=16:X=X3+11:Y=Y2+26:GOSUB 260:RV=0:X=X3:Y=Y2+20:
     GOSUB 260:NEXT
2340 XDRAW F AT X3,Y3:XDRAW 2 AT X4,Y4:GOSUB 200:F=2:G=
     3:GOSUB 370:F=3
2350 X6=X4:GOSUB 470:X1=X4:Y1=35:RV=48:X=177:Y=51:G=2
2360 GOSUB 260:RV=32:X=189:Y=66:F=2:G=3:GOSUB 260:F=3
2370 G=1:FOR Y=66 TO 166 STEP 10:Y1=Y+5:Y2=Y+10:GOSUB
     250
2380 GOSUB 500:GOSUB 280:GOSUB 500:NEXT
2390 XDRAW F AT X,Y2:ROT=0:XDRAW 2 AT X3,Y4
2400 GOSUB 220:ROT=32:DRAW 2 AT X4,187:ROT=0:DRAW 1 AT
     X3,154:PRINT BL$
2800 X=X3:F=1:G=1:FOR Y=154 TO 14 STEP -10:Y1=Y-5:X1=X+
     3:GOSUB 250:GOSUB 530
2810 X=X1+3:Y2=Y1-5:GOSUB 280:GOSUB 530:NEXT:G=2:X=182
2820 Y=4:X1=X4:Y1=8:GOSUB 250:GOSUB 500:F=2:X=194
2830 Y2=12:GOSUB 280:GOSUB 500:Y=Y2:X1=200:Y1=17
2840 GOSUB 250:GOSUB 620:F=1:GOSUB 280:GOSUB 500:G=1
2850 X1=X4:Y1=8:GOSUB 250:GOSUB 500:X=182:Y2=4:F=2
2860 GOSUB 280:GOSUB 500:G=2:FOR Y=4 TO 144 STEP 10:F=2
2870 Y1=Y+5:X1=X-3:GOSUB 250:G=3:GOSUB 450:X=X1-3
2880 Y2=Y1+5:G=2:GOSUB 280:F=3:GOSUB 450:NEXT
3000 XDRAW 2 AT X3,154:ROT=32:XDRAW 2 AT X4,187:ROT=0:
     GOSUB 200
3010 DRAW 2 AT X3,Y4:ROT=32:DRAW 2 AT X4,176:X=X4
3020 FOR Y=176 TO 56 STEP -10:X1=X-5:Y1=Y-5:F=2
3030 G=3:GOSUB 250:GOSUB 500:X=X1-5:Y2=Y-10:GOSUB 280
3040 GOSUB 500:NEXT:X=58:X1=X:Y=46:Y1=51:G=1
3050 GOSUB 250:F=1:FOR Y=51 TO 181 STEP 5:Y1=Y+5
3060 GOSUB 250:GOSUB 520:NEXT:Y2=189:GOSUB 280
3070 FOR Y=189 TO 169 STEP -5:Y1=Y-5:GOSUB 250:GOSUB
     530
3080 NEXT:FOR Y=164 TO 184 STEP 5:Y1=Y+5:GOSUB 250
3090 GOSUB 530:NEXT:PRINT BL$
3500 GOSUB 600:Y=187:XDRAW 1 AT X,189:ROT=16
3510 DRAW 4 AT X,Y:GOSUB 620:F=4:G=5:GOSUB 320
3520 GOSUB 620:GOSUB 330:GOSUB 620:ROT=0:X=X3:Y=Y4
3530 F=2:G=4:GOSUB 320:GOSUB 620:GOSUB 600:F=1:GOSUB
     330
3540 GOSUB 620:GOSUB 600:G=2:GOSUB 320
```

```
3550 PRINT BL$;BL$;BL$:GOSUB 620:RETURN
4000 HTAB 17:VTAB 10:PRINT"F I N I S"
4010 GOSUB 620:GOSUB 620:HTAB 1:VTAB 20:RETURN
5000 X6=25600
5010 RESTORE:F=INT(X6/256):G=X6-F*256:POKE 232,G:POKE
     233,F:X=X6-1
5100 READ Y:IF Y=999 THEN 5300
5110 IF Y>=0 THEN X=X+1:POKE X,Y:GOTO 5100
5120 READ F:FOR J=1 TO -Y:X=X+1:POKE X,F:NEXT
5130 GOTO 5100
5300 FOR J=208 TO 278:Y=PEEK(X6+J):POKE X6-100+J,Y:NEXT
5400 FOR J=79 TO 107:Y=PEEK(X6+J):POKE X6+100+J,Y:NEXT:
     RETURN
6000 DATA  6,0,14,0,108,0,208,0,69,1,109,1,175,1
6010 DATA  173,63,55,45,53,63,119,109,58,63,63
6020 DATA  159,-4,45,173,-5,63,55,-5,45,173,-6,63
6030 DATA  55,109,9,45,109,9,173,63,223,59,63,223,59,55,
     109
6040 DATA  73,45,109,73,173,63,223,59,63,63,223,59,119
6050 DATA  73,9,45,45,53,63,63,55,109,41,62,223,55
6060 DATA  109,41,62,223,55,109,41,21,63,223,63,23,45
6070 DATA  77,9,45,5,-101,0
6100 DATA  173,63,255,219,219,42,77,73,41,45
6110 DATA  77,73,41,30,63,223,27,63,255,219
6120 DATA  63,46,109,73,41,77,73,45,30,63,223,63,63
6130 DATA  255,59,55,-7,45,245,-6,63,119,-5,45
6140 DATA  245,59,-3,63,78,45,53,63,55,45,173,63,63
6150 DATA  55,45,45,173,-3,63,55,45,77,45,21,63,223,27
6160 DATA  63,23,45,77,73,41,173,63,223,219,219,63,46
6170 DATA  109,73,73,41,53,255,-3,219,255,42,109
6180 DATA  -3,73,9,45,5,0
6200 DATA  53,63,46,53,63,14,173,63,191,45,45
6210 DATA  62,63,55,45,45,62,63,55,45,45,30,63,46
6220 DATA  53,63,46,53,55,53,55,53,55,53,63,159,45,45,5,
     0
6300 DATA  53,63,46,53,63,14,173,63,255,42
6310 DATA  45,45,62,63,63,191,-3,45,53
6320 DATA  63,255,59,255,42,45,77,41,45,30
6330 DATA  63,223,219,119,73,73,45,62,191,45
6340 DATA  53,255,191,45,13,53,255,59,55,109
6350 DATA  9,53,255,219,255,42,45,77,9,53,63
6360 DATA  159,45,45,5,0
6400 DATA  21,63,23,45,45,21,-3,63,23
6410 DATA  -4,45,21,-5,63,23,-6,45,5,0
6420 DATA  999
```

EASY CHANGES

1. If you wish to have the Walloons perform more (or less) jumps during their performance, change the loop bound value of 2 in line 2100 accordingly. To get four jumps, use

    2100 FOR K=1 TO 4

2. The title placard is currently bordered by asterisks. To get another character, change the string value of C$ in line 830. For example, to have the title placard bordered by plus signs (+), alter line 830 to read:

    830 B$=CHR$(32):C$="+":BL$=CHR$(7)

3. You might want to personalize the title placard and make yourself the presenter of the Walloons. This can be done by altering the string literal, "APPLE ARENA", in line 1010 to something else. However, you cannot use a string with a length of more than 22 characters or it will be clipped by the end of the placard. To say, for example, that Mr. Simon Q. Fenster presents the Walloons, change line 1010 to read:

    1010 PRINT"MR. SIMON Q. FENSTER"

4. As currently written, the program uses page 2 of high-resolution graphics and stores the shape table at decimal address 25600. If your system has 16K of RAM and Applesoft in ROM (see Appendix 1), you should be able to run Walloons with the following changes:

    900 HGR:TEXT:HOME:GOSUB 1000
    910 GOSUB 5000:GOSUB 1100:HGR:POKE –16302,0
    5000 X6=7690

MAIN ROUTINES

200 - 490	Subroutines to draw (and erase) Walloons and their performing apparatus.
500 - 620	Time-delay subroutines.
700 - 750	Utility subroutines.
800 - 830	Initializes variables.
900 - 990	Drives text and graphics displays.
1000 - 1060	Subroutine to display placard.
1100 - 1170	The performers are announced.
1500 - 1570	The Walloons make their entrance.

1600 - 2880   Flying Walloons perform.
3000 - 3550   Concludes Walloons performance.
4000 - 4010   Displays final message.
5000 - 6420   Subroutine to store shape table at address X6.

MAIN VARIABLES

X,Y   Current X,Y location of Walloon; also shape table data values and locations.

X1,Y1;

X2,Y2;   Reference X, Y locations for Walloons.

X3,Y3;

X4,Y4

F,G   Current shapes to draw and/or erase; also shape table index values.

X6   Starting address of shape table.

RV   Graphics rotation factor.

K,J   Loop indices.

B$ Blank character.

C$ Title placard border character.

BL$ ASCII value to ring bell.

Z   Zero.

SUGGESTED PROJECTS

1. There are many possibilities for "spicing up" the Walloons' act with extra tricks or improved ones. Perhaps you would like to change their finish. To get you started, here are changes to produce one alternate ending:
   ```
   3020 FOR Y=176 TO 96 STEP -10:X1=X-5:Y1=Y-5:F=2
   3040 GOSUB 500:NEXT:Y=Y2:X1=X-5:Y1=Y-5:GOSUB 250
   3050 F=3:X=X1:FOR Y=81 TO 161 STEP 5:Y1=Y+5
   3060 GOSUB 250:GOSUB 520:NEXT:GOTO 3550
   ```

2. If you add some alternate tricks or endings as suggested in the previous project, try randomizing if and when they will be done. Thus, the Walloons' performance will be different each time the program is run. At least their ending may be variable.

3. Scour the world yourself for other acts to include in the Apple Arena. Maybe someday we will have a complete software library of performing artists.

Section 5

Mathematics Programs

INTRODUCTION TO MATHEMATICS PROGRAMS

Since their invention, computers have been used to solve mathematical problems. Their great speed and reliability render solvable many otherwise difficult (or impossible) calculations. Several different numerical techniques lend themselves naturally to computer solution. The following programs explore some of them. They will be of interest mainly to engineers, students, mathematicians, statisticians, and others who encounter such problems in their work.

GRAPH takes advantage of the Apple's graphic powers to draw the graph of a function $Y = f(X)$. The function is supplied by you. INTEGRATE calculates the integral, or "area under the curve," for any such function.

Experimental scientific work frequently results in data at discrete values of X and Y. CURVE finds a polynomial algebraic expression to express this data with a formula.

Theoretical scientists (and algebra students) often must find the solution to a set of simultaneous linear algebraic equations. SIMEQN does the trick.

Much modern engineering work requires the solution of differential equations. DIFFEQN will solve any first-order ordinary differential equation that you provide.

STATS will take a list of data and derive standard statistical information describing it. In addition, it will sort the data list into ranking numerical order.

CURVE

PURPOSE AND DISCUSSION

CURVE fits a polynomial function to a set of data. The data must be in the form of pairs of X-Y points. This type of data occurs frequently as the result of some experiment, or perhaps from sampling tabular data in a reference book.

There are many reasons why you might want an analytic formula to express the functional relationship inherent in the data. Often you will have experimental errors in the Y values. A good formula expression tends to smooth out these fluctuations. Perhaps you want to know the value of Y at some X not obtained exactly in the experiment. This may be a point between known X values (interpolation) or one outside the experimental range (extrapolation). If you wish to use the data in a computer program, a good formula is a convenient and efficient way to do it.

This program fits a curve of the form

$$Y = C_0 + C_1 X^1 + C_2 X^2 + \ldots + C_D X^D$$

to your data. You may select D, the degree (or power) of the highest term, to be as large as 7. The constant coefficients, $C_0 - C_D$, are the main output of the program. Also calculated is the goodness of fit, a guide to the accuracy of the fit. You may fit different degree polynomials to the same data and also ask to have Y calculated for specific values of X.

The numerical technique involved in the computation is known as least squares curve fitting. It minimizes the sum of the squares of the errors. The least squares method reduces the problem to a set of simultaneous algebraic equations. Thus these equations could be solved by the algorithm used in SIMEQN. In fact, once the proper equations are set up, CURVE uses the identical subroutine found in SIMEQN to solve the equations. For more information, the bibliography contains references to descriptions of the numerical technique.

HOW TO USE IT

The first thing you must do, of course, is enter the data into the program. This consists of typing in pairs of numbers. Each pair represents an X value and its corresponding Y value. The two numbers (of each pair) are separated by a comma. A question mark will prompt you for each data pair. After you have entered them all, type

$$999,999$$

to signal the end of the data. When you do this, the program will respond by indicating how many data pairs have been entered. A maximum of 75 data pairs is allowed.

Next, you must input the degree of the polynomial to be fitted. This can be any non-negative integer subject to certain constraints. The maximum allowed is 7. Also, D must be less than the number of data pairs.

A few notes regarding the selection of D may be of interest. If $D=0$, the program will output the mean value of Y as the coefficient C_0. If $D=1$, the program will be calculating the best straight line through the data. This special case is known as "linear regression." If D is one less than the number of data pairs, the program will find an exact fit to the data (barring round-off and other numerical errors). This is a solution which passes exactly through each data point.

Once you have entered the desired degree, the program will begin calculating the results. There will be a pause while this calculation is performed. The time involved depends on the number of data pairs and the degree selected. For 25 data pairs and a third degree fit, the pause will be less than half a minute. Fifty data pairs and a fifth degree fit will take about a minute.

The results are displayed in a table. It gives the values of the coefficients for each power of X from 0 to D. That is, the values of $C_0 - C_D$ are output. Also shown is the percent goodness of fit. This is a measure of how accurately the program was able to fit the given case. A value of 100 percent means perfect fit, lesser values indicate correspondingly poorer fits. It is hard to say what value denotes *satisfactory* fit since much depends on the accuracy of data and the purpose at hand. But as a rule of thumb, anything in the high nineties is quite good. For those interested, the formula to calculate the percent goodness of fit is

$$\text{P.G.F.} = 100 * \sqrt{ 1 - \frac{\sum\limits_i (Y_i - \hat{Y}_i)^2}{\sum\limits_i (Y_i - \bar{Y})^2} }$$

where Y_i are the actual Y data values, $\hat{Y}_i$ are the calculated Y values (through the polynomial expression), and $\bar{Y}$ is the mean value of Y.

Next, you are presented with three options for continuing the run. These are 1) determining specific points, 2) fitting another degree, 3) ending the program. Simply type **1**, **2**, or **3** to make your selection. A description of each choice now follows.

Option 1 allows you to see the value of Y that the current fit will produce for a given value of X. In this mode you are continually prompted to supply any value of X. The program then shows what the polynomial expression produces as the value for Y. Input 999 for an X value to leave this mode.

Option 2 allows you to fit another degree polynomial to the same data. Frequently, you will want to try successively higher values of D to improve the goodness of fit., Unless round-off errors occur, this will cause the percent goodness of fit to increase.

Option 3 simply terminates the program and with that we will terminate this explanation of how to use CURVE.

SAMPLE PROBLEM AND RUN

Problem: An art investor is considering the purchase of Primo's masterpiece, "Frosted Fantasy." Since 1940, the painting has been for sale at auction seven times. Here is the painting's sales record from these auctions.

Year	Price
1940	$ 8000.
1948	$13000.
1951	$16000.
1956	$20000.
1962	$28000.
1968	$39000.
1975	$53000.

The painting is going to be sold at auction in 1981. What price should the investor expect to have to pay to purchase the painting? If he resold it in 1985, how much profit should he expect to make?

Solution: The investor will try to get a polynomial function that expresses the value of the painting as a function of the year. This is suitable for CURVE. The year will be represented by the variable X, and the price is shown by the variable Y. To keep the magnitude of the numbers small, the years will be expressed as elapsed years since 1900, and the price will be in units of $1000. (Thus a year of 40 represents 1940, a price of 8 represents $8000.)

SAMPLE RUN

```
    - LEAST SQUARES CURVE FITTING -

ENTER A DATA PAIR IN RESPONSE TO EACH
QUESTION MARK.   EACH PAIR IS AN X VALUE
AND A Y VALUE SEPARATED BY A COMMA.

AFTER ALL DATA IS ENTERED, TYPE
 999,999
IN RESPONSE TO THE LAST QUESTION MARK.

THE PROGRAM IS CURRENTLY SET TO
ACCEPT A MAXIMUM OF 75 DATA PAIRS.

X,Y=? 40,8
X,Y=? 48,13
X,Y=? 51,16
```

```
X,Y=? 56,20
X,Y=? 62,28
X,Y=? 68,39
X,Y=? 75,53
X,Y=? 999,999
```

7 DATA PAIRS ENTERED

DEGREE OF POLYNOMIAL TO BE FITTED? 1

X POWER	COEFFICIENT
0	-48.2701205
1	1.28722711

PERCENT GOODNESS OF FIT= 97.5302068

-- CONTINUATION OPTIONS --

```
1 - DETERMINE SPECIFIC POINTS
2 - FIT ANOTHER DEGREE TO SAME DATA
3 - END PROGRAM
```

WHAT NEXT? 2

DEGREE OF POLYNOMIAL TO BE FITTED?2

X POWER	COEFFICIENT
0	38.475481
1	-1.83492574
2	.0270347151

PERCENT GOODNESS OF FIT= 99.9485752

⋮

(continuation options displayed again)

⋮

WHAT NEXT? 1

ENTER 999 TO LEAVE THIS MODE

```
X=? 81
Y= 67.2212621
```

X=? 85
Y= 77.8326099

X=? 999

                                •
                                •
    (continuation options displayed again)
                                •
                                •

WHAT NEXT? 3

Initially, a first degree fit was tried and a goodness of fit of
about 97.5% was obtained. The investor wanted to do better,
so he tried a second degree fit next. This had a very high goodness of fit. He then asked for the extrapolation of his data to
the years 1981 and 1985. He found that he should expect to
pay about $67200 to buy the painting in 1981. Around a
$10500 profit could be expected upon resale in 1985.

Of course, the investor did not make his decision solely on
the basis of this program. He used it only as one guide to his
decision. There is never any guarantee that financial data will
perform in the future as it has done in the past. Though CURVE
is probably as good a way as any, extrapolation of data can
never be a totally reliable process.

PROGRAM LISTING

```
100 REM: CURVE
110 REM: COPYRIGHT 1980 BY PHIL FELDMAN AND TOM RUGG
130 TEXT
150 MX=75
160 EF=999
170 MD=7
200 DIM X(MX),Y(MX)
210 Q=MD+1:DIM A(Q,Q),R(Q),V(Q)
220 Q=MD*2:DIM P(Q)
300 HOME:PRINT"   - LEAST SQUARES CURVE FITTING -":PRINT
310 PRINT"ENTER A DATA PAIR IN RESPONSE TO EACH"
320 PRINT"QUESTION MARK.  EACH PAIR IS AN X VALUE"
330 PRINT"AND A Y VALUE SEPARATED BY A COMMA.":PRINT
340 PRINT:PRINT"AFTER ALL DATA IS ENTERED, TYPE"
350 PRINT SPC(1);EF;",";EF
```

```
360 PRINT"IN RESPONSE TO THE LAST QUESTION MARK.":PRINT
370 PRINT:PRINT"THE PROGRAM IS CURRENTLY SET TO"
380 PRINT"ACCEPT A MAXIMUM OF ";MX;" DATA PAIRS."
400 PRINT:PRINT:J=0
410 J=J+1:INPUT"X,Y=? ";X(J),Y(J)
420 IF X(J)=EF AND Y(J)=EF THEN J=J-1:GOTO 450
430 IF J=MX THEN PRINT:PRINT"NO MORE DATA ALLOWED":GOTO
    450
440 GOTO 410
450 NP=J:PRINT
460 IF NP=0 THEN GOSUB 1600:PRINT"NO DATA ENTERED":STOP
470 PRINT NP;" DATA PAIRS ENTERED":PRINT
500 PRINT:INPUT"DEGREE OF POLYNOMIAL TO BE FITTED? ";D:
    PRINT
510 IF D<0 THEN GOSUB 1500:PRINT"DEGREE MUST BE >= 0":
    GOTO 500
520 D=INT(D):IF D<NP THEN 540
530 GOSUB 1500:PRINT"NOT ENOUGH DATA":GOTO 500
540 D2=2*D:IF D>MD THEN GOSUB 1500:PRINT
    "DEGREE TOO HIGH":GOTO 500
550 N=D+1
600 FOR J=1 TO D2:P(J)=0:FOR K=1 TO NP
610 P(J)=P(J)+X(K)↑J:NEXT:NEXT:P(0)=NP
620 R(1)=0:FOR J=1 TO NP:R(1)=R(1)+Y(J)
630 NEXT:IF N=1 THEN 660
640 FOR J=2 TO N:R(J)=0:FOR K=1 TO NP
650 R(J)=R(J)+Y(K)*X(K)↑(J-1):NEXT:NEXT
660 FOR J=1 TO N:FOR K=1 TO N:A(J,K)=P(J+K-2):NEXT:NEXT
670 GOSUB 2000
700 PRINT:PRINT TAB(1);"X POWER            COEFFICIENT"
710 PRINT TAB(1);:FOR J=1 TO 7:PRINT"-";:NEXT:PRINT
    TAB(17);
720 FOR J=1 TO 11:PRINT"-";:NEXT:PRINT
730 FOR J=1 TO N:PRINT"   ";J-1,V(J):NEXT:PRINT:PRINT
740 Q=0:FOR J=1 TO NP:Q=Q+Y(J):NEXT:M=Q/NP:T=0:G=0:FOR
    J=1 TO NP
750 Q=0:FOR K=1 TO N:Q=Q+V(K)*X(J)↑(K-1):NEXT:T=T+(Y(J)-
    Q)↑2
760 G=G+(Y(J)-M)↑2:NEXT:IF G=0 THEN T=100:GOTO 780
770 T=100*SQR(1-T/G)
780 PRINT"PERCENT GOODNESS OF FIT= ";T
800 PRINT:PRINT"-- CONTINUATION OPTIONS --":PRINT
810 PRINT"  1 - DETERMINE SPECIFIC POINTS"
820 PRINT"  2 - FIT ANOTHER DEGREE TO SAME DATA"
830 PRINT"  3 - END PROGRAM":PRINT
```

```
840 INPUT"WHAT NEXT? ";Q:Q=INT(Q):IF Q=3 THEN END
850 IF Q=2 THEN 500
860 IF Q<>1 THEN 800
900 PRINT:PRINT:PRINT"ENTER ";EF;" TO LEAVE THIS MODE"
910 PRINT:INPUT"X=? ";XV:IF XV=EF THEN 800
920 YV=0:FOR K=1 TO N
930 YV=YV+V(K)*XV↑(K-1):NEXT:PRINT"Y= ";YV
940 GOTO 910
1500 PRINT"** ";:FLASH:PRINT"ERROR!";:NORMAL
1510 PRINT" ** -- ";:RETURN
1600 PRINT"** ";:FLASH:PRINT"FATAL ERROR!";:NORMAL
1610 PRINT" ** -- ";:RETURN
2000 IF N=1 THEN V(1)=R(1)/A(1,1):RETURN
2010 FOR K=1 TO N-1
2020 I=K+1
2030 L=K
2040 IF ABS(A(I,K))>ABS(A(L,K)) THEN L=I
2050 IF I<N THEN I=I+1:GOTO 2040
2060 IF L=K THEN 2100
2070 FOR J=K TO N:Q=A(K,J):A(K,J)=A(L,J)
2080 A(L,J)=Q:NEXT
2090 Q=R(K):R(K)=R(L):R(L)=Q
2100 I=K+1
2110 Q=A(I,K)/A(K,K):A(I,K)=0
2120 FOR J=K+1 TO N:A(I,J)=A(I,J)-Q*A(K,J):NEXT
2130 R(I)=R(I)-Q*R(K):IF I<N THEN I=I+1:GOTO 2110
2140 NEXT
2150 V(N)=R(N)/A(N,N):FOR I=N-1 TO 1 STEP -1
2160 Q=0:FOR J=I+1 TO N:Q=Q+A(I,J)*V(J)
2170 V(I)=(R(I)-Q)/A(I,I):NEXT:NEXT
2180 RETURN
```

EASY CHANGES

1. The program uses 999 as the flag number to terminate various input modes. This may cause a problem if your data include 999. You can easily change the flag number by modifying the value of EF in line 160 to any value not needed in your data. To use 10101, for example, make this change:

160 EF=10101

2. Currently a maximum value of 75 data pairs is allowed. If you need more, change the value of MX in line 150 to the

number required. For example, to allow up to 200 data pairs, use

$$150 \ MX = 200$$

3. To allow fits of higher degrees than seven, set MD in line 170 to the maximum degree desired. To achieve up to tenth degree fits, set the value of MD appropriately:

$$170 \ MD = 10$$

However, it must be stressed that it can be unreliable to attempt high degree fits. Unless your data is well behaved (X and Y values close to 1), the program will often not produce accurate results if D is greater than five or so. This is because sums of powers of X and Y are calculated up to powers of 2*D. These various sums are several orders of magnitude different from each other. Errors result because of the numerous truncation and round-off operations involved in doing arithmetic with them. A practical limit for MD is seven.

4. The demand on available RAM memory is increased if you raise the values of MX or MD as described in the above two Easy Changes. As written, the program should run on an Apple with 4K bytes free (see Appendix 1). If your system has less, you may need to decrease MX and/or MD to enable the program to run. Should MX or MD be set too large for your available memory, an out-of-memory or illegal-quantity error will result after execution begins.

MAIN ROUTINES

150 - 170	Initializes constants.
200 - 220	Dimensions arrays.
300 - 380	Displays introductory messages.
400 - 470	Gets X–Y input data from the user.
500 - 550	Gets degree of polynomial from the user, determines if it is acceptable.
600 - 670	Sets up equations for the simultaneous equation solver and calls it.
700 - 780	Calculates percent goodness of fit, displays all results.
800 - 860	Gets user's continuation option and branches to it.
900 - 940	Determines Y value corresponding to any X value.
1500 - 1610	Subroutines to print flashing error messages.

2000 - 2180 Subroutine to solve simultaneous linear algebraic
              equations.

MAIN VARIABLES

MX	Maximum number of data pairs allowed.
MD	Maximum degree allowed to fit.
EF	Ending flag value for data input and X point mode.
X,Y	Arrays of X and Y data points.
NP	Number of data pairs entered.
D	Degree of polynomial to fit.
D2	2*D, the maximum power sum to compute.
N	D+1, number of simultaneous equations to solve.
A,R,V	Arrays for simultaneous linear equation solver.
P	Array for holding sums of various powers of X.
I,J,K,L	Loop indices.
Q,G	Work variables.
M	Mean value of Y.
T	Percent goodness of fit.
XV	Specific X point for which to calculate Y.
YV	Y value corresponding to XV.

SUGGESTED PROJECTS

1. No provision for modifying the data is incorporated into the
   program. Often it would be nice to add, subtract, or modify
   parts of the data after some results are seen. Build in a
   capability to do this.
2. You may desire other forms of output. A useful table for
   many applications might include the actual X values, calculated Y values, and/or percentage errors in Y.
3. Sometimes certain points (or certain regions of points) are
   known to be more accurate than others. Then you would
   like to weight these points as being more important than
   others to be fit correctly. The least squares method can be
   modified to include such a weighting parameter with each
   data pair. Research this technique and incorporate it into the
   program. (Note: you can achieve some weighting with the
   current program by entering important points two or more
   times. There is a certain danger to this, however. You must
   only ask for a solution with D less than the number of *unique*
   data points. A division by zero error may result otherwise.)

4. Often you wish to try successively higher degree polynomials until a certain minimum percent goodness of fit is obtained. Modify the program to accept a minimally satisfactory percent goodness of fit from the user. Then have the program automatically try various polynomial fits until it finds the lowest degree fit, if any, with a satisfactory goodness of fit.

DIFFEQN

PURPOSE

Differential equations express functions by giving the rate of change of one variable with respect to another. This type of relation occurs regularly in almost all the physical sciences. The solution of these equations is necessary in many practical engineering problems.

For many such equations, a closed form (or exact analytical expression) solution can be obtained. However, for just as many, no such "simple" solution exists. The equation must then be solved numerically, usually by a computer program such as this.

There are many types and classes of differential equations. This program solves those of a simple type; namely, first order, ordinary differential equations. This means that the equation to be solved can be written in the form

$$\frac{dY}{dX} = \text{(any function of X,Y)}$$

Here, X is the independent variable and Y is the dependent variable. The equation expresses the derivative (or rate of change) of Y with respect to X. The right-hand side is an expression which may involve X and/or Y.

To use the program, you must supply it with the differential equation to be solved. The procedure used to do this is explained in the "How To Use It" section.

A technique known as the "fourth-order, Runge-Kutta" method is used to solve the equation. Space limitations prevent any detailed explanation of it here. However, it is discussed well in the numerical analysis books referenced in the bibliography.

The program allows two forms of output. You can have the answers tabulated in columns or plotted graphically.

HOW TO USE IT

The first thing you must do is enter the differential equation into the program. This must be done at line 200. Currently this line contains a GOTO statement. This GOTO will cause an error message to be displayed if the program is run before you have changed line 200. The form of line 200 should be:

200 D = (your function of X,Y)

D represents dY/dX. GOSUBs are made to line 200 with X and Y set to their current values. Thus, when each RETURN is made, D will be set to the appropriate value of dY/dX for that given X and Y. If necessary, you may use the lines between 200 and 899 to complete the definition of D. Line 899 already contains a RETURN statement so you do not need to add another one.

The program begins by warning you that you should have already entered the equation at line 200. You acknowledge that this has been done by hitting the C key to continue.

Now the various initial conditions are input. You are prompted for them one at a time. They consist of: the initial values of X and Y, the stepsize interval in X at which to display the output, and the final value of X.

You now have a choice between two types of output. Enter a T for tabular output or a G for graphical output. The tabular form is simply a two-column display of the corresponding values of X and Y.

The graphical output plots the values of Y along a horizontal axis as each corresponding X value is displayed on successive lines of the screen. This graphical display requires you to input the minimum and maximum values of Y that will be used on the Y axis. You will be prompted for them if this output form is chosen. An asterisk (*) is used to plot the value of Y. If, however, the value of Y is "off-scale," an open circle is plotted at the appropriate edge of the graph.

With the input phase completed, the program initializes things to begin the output. A question mark will be displayed in the lower left of the screen, telling you the program is waiting for you to hit any key to begin the output.

The output is displayed at each interval of the stepsize until the final value of X is reached. Output may temporarily be halted at any time by simply hitting any key. This will stop the display until you hit any key to resume the output. The output may be started and stopped as often as desired, thus enabling you to leisurely view intermediate results before they scroll off the screen. It is applicable to both the tabular and graphical forms of output.

SAMPLE PROBLEM AND RUN

Problem: A body, originally at rest, is subjected to a force of 2000 dynes. Its initial mass is 200 grams. However, while it moves, it loses mass at the rate of 1 gram/sec. There is also an air resistance equal to twice its velocity retarding its movement. The differential equation expressing this motion is:

$$\frac{dY}{dX} = \frac{(2000 - 2Y)}{(200 - X)} \qquad \text{where } Y = \text{velocity (cm./sec.)}$$
$$X = \text{time (sec.)}$$

Find the velocity of the body every ten seconds up through two and one-half minutes. Also, plot this velocity as a function of time.

Solution and Sample Run: The solution and sample run are illustrated in the accompanying photographs.

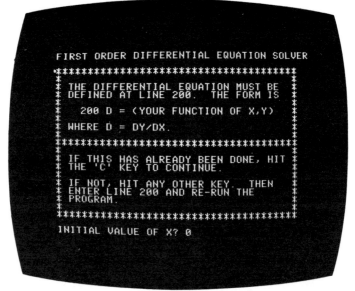

```
******************************************
*                                        *
* THE DIFFERENTIAL EQUATION MUST BE       *
* DEFINED AT LINE 200.  THE FORM IS       *
*                                        *
*   200 D = (YOUR FUNCTION OF X,Y)        *
*                                        *
* WHERE D = DY/DX.                        *
*                                        *
******************************************
*                                        *
* IF THIS HAS ALREADY BEEN DONE, HIT      *
* THE 'C' KEY TO CONTINUE.                *
*                                        *
* IF NOT, HIT ANY OTHER KEY.  THEN        *
* ENTER LINE 200 AND RE-RUN THE           *
* PROGRAM.                                *
*                                        *
******************************************

]200 D=(2000-2*Y)/(200-X)
]RUN
```

The operator hits a key to exit from the program. Then he enters
the differential equation into line 200. He types RUN to restart
the program.

```
    FIRST ORDER DIFFERENTIAL EQUATION SOLVER
******************************************
*                                        *
* THE DIFFERENTIAL EQUATION MUST BE       *
* DEFINED AT LINE 200.  THE FORM IS       *
*                                        *
*   200 D = (YOUR FUNCTION OF X,Y)        *
*                                        *
* WHERE D = DY/DX.                        *
*                                        *
******************************************
*                                        *
* IF THIS HAS ALREADY BEEN DONE, HIT      *
* THE 'C' KEY TO CONTINUE.                *
*                                        *
* IF NOT, HIT ANY OTHER KEY.  THEN        *
* ENTER LINE 200 AND RE-RUN THE           *
* PROGRAM.                                *
*                                        *
******************************************

INITIAL VALUE OF X? 0
```

The operator has hit the "C" key. The program responds by beginning the input phase. The operator has responded to the first
request.

```
INITIAL VALUE OF Y? 0
STEPSIZE IN X? 10
FINAL VALUE OF X? 150
OUTPUT FORM (T=TABLE, G=GRAPH) ? T
*****************************************
    THE FOLLOWING OUTPUT CAN BE HALTED
BY HITTING ANY KEY.  IT CAN THEN BE
RESUMED BY HITTING ANY KEY.  THIS MAY
BE DONE AS OFTEN AS DESIRED.

    WHEN THE QUESTION MARK (?) APPEARS,
HIT ANY KEY TO BEGIN THE OUTPUT.
*****************************************
X                    Y

?
```

The operator has completed the input and requested tabular output.
The program signals with a question mark that it is waiting for him
to hit any key. It will not continue the run until he does so.

```
*****************************************
X                    Y

0                    0
10                   97.4999135
20                   189.999821
30                   277.49972
40                   359.999609
50                   437.499483
60                   509.999337
70                   577.499165
80                   639.998955
90                   697.498692
100                  749.998352
110                  797.497896
120                  839.997256
130                  877.496312
140                  909.994825
150                  937.492274
```

The operator has hit a key and the program responds with the
tabulated output. X is time in seconds and Y is velocity in cm/sec.

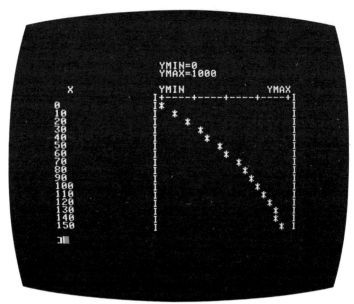

The program is rerun requesting graphical output. Before this photo,
the program requested a minimum and maximum value of Y to use
on the Y axis. Values of 0 and 1000 respectively were entered.
The program displays the desired graph.

PROGRAM LISTING

```
100 REM: DIFFEQN
110 REM: COPYRIGHT 1980 BY PHIL FELDMAN AND TOM RUGG
130 TEXT
150 GOTO 1200
190 REM
200 GOTO 3000:REM  REDEFINE THIS LINE TO BE D=(YOUR
    FUNCTION OF X,Y)
899 RETURN
900 REM  ***********************
910 REM  DEFINE THE DIFFERENTIAL
920 REM  EQUATION BETWEEN LINES
930 REM  200 AND 899
940 REM
950 REM  LINE 200 MUST BE
960 REM  OVERWRITTEN, MAKING IT
970 REM  THE FIRST LINE OF THE
980 REM  EQUATION.
990 REM  ***********************
```

```
1000 IF F$="T" THEN PRINT XX,YY:GOSUB 1160:RETURN
1010 F=(YY-YL)/(YH-YL):V=INT(17+20*F+0.5)
1020 C=42:IF YY<YL THEN V=17:C=79
1030 IF YY>YH THEN V=37:C=79
1040 PRINT XX;TAB(16);CHR$(73);TAB(V);CHR$(C);TAB(38);
     CHR$(73)
1050 GOSUB 1160:RETURN
1100 PRINT TAB(1);:FOR Q=1 TO 38:PRINT"*";:NEXT:PRINT:
     RETURN
1110 PRINT TAB(1);"*";TAB(38);"*":RETURN
1120 PRINT TAB(38);"*":RETURN
1160 Q=PEEK(-16384):IF Q<128 THEN RETURN
1170 POKE -16368,0
1180 Q=PEEK(-16384):IF Q<128 THEN 1180
1190 POKE -16368,0:RETURN
1200 HOME
1210 PRINT"FIRST ORDER DIFFERENTIAL EQUATION SOLVER"
1220 GOSUB 1100:GOSUB 1110
1230 PRINT TAB(1);"* THE DIFFERENTIAL EQUATION MUST BE";
     :GOSUB 1120
1240 PRINT TAB(1);"* DEFINED AT LINE 200.  THE FORM IS";
     :GOSUB 1120
1250 GOSUB 1110:PRINT TAB(1);
     "*    200 D = (YOUR FUNCTION OF X,Y)";:GOSUB 1120
1260 GOSUB 1110:PRINT TAB(1);"* WHERE D = DY/DX.";:
     GOSUB 1120
1270 GOSUB 1110:GOSUB 1100:GOSUB 1110
1280 PRINT TAB(1);"* IF THIS HAS ALREADY BEEN DONE, HIT"
     ;:GOSUB 1120
1290 PRINT TAB(1);"* THE 'C' KEY TO CONTINUE.";:GOSUB
     1120
1300 GOSUB 1110:PRINT TAB(1);
     "* IF NOT, HIT ANY OTHER KEY.  THEN";:GOSUB 1120
1310 PRINT TAB(1);"* ENTER LINE 200 AND RE-RUN THE";:
     GOSUB 1120
1320 PRINT TAB(1);"* PROGRAM.";:GOSUB 1120
1330 GOSUB 1110:GOSUB 1100
1400 PRINT:GET R$:IF R$<>"C" THEN END
1410 INPUT"INITIAL VALUE OF X? ";XX
1420 PRINT:INPUT"INITIAL VALUE OF Y? ";YY:Y=YY:X=XX:
     GOSUB 200
1430 PRINT:INPUT"STEPSIZE IN X? ";DX
1440 PRINT:INPUT"FINAL VALUE OF X? ";XF
1450 PRINT:INPUT"OUTPUT FORM (T=TABLE, G=GRAPH) ? ";F$
1460 F$=LEFT$(F$,1):IF F$<>"T" AND F$<>"G" THEN 1450
```

```
1470 IF F$="T" THEN 1600
1480 PRINT:INPUT"MINIMUM Y FOR THE GRAPH AXIS? ";YL
1490 PRINT:INPUT"MAXIMUM Y FOR THE GRAPH AXIS? ";YH
1500 IF YH>YL THEN 1600
1510 PRINT
1520 PRINT"*** ERROR! -- MAX Y MUST BE > MIN Y ***"
1530 GOTO 1480
1600 PRINT:GOSUB 1100:PRINT
1610 PRINT"   THE FOLLOWING OUTPUT CAN BE HALTED"
1620 PRINT"BY HITTING ANY KEY.  IT CAN THEN BE"
1630 PRINT"RESUMED BY HITTING ANY KEY.  THIS MAY"
1640 PRINT"BE DONE AS OFTEN AS DESIRED.":PRINT
1650 PRINT"   WHEN THE QUESTION MARK (?) APPEARS,"
1660 PRINT"HIT ANY KEY TO BEGIN THE OUTPUT."
1670 PRINT:GOSUB 1100:PRINT
1700 IF F$="T" THEN PRINT"X","Y":PRINT:GOTO 1800
1720 PRINT TAB(17);"YMIN=";YL:PRINT TAB(17);"YMAX=";YH
1730 PRINT:PRINT"   X";TAB(17);"YMIN";TAB(34);"YMAX"
1740 PRINT TAB(16);
1750 PRINT"I+----+----+----+----+I";
1800 PRINT:PRINT"?";
1810 GET R$
1820 PRINT CHR$(8);CHR$(32);CHR$(8);
1830 POKE -16368,0:GOSUB 1000
1900 Q=XX+DX:IF Q>XF+1.E-5 THEN END
1910 X=XX:Y=YY:GOSUB 200:K0=D:X=XX+DX/2:Y=YY+K0*DX/2
1920 GOSUB 200:K1=D:Y=YY+K1*DX/2:GOSUB 200:K2=D
1930 X=XX+DX:Y=YY+K2*DX:GOSUB 200:K3=D
1940 DY=DX*(K0+2*K1+2*K2+K3)/6
1950 YY=YY+DY:XX=XX+DX:GOSUB 1000
1960 GOTO 1900
3000 PRINT:PRINT"*** ERROR! -- YOU HAVE NOT DEFINED"
3010 PRINT SPC(11);"THE DIFFERENTIAL EQUATION"
3020 PRINT SPC(11);"IN LINE 200."
3030 END
```

EASY CHANGES

1. If you have already entered the differential equation and
   wish to skip the introductory output, add this line:

   1215 PRINT:GOTO 1410

   This will immediately begin the input dialog.

2. If you wish to use negative stepsizes, line 1900 must be changed to:

    1900 Q=XX+DX:IF Q < XF-1.E-5 THEN END

MAIN ROUTINES

150	Begins execution.
200 - 899	User-supplied subroutine to define D.
1000 - 1050	Displays output.
1100 - 1120	Subroutines to format messages.
1160 - 1190	Subroutine to stop and start output.
1200 - 1330	Displays initial messages.
1400 - 1530	Gets user's inputs.
1600 - 1670	Displays additional messages.
1700 - 1750	Initializes output display.
1800 - 1830	Waits for user to hit a key to start the output.
1900 - 1960	Computes each step.
3000 - 3030	Error message.

MAIN VARIABLES

D	Value of dY/dX.
X,Y	Values of X,Y on current step.
XX,YY	Values of X,Y on last step.
DX	Stepsize in X.
XF	Final value of X.
F$	Output flag string (T=table, G=graph).
YL,YH	Minimum, maximum values of Y plot axis.
F	Fractional distance of graphical point along Y axis.
V	Tab position for graphical output.
C	CHR$ argument for graphical output.
K0,K1, K2,K3	Runge-Kutta coefficients.
R$	User-entered string.
Q	Work variable.
J	Loop index.

SUGGESTED PROJECTS

1. Modify the program to display the tabular output followed by the graphical output. During the tabular phase, the mini-

mum and maximum values of Y can be saved and automatically used as the plot limits for the graphical output.

2. The value of dY/dX as a function of X is often a useful quantity to know. Modify the program to add it to the columnar display and/or the graphical display.

3. The inherent error in the calculation depends on the stepsize chosen. Most cases should be run with different stepsizes to insure that the errors are not large. If the answers do not change much, you can be reasonably certain that your solutions are accurate. Better yet, techniques exist to vary the stepsize during the calculation to insure that the error is sufficiently small during each step. Research these methods and incorporate them into the program.

4. The program can be easily broadened to solve a set of coupled, first order, differential equations simultaneously. This would greatly increase the types of problems that could be solved. Research this procedure and expand the program to handle it.

GRAPH

PURPOSE

Is a picture worth a thousand words? In the case of mathematical functions, the answer is often "yes." A picture, i.e. a graph, enables you to see the important behavior of a function quickly and accurately. Trends, minima, maxima, etc. become easy and convenient to determine.

GRAPH produces a two-dimensional plot of a function that you supply. The function must be in the form Y = (any function of X). The independent variable X will be plotted along the abscissa (horizontal axis). The dependent variable Y will be plotted along the ordinate (vertical axis). You have complete control over the scaling that is used on the X and Y axes.

HOW TO USE IT

Before running the program, you must enter into it the function to be plotted. This is done as a subroutine beginning at line 200. It must define Y as a function of X. The subroutine will be called with X set to various values. It must then set the variable Y to the correct corresponding value. The subroutine may be as simple or as complex as necessary to define the function. It can take one line or several hundred lines. Line 999 is already set as a RETURN statement, so you need not add another one.

Having entered this subroutine, you are ready to run the program. The program begins by warning you that it assumes the function has already been entered at line 200. It will then ask you for the domain of X, i.e. the lowest and highest values of X that you wish to have plotted. Values can be positive or negative as long as two conditions are met: the highest value must be algebraically larger than the lowest value and the number of characters the Apple uses to express each value must be no more than eight.

Now you must choose the scale for Y. To do this intelligently, you probably need to know the minimum and maximum values of Y over the domain of X selected. The program finds these values and displays them for you. You must then choose the minimum and maximum values you wish to have on the Y scale. Again, any two values are acceptable as long as they satisfy the two conditions given above.

The program will now request that you hit any key to display the plot of your function. Each axis is 20 tick-marks long, with the origin defined as the minimum scale values of both X and Y. The minimum, middle, and maximum values on each scale are displayed appropriately. (Note: in certain cases, the program will not display the middle scaling value for one or both axes. However, the highest and lowest scaling values for each axis will always be present.)

The actual plot is drawn with eight times the resolution shown by the axes' tick-marks. That is, 160 values of X and Y are plotted. This is accomplished by taking advantage of the Apple's high-resolution graphics capabilities.

If a value for Y should be off-scale, a special "enlarged line" will be displayed at the appropriate value of X. If the actual value of Y is too large, it will be plotted at the maximum Y value. Similarly, it will be drawn at the minimum Y value if it is too low or if its value is exactly the minimum Y value.

After the plot is drawn, you can exit the program and return to text mode by hitting any key.

GRAPH   223

SAMPLE RUN

After loading the program, the operator enters line 200 to request
the graph Y=SIN(X). RUN is typed to begin the program.

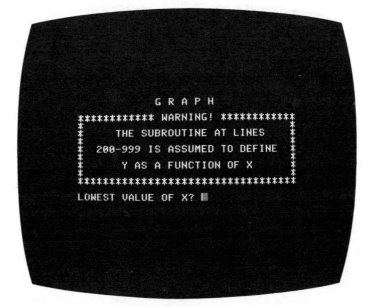

The program initiates the input dialog.

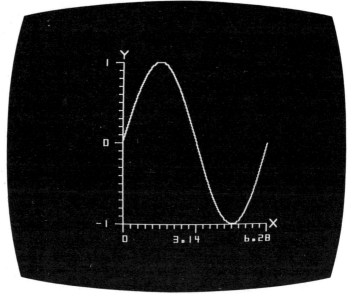

```
*  200-999 IS ASSUMED TO DEFINE  *
*       Y AS A FUNCTION OF X      *
*********************************
LOWEST VALUE OF X? 0

HIGHEST VALUE OF X? 6.28

OVER THIS RANGE OF X:
   MAXIMUM Y = .999999683
   MINIMUM Y = -.999997146

NOW CHOOSE THE SCALE FOR Y

MINIMUM Y SCALE VALUE? -1

MAXIMUM Y SCALE VALUE? 1

     HIT ANY KEY TO SEE THE GRAPH, THEN
HIT ANY KEY TO RETURN TO TEXT MODE.
```

The input dialog transpires. The operator asks that the domain of X be 0-6.28. The program responds by showing the maximum and minimum values of Y over this domain. The operator chooses an appropriate scale for the Y axis.

The graph is displayed as requested. The program waits for the operator to hit any key to return to text mode.

GRAPH   225

PROGRAM LISTING

```
100 REM: GRAPH
110 REM: COPYRIGHT 1980 BY PHIL FELDMAN AND TOM RUGG
150 GOTO 1200
170 REM
180 REM   ** ENTER SUBROUTINE AT 200 **
190 REM
200 REM   ***** Y=F(X) GOES HERE
999 RETURN
1200 TEXT:HOME:PRINT TAB(13);"G R A P H":PRINT
1210 PRINT TAB(1);:FOR J=1 TO 12:PRINT"*";:NEXT
1220 PRINT" WARNING! ";:FOR J=1 TO 12
1230 PRINT TAB(1);"*";:NEXT:PRINT:GOSUB 1290:PRINT
     TAB(1);"*";TAB(7);
1240 PRINT"THE SUBROUTINE AT LINES";TAB(34);"*":GOSUB
     1290
1250 PRINT TAB(1);"*   200-999 IS ASSUMED TO DEFINE  *":
     GOSUB 1290
1260 PRINT TAB(1);"*";TAB(8);"Y AS A FUNCTION OF X";
     TAB(34);"*":GOSUB 1290
1270 PRINT TAB(1);:FOR J=1 TO 34:PRINT"*";:NEXT
1280 PRINT:GOTO 1300
1290 PRINT TAB(1);"*";TAB(34);"*":RETURN
1300 PRINT:INPUT"LOWEST VALUE OF X? ";XL
1310 XL$=STR$(XL):L=LEN(XL$)
1320 IF L>8 THEN PRINT:PRINT
     " *** TOO MANY DIGITS - PLEASE REDUCE":GOTO 1300
1330 PRINT:INPUT"HIGHEST VALUE OF X? ";XU
1340 IF XU<=XL THEN PRINT:PRINT" *** BAD X RANGE ***":
     GOTO 1300
1350 XU$=STR$(XU):L=LEN(XU$)
1360 IF L>8 THEN PRINT:PRINT
     " *** TOO MANY DIGITS - PLEASE REDUCE":GOTO 1330
1370 XM=(XL+XU)/2:XM$=STR$(XM)
1380 IF LEN(XM$)>9 THEN XM$=" "
1400 DX=(XU-XL)/160:X=XL:GOSUB 200:MN=Y:MX=Y
1410 FOR J=1 TO 160:X=XL+J*DX:GOSUB 200
1420 IF Y>MX THEN MX=Y
1430 IF Y<MN THEN MN=Y
1440 NEXT
1450 PRINT:PRINT"OVER THIS RANGE OF X:"
1460 PRINT" MAXIMUM Y = ";MX
1470 PRINT" MINIMUM Y = ";MN:PRINT
```

```
1480 PRINT"NOW CHOOSE THE SCALE FOR Y":PRINT
1490 INPUT"MINIMUM Y SCALE VALUE? ";YL:PRINT
1500 YL$=STR$(YL):L=LEN(YL$)
1510 IF L>8 THEN PRINT
     " *** TOO MANY DIGITS - PLEASE REDUCE":PRINT:GOTO
     1490
1520 INPUT"MAXIMUM Y SCALE VALUE? ";YU:PRINT
1530 IF YU<=YL THEN PRINT" *** BAD Y RANGE ***":GOTO
     1450
1540 YU$=STR$(YU):L=LEN(YU$)
1550 IF L>8 THEN PRINT
     "*** TOO MANY DIGITS - PLEASE REDUCE":PRINT:GOTO
     1520
1560 YM=(YU+YL)/2:YM$=STR$(YM)
1570 IF LEN(YM$)>9 THEN YM$=" "
1600 PRINT"   HIT ANY KEY TO SEE THE GRAPH, THEN"
1610 PRINT"HIT ANY KEY TO RETURN TO TEXT MODE."
1620 PRINT:GET D$
2000 HGR2:HCOLOR=3
2100 HP=107:VP=172
2110 HPLOT HP,VP-160 TO HP,VP:HPLOT TO HP+160,VP
2120 FOR J=VP-160 TO VP STEP 8
2130 HPLOT HP-4,J TO HP,J:NEXT
2140 FOR J=VP-160 TO VP STEP 80
2150 HPLOT HP-8,J TO HP,J:NEXT
2160 FOR J=HP TO HP+160 STEP 8
2170 HPLOT J,VP TO J,VP+4:NEXT
2180 FOR J=HP TO HP+160 STEP 80
2190 HPLOT J,VP TO J,VP+8:NEXT
2200 HPLOT HP+164,VP-4 TO HP+172,VP+4
2210 HPLOT HP+164,VP+4 TO HP+172,VP-4
2220 HPLOT HP-4,VP-172 TO HP,VP-168
2230 HPLOT TO HP+4,VP-172
2240 HPLOT HP,VP-168 TO HP,VP-164
2300 H=HP-20:V=VP-163:A$=YU$:GOSUB 5000
2310 H=HP-20:V=VP-83:A$=YM$:GOSUB 5000
2320 H=HP-20:V=VP-3:A$=YL$:GOSUB 5000
2340 H=HP:V=VP+12:A$=XL$:GOSUB 5000
2350 H=HP+80:V=VP+12:A$=XM$:GOSUB 5000
2360 H=HP+160:V=VP+12:A$=XU$:GOSUB 5000
2400 DX=(XU-XL)/160:DY=(YU-YL)/160
2410 AF=0:X=XL:GOSUB 200
2420 IF Y>YU THEN Y=YU:AF=1
2430 IF Y<YL THEN Y=YL:AF=1
```

GRAPH   227

```
2440 YY=(Y-YL)/DY:H=HP:V=VP-YY
2450 HPLOT H,V
2460 IF AF=1 THEN GOSUB 3500
2500 FOR J=1 TO 160:X=XL+J*DX:GOSUB 200
2510 IF Y>YU THEN Y=YU:AF=1
2520 IF Y<=YL THEN Y=YL:AF=1
2530 YY=(Y-YL)/DY:H=HP+J:V=VP-YY
2540 HPLOT TO H,V
2550 IF AF=1 THEN GOSUB 3500
2560 NEXT
2570 GET D$:TEXT:END
3000 HPLOT H,V TO H4,V:HPLOT TO H4,V6
3010 HPLOT TO H,V6:HPLOT TO H,V
3020 RETURN
3100 HPLOT H4,V TO H,V:HPLOT TO H,V6
3110 HPLOT TO H4,V6:HPLOT H,V3 TO H4,V3
3120 RETURN
3200 HPLOT H,V3 TO H4,V3:HPLOT H+2,V+1 TO H+2,V+5
3210 RETURN
3300 HPLOT H,V3 TO H4,V3:RETURN
3400 HPLOT H+1,V+4 TO H+3,V+4
3410 HPLOT TO H+3,V6:HPLOT TO H+1,V6
3420 HPLOT TO H+1,V+4:RETURN
3500 HPLOT TO H-1,V-1:HPLOT TO H-1,V+1
3510 HPLOT TO H+1,V+1:HPLOT TO H+1,V-1
3520 HPLOT TO H-1,V-1:HPLOT TO H,V
3530 AF=0:RETURN
4100 HPLOT H+2,V TO H+2,V6
4110 RETURN
4200 HPLOT H,V TO H4,V
4210 HPLOT TO H4,V3:HPLOT TO H,V3
4220 HPLOT TO H,V6:HPLOT TO H4,V6:RETURN
4300 HPLOT H,V TO H4,V
4310 HPLOT TO H4,V6:HPLOT TO H,V6
4320 HPLOT H,V3 TO H4,V3:RETURN
4400 HPLOT H,V TO H,V3:HPLOT TO H4,V3
4410 HPLOT H+3,V TO H+3,V6:RETURN
4500 HPLOT H4,V TO H,V
4510 HPLOT TO H,V3:HPLOT TO H4,V3
4520 HPLOT TO H4,V6:HPLOT TO H,V6:RETURN
4600 HPLOT H,V TO H,V6:HPLOT TO H4,V6
4610 HPLOT TO H4,V3:HPLOT TO H,V3:RETURN
4700 HPLOT H,V TO H4,V:HPLOT TO H4,V+2
4710 HPLOT TO H,V6:RETURN
```

```
4800 HPLOT H,V TO H4,V:HPLOT TO H4,V6
4810 HPLOT TO H,V6:HPLOT TO H,V
4820 HPLOT H,V3 TO H4,V3:RETURN
4900 HPLOT H4,V6 TO H4,V:HPLOT TO H,V
4910 HPLOT TO H,V3:HPLOT TO H4,V3:RETURN
5000 FOR J=LEN(A$) TO 1 STEP -1:H4=H+4:V3=V+3:V6=V+6
5010 D$=MID$(A$,J,1):D=VAL(D$)
5020 IF D=0 THEN 5040
5030 ON D GOSUB 4100,4200,4300,4400,4500,4600,4700,4800,
     4900:GOTO 5090
5040 IF D$="0" THEN GOSUB 3000:GOTO 5090
5050 IF D$="E" THEN GOSUB 3100:GOTO 5090
5060 IF D$="+" THEN GOSUB 3200:GOTO 5090
5070 IF D$="-" THEN GOSUB 3300:GOTO 5090
5080 IF D$="." THEN GOSUB 3400
5090 H=H-8:NEXT:RETURN
```

EASY CHANGES

1. You may want the program to self-scale the Y axis for you.
That is, you want it to use the minimum and maximum Y
values that it finds as the limits on the Y axis. This can be
accomplished by adding the following lines:

1443 IF LEN(STR$(MX)) > 8 OR LEN(STR$(MN)) > 8
     THEN 1450
1444 IF MX <= MN THEN 1450
1445 YU=MX:YL=MN:PRINT
1447 YU$=STR$(YU):YL$=STR$(YL):GOTO 1560

(Note: on rare occasions, the program will not be able to
perform the desired self-scaling. In these cases, the program
will revert to requesting the Y scaling from you.)

2. Do you sometimes forget to enter the subroutine at line 200
despite the introductory warning? As is, the program will
plot the straight line Y=0 if you do this. If you want a more
drastic reaction to prevent this, change line 200 to read:

$$200 \ Y=1/0$$

Now, if you don't enter the actual subroutine desired, the
program will stop and print the following message after you
enter the X scaling values:

?DIVISION BY ZERO ERROR IN 200

GRAPH 229

3. As written, the program uses page 2 of high-resolution graphics. To accommodate a 16K system with Applesoft in ROM, or a 32K Disk Applesoft system (see Appendix 1), page 1 may be used instead with this change:

2000 HGR:POKE–16302,0:HCOLOR=3

MAIN ROUTINES

150	Begins execution.
200 - 999	User-supplied subroutine to evaluate Y as a function of X.
1200 - 1290	Displays introductory warning.
1300 - 1380	Gets X scaling from user.
1400 - 1570	Determines the minimum, maximum Y values; gets Y scale from user.
1600 - 1620	Waits for user to hit any key.
2000 - 2240	Draws plot axes.
2300 - 2360	Labels each axis.
2400 - 2570	Draws plot and terminates program.
3000 - 3420	Subroutines to draw characters O, E, +, – in hi-res.
3500 - 3530	Subroutine to draw off-axis line at H,V.
4100 - 4910	Subroutines to draw digits 1–9 in hi-res.
5000 - 5090	Subroutine to draw scaling values.

MAIN VARIABLES

XL,XM, XU	Lower, middle, upper scale values of X.
YL,YM, YU	Lower, middle, upper scale values of Y.
DX,DY	Scale increments of X,Y.
X,Y	Current values of X,Y.
XL$, XM$, XU$	String representation of XL, XM, XU.
YL$, YM$, YU$	String representation of YL, YM, YU.
D$	Temporary string variable.
D	Numeric value of D$.
H,V	Horizontal, vertical position in hi-res units.

HP,VP   Horizontal, vertical position of axes origin.
YY   Y direction offset in hi-res units.
AF   Y position flag (0=in bounds, 1=out of bounds).
H4,V3,   H, V offsets.
V6

SUGGESTED PROJECTS

1. Determine and display the values of X at which the minimum
   and maximum values of Y occur.
2. After the graph is plotted, allow the user to obtain the exact
   value of Y for any given X.

INTEGRATE

PURPOSE AND DEFINITION

The need to evaluate integrals occurs frequently in much scientific and mathematical work. This program will numerically integrate a function that you supply using a technique known as Simpson's rule. It will continue to grind out successive approximations of the integral until you are satisfied with the accuracy of the solution.

Mathematical integration will probably be a familiar term to those who have studied some higher mathematics. It is a fundamental subject of second-year calculus. The integral of a function between the limits $x = \ell$ (lower limit) and $x = u$ (upper limit) represents the area under its curve; i.e., the shaded area in Figure 1.

We may approximate the integral by first dividing up the area into rectangular strips or segments. We can get a good estimate of the total integral by summing the areas of these segments by using a parabolic fit across the top. For those who understand some mathematical theory, Simpson's rule may be expressed as

$$\int_{x=\ell}^{x=u} f(x)\,dx \cong \frac{\Delta}{3} \left\{ f(\ell) + f(u) + 4 \sum_{j=1}^{N/2} f[\ell + \Delta(2j-1)] + 2 \sum_{j=1}^{(N-2)/2} f[\ell + 2\Delta j] \right\}$$

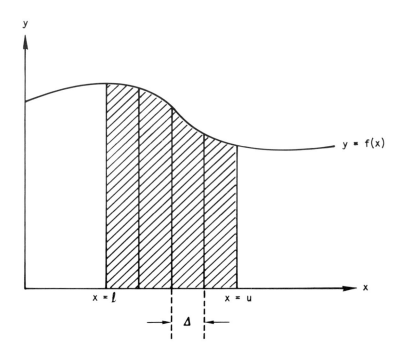

Figure 1. The Integral of f(x)

Here N is the number of segments into which the total interval is divided. N is 4 in the diagram.

For a good discusson of the numerical evaluation of integrals see: McCracken, Dorn, *Numerical Methods and FORTRAN Programming*, New York, Wiley, 1964, p. 160. Don't let the word "FORTRAN" scare you away. The discussions in the book are independent of programming language with only some program examples written in FORTRAN.

HOW TO USE IT

The program begins with a warning! This is to remind you that you should have already entered the subroutine to evaluate Y as a function of X. This subroutine must start at line 200. More about it shortly.

You will then be asked to provide the lower and upper limits of the integration domain. Any numerical values are acceptable.

It is not even necessary that the lower limit of X be smaller than the upper one.

The program will now begin displaying its numerical evaluations of the integral. The number of segments used in the calculation continually doubles. This causes the accuracy of the integral to increase at the expense of additional computation time. For most functions, you should see the value of the integral converging quickly to a constant (or near constant) value. This, of course, will be the best numerical evaluation of the integral at hand.

When you are satisfied with the accuracy of the solution, you must hit control C to terminate the program. If not, the program will run forever (assuming you can pay the electric bills). The amount of computation is approximately doubled each step. This means it will take the computer about the same amount of time to compute the next step that it took to compute *all* the previous steps. Thus, it will soon be taking the Apple hours, days, and weeks to compute steps. Eventually, round-off errors begin degrading the results, causing a nice, constant, converged solution to change. However, the high precision of the computer's floating point arithmetic will postpone this for quite a while. You will probably lose patience before seeing it.

The function to be integrated can be as simple or as complicated as you desire. It may take one line or a few hundred lines of code. In any case, the subroutine to express it must start at line 200. This subroutine will be continually called with the variable X set. When it returns, it should have set the variable Y to the corresponding value of the function for the given X. The subroutine must be able to evaluate the function at any value of X between the lower and upper bounds of the integration domain.

If your function consists of experimental data at discrete values of X, you must do something to enable the subroutine to evaluate the function at intermediate values of X. We recommend one of two approaches. First, you could write the subroutine to linearly interpolate the value of Y between the appropriate values of X. This will involve searching your data table for the pair of experimental X values that bound the value of X where the function is to be evaluated. Secondly, the program CURVE presented elsewhere in this section can produce an approximate polynomial expression to fit your experimental data. This expression can then be easily entered as the subroutine at line 200.

By the way, Simpson's rule is *exact* for any polynomial of degree three or less. This means that if the function can be written in the form

$$Y = A*X\uparrow3 + B*X\uparrow2 + C*X + D$$

where A, B, C, and D are constants, the program will calculate the integral exactly even with only two segments.

SAMPLE RUN

The sample run illustrates the following integration:

$$\int_{x=0}^{x=1} \frac{4}{1+x^2}\ dx$$

This integral has the theoretical value of π (pi) as the correct answer! Pi, as you may know, has the value 3.1415926535. . . Before the run is started, the above function is entered at line 200. For reference, the elapsed time since the beginning of the run is given in parentheses after each line of output. It is in hours, minutes, and seconds. This gives you an idea of how long the program took to compute each step. However, these times are not displayed in the actual program output.

INTEGRATE - SAMPLE RUN

]200 Y=4/(1+X*X)

]RUN

          INTEGRAL BY SIMPSON'S RULE

```
*********** WARNING! ***********
*                              *
*    THE SUBROUTINE AT LINES   *
*                              *
*  200-999 IS ASSUMED TO DEFINE *
*                              *
*     Y AS A FUNCTION OF X     *
*                              *
********************************
```

LOWER LIMIT OF X? <u>O</u>

UPPER LIMIT OF X? <u>1</u>

#SEGMENTS	INTEGRAL	
2	3.13333334	(00:00:00)
4	3.14156863	(00:00:00)
8	3.1415925	(00:00:00)
16	3.14159265	(00:00:01)
32	3.14159266	(00:00:02)
64	3.14159265	(00:00:03)
128	3.14159266	(00:00:06)
256	3.14159266	(00:00:12)
512	3.14159265	(00:00:23)
1024	3.14159266	(00:00:46)
2048	3.14159265	(00:01:32)
4096	3.14159266	(00:03:04)
8192	3.14159267	(00:06.09)
16384	3.14159265	(00:12:21)
32768	3.14159267	(00:24:48)
65536	3.14159265	(00:50:04)

(control C key pressed)

PROGRAM LISTING

```
100 REM: INTEGRATE
110 REM: COPYRIGHT 1980 BY PHIL FELDMAN AND TOM RUGG
130 TEXT
150 N=2:GOTO 1200
170 REM
```

```
180 REM  ** ENTER SUBROUTINE AT 200 **
190 REM
200 REM  ***** Y=F(X) GOES HERE
999 RETURN
1200 HOME:PRINT SPC(4);"INTEGRAL BY SIMPSON'S RULE":
     PRINT:PRINT
1210 PRINT TAB(1);:FOR J=1 TO 12:PRINT"*";:NEXT
1220 PRINT" WARNING! ";:FOR J=1 TO 12
1230 PRINT"*";:NEXT:PRINT:GOSUB 1290:PRINT TAB(1);"*";
     TAB(6);
1240 PRINT"THE SUBROUTINE AT LINES";TAB(34);"*":GOSUB
     1290
1250 PRINT TAB(1);"*  200-999 IS ASSUMED TO DEFINE  *":
     GOSUB 1290
1260 PRINT TAB(1);"*";TAB(8);"Y AS A FUNCTION OF X";
     TAB(34);"*":GOSUB 1290
1270 PRINT TAB(1);:FOR J=1 TO 34:PRINT"*";:NEXT
1280 PRINT:GOTO 1300
1290 PRINT TAB(1);"*";TAB(34);"*":RETURN
1300 PRINT:INPUT"LOWER LIMIT OF X? ";L
1310 PRINT:INPUT"UPPER LIMIT OF X? ";U
1360 PRINT:PRINT:PRINT
1370 PRINT"# SEGMENTS","INTEGRAL"
1380 PRINT
1400 DX=(U-L)/N:T=0
1410 X=L:GOSUB 200:T=T+Y
1420 X=U:GOSUB 200:T=T+Y
1450 M=N/2:Z=0
1460 FOR J=1 TO M
1470 X=L+DX*(2*J-1):GOSUB 200:Z=Z+Y
1480 NEXT:T=T+4*Z
1500 M=M-1:IF M=0 THEN 1600
1510 Z=0:FOR J=1 TO M
1520 X=L+DX*2*J:GOSUB 200:Z=Z+Y
1530 NEXT:T=T+2*Z
1600 A=DX*T/3
1610 PRINT N,A
1620 N=N*2
1630 GOTO 1400
```

EASY CHANGES

1. You might want the program to stop calculation after the
   integral has been evaluated for a given number of segments.
   Adding the following line will cause the program to stop after

the integral is evaluated for a number of segments greater than or equal to 100.

1615 IF N $>=$ 100 THEN END

Of course, you may use any value you wish instead of 100.

2. Perhaps you would like to see the number of segments change at a different rate during the course of the calculation. This can be done by modifying line 1620. To increase the rate of change, try

1620 N=N*4

To change it at a constant (and slower) rate, try

1620 N=N+50

Be sure, however, that the value of N is always even.

MAIN ROUTINES

150	Initializes and calls mainline routine.
200 - 999	User-supplied subroutine to evaluate f(X).
1200 - 1290	Displays introductory messages and warning.
1300 - 1310	Gets integration limits from operator.
1360 - 1380	Displays column headings.
1400 - 1420	Computes integral contribution from end points.
1450 - 1480	Adds contribution from one summation.
1500 - 1530	Adds contribution from other summation.
1600 - 1630	Completes integral calculation and displays it. Increases number of segments and restarts calculation.

MAIN VARIABLES

N	Number of segments.
J	Loop index.
L,U	Lower, upper integration limit of x.
DX	Width of one segment.
T	Partial result of integral.
M	Number of summations.
Z	Subtotal of summations.
A	Value of integral.
X	Current value of x.
Y	Current value of the function y = f(x).

SUGGESTED PROJECTS

1. Research other similar techniques for numerical integration such as the simpler trapezoid rule. Then add a column of output computing the integral with this new method. Compare how the two methods converge toward the (hopefully) correct answer.
2. Modify the program to compute answers to "double precision" or greater; i.e. at least fifteen significant digits. Try the function used in the Sample Run to see if you can calculate pi to this high degree of precision.

SIMEQN

PURPOSE

This program solves a set of simultaneous linear algebraic equations. This type of problem often arises in scientific and numerical work. Algebra students encounter them regularly —many "word" problems can be solved by constructing the proper set of simultaneous equations.

The program can handle up to 20 equations in 20 unknowns. This should prove more than sufficient for any practical application.

The equations to be solved can be written mathematically as follows:

$$A_{11}X_1 + A_{12}X_2 + \ldots + A_{1N}X_N = R_1$$
$$A_{21}X_1 + A_{22}X_2 + \ldots + A_{2N}X_N = R_2$$
$$\vdots \qquad \vdots \qquad \qquad \vdots \qquad \vdots$$
$$A_{N1}X_1 + A_{N2}X_2 + \ldots + A_{NN}X_N = R_N$$

N is the number of equations and thus the number of unknowns also. The unknowns are denoted X_1 through X_N.

Each equation contains a coefficient multiplier for each unknown and a right-hand-side term. These coefficients (the A matrix) and the right-hand-sides (R_1 through R_N) must be constants—positive, negative, or zero. The A matrix is denoted with double subscripts. The first subscript is the equation number and the second one is the unknown that the coefficient multiplies.

HOW TO USE IT

The program will prompt you for all necessary inputs. First, it asks how many equations (and thus how many unknowns) comprise your set. This number must be at least 1 and no more than 20.

Next, you must enter the coefficients and right-hand-sides for each equation. The program will request these one at a time, continually indicating which term it is expecting next.

Once it has all your inputs, the program begins calculating the solution. This may take a little while if the value of N is high. The program ends by displaying the answers. These, of course, are the values of each of the unknowns, X_1 through X_N.

If you are interested, the numerical technique used to solve the equations is known as Gaussian elimination. Row interchange to achieve pivotal condensation is employed. (This keeps maximum significance in the numbers.) Then back substitution is used to arrive at the final results. This technique is much simpler than it sounds and is described well in the numerical analysis books referenced in the bibliography.

SAMPLE PROBLEM AND RUN

Problem: A painter has a large supply of three different colors of paint: dark green, light green, and pure blue. The dark green is 30% blue pigment, 20% yellow pigment, and the rest base. The light green is 10% blue pigment, 35% yellow pigment, and the rest base. The pure blue is 90% blue pigment, no yellow pigment, and the rest base. The painter, however, needs a medium green to be composed of 25% blue pigment, 25% yellow pigment, and the rest base. In what percentages should he mix his three paints to achieve this mixture?

Solution: Let X_1 = percent of dark green to use,

X_2 = percent of light green to use,

X_3 = percent of pure blue to use.

The problem leads to these three simultaneous equations to solve:

$$0.3\,X_1 + 0.1\;\;X_2 + 0.9\,X_3 = 0.25$$
$$0.2\,X_1 + 0.35\,X_2 \qquad\quad = 0.25$$
$$X_1 + \quad\;\; X_2 + \quad\;\; X_3 = 1.0$$

The first equation expresses the amount of blue pigment in the mixture. The second equation is for the yellow pigment. The third equation states that the mixture is composed entirely of the three given paints. (Note that all the percentages are expressed as numbers from 0–1.) The problem leads to the following use of SIMEQN.

SAMPLE RUN

```
A SIMULTANEOUS LINEAR EQUATION SOLVER

HOW MANY EQUATIONS IN THE SET? 3

THE 3   UNKNOWNS WILL BE DENOTED
X1 THROUGH X3
-----------------------------------

ENTER THE PARAMETERS FOR EQUATION 1

COEFFICIENT OF X1? .3
COEFFICIENT OF X2? .1
COEFFICIENT OF X3? .9
RIGHT HAND SIDE? .25
-----------------------------------

ENTER THE PARAMETERS FOR EQUATION 2

COEFFICIENT OF X1? .2
COEFFICIENT OF X2? .35
COEFFICIENT OF X3? 0
RIGHT HAND SIDE? .25
-----------------------------------

ENTER THE PARAMETERS FOR EQUATION 3
```

```
COEFFICIENT OF X1? 1
COEFFICIENT OF X2? 1
COEFFICIENT OF X3? 1
RIGHT HAND SIDE? 1
----------------------------------

THE SOLUTION IS

   X1= .55
   X2= .4
   X3= .05
```

Thus, the painter should use a mixture of 55%
dark green, 40% light green, and 5% pure blue.

PROGRAM LISTING

```
100 REM: SIMEQN
110 REM: COPYRIGHT 1980 BY PHIL FELDMAN AND TOM RUGG
130 TEXT
150 M=20
200 HOME
210 PRINT"A SIMULTANEOUS LINEAR EQUATION SOLVER"
220 PRINT:PRINT
300 INPUT"HOW MANY EQUATIONS IN THE SET? ";N
310 PRINT:N=INT(N):IF N>0 AND N<=M THEN 330
320 PRINT"** ERROR! ** IT MUST BE BETWEEN 1-";M:PRINT:
    GOTO 300
330 DIM A(N,N),R(N),V(N)
340 PRINT"THE ";N;" UNKNOWNS WILL BE DENOTED"
350 PRINT"X1 THROUGH X";STR$(N)
360 GOSUB 900:FOR J=1 TO N
370 PRINT"ENTER THE PARAMETERS FOR EQUATION ";J
380 PRINT:FOR K=1 TO N
390 PRINT"COEFFICIENT OF X";STR$(K);
400 INPUT"? ";A(J,K):NEXT
410 INPUT"RIGHT HAND SIDE? ";R(J)
420 GOSUB 900:NEXT
430 GOSUB 2000
500 PRINT"THE SOLUTION IS":PRINT
510 FOR J=1 TO N
520 PRINT"  X";STR$(J);" = ";V(J)
530 NEXT:END
900 PRINT:PRINT"--------------------------------"
```

```
910 PRINT:RETURN
2000 IF N=1 THEN V(1)=R(1)/A(1,1):RETURN
2010 FOR K=1 TO N-1
2020 I=K+1
2030 L=K
2040 IF ABS(A(I,K))>ABS(A(L,K)) THEN L=I
2050 IF I<N THEN I=I+1:GOTO 2040
2060 IF L=K THEN 2100
2070 FOR J=K TO N:Q=A(K,J):A(K,J)=A(L,J)
2080 A(L,J)=Q:NEXT
2090 Q=R(K):R(K)=R(L):R(L)=Q
2100 I=K+1
2110 Q=A(I,K)/A(K,K):A(I,K)=0
2120 FOR J=K+1 TO N:A(I,J)=A(I,J)-Q*A(K,J):NEXT
2130 R(I)=R(I)-Q*R(K):IF I<N THEN I=I+1:GOTO 2110
2140 NEXT
2150 V(N)=R(N)/A(N,N):FOR I=N-1 TO 1 STEP -1
2160 Q=0:FOR J=I+1 TO N:Q=Q+A(I,J)*V(J)
2170 V(I)=(R(I)-Q)/A(I,I):NEXT:NEXT
2180 RETURN
```

EASY CHANGES

1. The program is currently set to allow a maximum of 20
   equations. If you should somehow need more, and your
   system has the available memory to handle it, change the
   value of M in line 150 to the maximum number of equations
   needed. For example, to allow up to 50 equations in 50
   unknowns, change line 150 to read

$$150\ M = 50$$

2. You may be surprised sometime to see the program fail
   completely and display this message:

   ?DIVISION BY ZERO ERROR IN 2150

   This means your input coefficients (the A array) were ill-
   conditioned and no solution was possible. This can arise from
   a variety of causes; e.g. if one equation is an exact multiple
   of another, or if *every* coefficient of one particular unknown
   is zero. If you would like the program to print a diagnostic
   message in these cases, add this line:

   2145 IF A(N,N)=0 THEN PRINT
        "ILL-CONDITIONED INPUT":STOP

MAIN ROUTINES

200 - 220	Clears screen and displays program title.
300 - 430	Gets input from user and calculates the solution.
500 - 530	Displays the solution.
900 - 910	Subroutine to space and separate the output.
2000 - 2180	Subroutine to calculate the solution; consisting of the following parts:
2000	Forms solution if $N=1$.
2010 - 2140	Gaussian elimination.
2030 - 2100	Interchanges rows to achieve pivotal condensation.
2150 - 2180	Back substitution.

MAIN VARIABLES

I,J,K,L	Loop indices and subscripts.
N	Number of equations (thus number of unknowns also).
A	Doubly dimensioned array of the coefficients.
R	Array of right-hand-sides.
V	Array of the solution.
Q	Work variable.
M	Maximum allowable number of equations.

SUGGESTED PROJECTS

1. The program modifies the A and R arrays while computing the answer. This means that the original input cannot be displayed after it is input. Modify the program to save the information and enable the user to retrieve it after the solution is given.
2. Currently, a mistake in typing input cannot be corrected once the **RETURN** key is pressed after typing a number. Modify the program to allow correcting previous input.

STATS

PURPOSE

Ever think of yourself as a statistic? Many times we lament at how we have become just numbers in various computer memories, or we simply moan at our insurance premiums. To most people, the word "statistics" carries a negative connotation. To invoke statistics is almost to be deceitful, or at least dehumanizing. But really, we all use statistical ideas regularly. When we speak of things like "she was of average height" or the "hottest weather in years," we are making observations in statistical terms. It is difficult not to encounter statistics in our lives, and this book is no exception.

Of course, when used properly, statistics can be a powerful, analytical tool. STATS analyzes a set of numerical data that you provide. It will compile your list, order it sequentially, and/or determine several statistical parameters which describe it.

This should prove useful in a wide variety of applications. Teachers might determine grades by analyzing a set of test scores. A businessman might determine marketing strategy by studying a list of sales to clients. Little leaguers always like to pore over the current batting and pitching averages. You can probably think of many other applications.

HOW TO USE IT

Before entering the data, the program will ask whether or not you wish to use identifiers with the data values. These identifiers can be anything associated with the data: e.g. names accompanying test scores, cities accompanying population values, corporations accompanying sales figures, etc. Hit the **Y** or **N** key to indicate yes or no regarding the use of identifiers. You do not need to hit the **RETURN** key.

Next, your data list must be entered. The program will prompt you for each value with a question mark. If identifiers are being used, you will be prompted for them before being asked for the associated data value. You may use any length character strings you desire for identifiers. However, if you limit them to a maximum of 18 characters, the formatting of later output will be "cleaner."

Two special inputs, *END and *BACK, may be used at any time during this data input phase. They are applicable whether or not identifiers are being used. To signal the end of data, input the four-character string, *END, in response to the (last) question mark. You must, of course, enter at least one data value.

If you discover that you have made a mistake, the five-character string, *BACK, can be used to back up the input process. This will cause the program to re-prompt you for the previous entry. By successive uses of *BACK you can return to any previous position.

With the input completed, the program enters a command mode. You have four options to continue the run:

          1) List the data in the order input
          2) List the data in ranking order
          3) Display statistical parameters
          4) End the program

Simply input the number **1**, **2**, **3**, or **4** to indicate your choice. If one of the first three is selected, the program will perform the selected function and return to this command mode to allow another choice. This will continue until you choose **4** to termi-nate the run. A description of the various options now follows.

Options 1 and 2 provide lists of the data. Option 1 does it in the original input order while option 2 sorts the data from highest value to lowest. In either case the identifiers, if used, will be shown alongside their associated values.

The lists are started by hitting any key when told to do so. Either list may be temporarily halted by hitting any key while the list is being displayed. This allows you to leisurely view data that might otherwise start scrolling off the screen. Simply hit any key to resume the display. This starting and stopping can be repeated as often as desired. When the display is completed, you must again hit a key to re-enter the command mode.

Option 3 produces a statistical analysis of your data. Various statistical parameters are calculated and displayed. The following is an explanation of some that may not be familiar to you.

Three measures of location, or central tendency, are provided. These are indicators of an "average" value. The *mean* is the sum of the values divided by the number of values. If the values are arranged in order from highest to lowest, the *median* is the middle value if the number of values is odd. If it is even, the median is the number halfway between the two middle values. The *midrange* is the number halfway between the largest and smallest values.

These measures of location give information about the average value of the data. However, they give no idea of how the data is dispersed or spread out around this "average." For that we need "measures of dispersion" or as they are sometimes called, "measures of variation." The simplest of these is the *range* which is just the difference between the highest and lowest data values. Two other closely related measures of dispersion are given: the *variance* and the *standard deviation*. The variance is defined as:

$$VA = \frac{\sum_{i=1}^{N} (V_i - M)^2}{N - 1}$$

Here N is the number of values, V_i is value i, and M is the mean value. The standard deviation is simply the square root of the variance. We do not have space to detail a lengthy discussion of their theoretical use. For this refer to the bibliography. Basically, however, the smaller the standard deviation, the more all the data tends to be clustered close to the mean value.

One word of warning—the first time option 2 or 3 is selected, the program must take some time to sort the data into numerical order. The time this requires depends upon how many items are on the list and how badly they are out of sequence. Average times are 15 seconds for 25 items, about one minute for 50

items, and about four and one-half minutes for 100 items. The
Apple will pause while this is occurring, so don't think it has
hung up or fallen asleep! If you have several items on your list,
this is the perfect chance to rob your refrigerator, make a quick
phone call, or whatever.

SAMPLE RUN

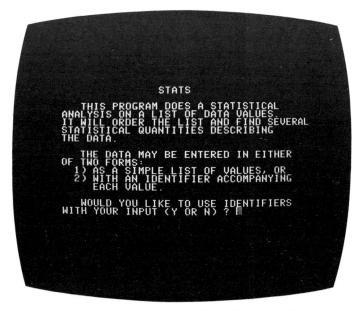

```
                    STATS

        THIS PROGRAM DOES A STATISTICAL
ANALYSIS ON A LIST OF DATA VALUES.
IT WILL ORDER THE LIST AND FIND SEVERAL
STATISTICAL QUANTITIES DESCRIBING
THE DATA.

        THE DATA MAY BE ENTERED IN EITHER
OF TWO FORMS:
    1) AS A SIMPLE LIST OF VALUES, OR
    2) WITH AN IDENTIFIER ACCOMPANYING
       EACH VALUE.

        WOULD YOU LIKE TO USE IDENTIFIERS
WITH YOUR INPUT (Y OR N) ?
```

The program describes its wares. It asks whether or not the operator
wishes to use identifiers with his or her input data.

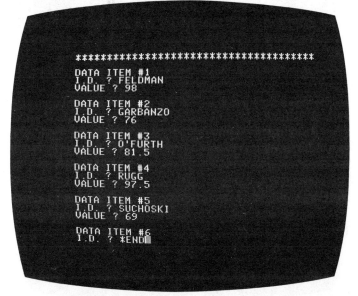

```
            EACH VALUE.
        WOULD YOU LIKE TO USE IDENTIFIERS
WITH YOUR INPUT (Y OR N) ? YES

*****************************************

    THE DATA MUST NOW BE ENTERED.

    FOR EACH DATA ITEM, ENTER ITS
IDENTIFIER (ABBREVIATED I.D.) AND ITS
VALUE IN RESPONSE TO THE SEPARATE
QUESTION MARKS.

    IF YOU MAKE A MISTAKE, TYPE
*BACK  TO RE-ENTER THE LAST DATUM.

    WHEN THE LIST IS COMPLETED, TYPE
*END  TO TERMINATE THE LIST.

*****************************************

DATA ITEM #1
I.D. ?
```

The operator wishes to use identifiers. The program explains how
data is to be entered; it is ready to receive the operator's input.

```
*****************************************

DATA ITEM #1
I.D. ? FELDMAN
VALUE ? 98

DATA ITEM #2
I.D. ? GARBANZO
VALUE ? 76

DATA ITEM #3
I.D. ? O'FURTH
VALUE ? 81.5

DATA ITEM #4
I.D. ? RUGG
VALUE ? 97.5

DATA ITEM #5
I.D. ? SUCHOSKI
VALUE ? 69

DATA ITEM #6
I.D. ? *END
```

The operator enters the names and scores of those who took a
programming aptitude test. The actual test was given to many
people, but for demonstration purposes, only five names are used
here. The special string, *END, is used to signal the end of the data.

The operator requests that the list be sorted into numerical order.
The program waits for a key to be pressed to continue the run.

```
WHAT NEXT (1, 2, 3, OR 4) ? 2
*****************************************
  THE DATA IN RANKING ORDER

  5 TOTAL ENTRIES

     WHILE THE LIST IS DISPLAYING, YOU
  CAN HIT ANY KEY TO CAUSE A TEMPORARY
  HALT.   THE DISPLAY WILL RESUME WHEN YOU
  HIT ANOTHER KEY.

     HIT ANY KEY TO START THE DISPLAY.
  #   VALUE                    I.D.
  1   98                       FELDMAN
  2   97.5                     RUGG
  3   81.5                     O'FURTH
  4   76                       GARBANZO
  5   69                       SUCHOSKI
HIT ANY KEY TO CONTINUE
```

The operator hits a key and is shown the data list in ranking order.
The program waits for the pressing of a key to continue.

Later in the run, the operator selects continuation option 3. This
calculates and displays the various statistical quantities.

PROGRAM LISTING

```
100 REM: STATS
110 REM: COPYRIGHT 1980 BY PHIL FELDMAN AND TOM RUGG
150 B$="*BACK":E$="*END"
160 MX=100
170 DIM D$(MX),V(MX),Z(MX)
180 Z(0)=0:N$=CHR$(32)
200 TEXT:HOME:PRINT:PRINT
210 PRINT TAB(16);"STATS":PRINT
220 PRINT"   THIS PROGRAM DOES A STATISTICAL"
230 PRINT"ANALYSIS ON A LIST OF DATA VALUES."
240 PRINT"IT WILL ORDER THE LIST AND FIND SEVERAL"
250 PRINT"STATISTICAL QUANTITIES DESCRIBING"
260 PRINT"THE DATA.":PRINT
270 PRINT"   THE DATA MAY BE ENTERED IN EITHER"
280 PRINT"OF TWO FORMS:"
290 PRINT" 1) AS A SIMPLE LIST OF VALUES, OR"
300 PRINT" 2) WITH AN IDENTIFIER ACCOMPANYING"
310 PRINT"      EACH VALUE.":PRINT
320 PRINT"   WOULD YOU LIKE TO USE IDENTIFIERS"
330 PRINT"WITH YOUR INPUT (Y OR N) ? ";
```

```
340 GET R$
350 IF R$="Y" THEN PRINT"YES":F=1:GOTO 400
360 IF R$="N" THEN PRINT"NO":F=0:GOTO 400
370 GOTO 340
400 GOSUB 2100:PRINT
410 PRINT"   THE DATA MUST NOW BE ENTERED."
420 PRINT:IF F=1 THEN 460
430 PRINT"   ENTER EACH VALUE SEPARATELY IN"
440 PRINT"RESPONSE TO THE QUESTION MARK."
450 GOSUB 2000:GOTO 500
460 PRINT"   FOR EACH DATA ITEM, ENTER ITS"
470 PRINT"IDENTIFIER (ABBREVIATED I.D.) AND ITS"
480 PRINT"VALUE IN RESPONSE TO THE SEPARATE"
490 PRINT"QUESTION MARKS.":GOSUB 2000
500 GOSUB 2100:POKE -16368,0:N=1
510 IF N<1 THEN N=1
520 PRINT:PRINT"DATA ITEM #";N
530 IF F=0 THEN D$(N)=N$:GOTO 570
540 INPUT"I.D. ? ";R$:IF R$=E$ THEN 700
550 IF R$=B$ THEN N=N-1:GOTO 510
560 D$(N)=R$
570 INPUT"VALUE ? ";R$:IF R$=E$ THEN 700
580 IF R$=B$ AND F=1 THEN 520
590 IF R$=B$ THEN N=N-1:GOTO 510
600 V(N)=VAL(R$)
610 IF N=MX THEN PRINT:PRINT
    "** NO MORE DATA ALLOWED! **":N=N+1:GOTO 700
620 N=N+1:GOTO 510
700 N=N-1: IF N=0 THEN PRINT
710 IF N=0 THEN PRINT"** NO DATA -- RUN ABORTED **":END
720 GOSUB 2100
730 PRINT:PRINT"-- CONTINUATION OPTIONS --":PRINT
740 PRINT" 1) LIST DATA IN ORIGINAL ORDER"
750 PRINT" 2) LIST DATA IN RANKING ORDER"
760 PRINT" 3) DISPLAY STATISTICS"
770 PRINT" 4) END PROGRAM"
780 PRINT:INPUT"WHAT NEXT (1, 2, 3, OR 4) ? ";R
790 R=INT(R):IF R<1 OR R>4 THEN 730
800 IF R=4 THEN END
810 ON R GOSUB 1000,1200,1500
820 GOTO 720
1000 GOSUB 2100:PRINT
1010 PRINT" THE ORIGINAL DATA ORDER":PRINT
1020 PRINT N;" TOTAL ENTRIES":GOSUB 2300
1030 PRINT:PRINT TAB(1);"#";TAB(5);"VALUE";
```

```
1040 IF F=0 THEN PRINT
1050 IF F=1 THEN PRINT TAB(22);"I.D"
1060 FOR J=1 TO N
1070 PRINT TAB(1);J;TAB(5);V(J);TAB(22);D$(J)
1080 GOSUB 2500
1090 NEXT:GOSUB 2900:RETURN
1200 GOSUB 2100:PRINT
1210 PRINT" THE DATA IN RANKING ORDER":PRINT
1220 PRINT N;" TOTAL ENTRIES"
1230 GOSUB 2700
1280 GOSUB 2300:PRINT:PRINT TAB(1);"N";TAB(5);"VALUE";
1290 IF F=0 THEN PRINT
1300 IF F=1 THEN PRINT TAB(22);"I.D."
1310 FOR J=1 TO N
1320 PRINT TAB(1);J;TAB(5);V(Z(J));TAB(22);D$(Z(J))
1330 GOSUB 2500
1340 NEXT:GOSUB 2900:RETURN
1500 GOSUB 2100:PRINT
1510 PRINT TAB(6);"STATISTICAL ANALYSIS":PRINT
1520 PRINT"YOUR LIST HAS ";N;" VALUES"
1530 NP=0:NN=0:NZ=0:SQ=0:W=0
1540 FOR J=1 TO N:W=W+V(J):SQ=SQ+V(J)*V(J)
1550 IF V(J)>0 THEN NP=NP+1
1560 IF V(J)<0 THEN NN=NN+1
1570 IF V(J)=0 THEN NZ=NZ+1
1590 NEXT:M=W/N:VA=0:IF N=1 THEN 1610
1600 VA=(SQ-N*M*M)/(N-1)
1610 SD=SQR(VA)
1620 PRINT NP;" POSITIVE; ";NN;" NEGATIVE; ";NZ;" ZERO":
     PRINT
1630 GOSUB 2700:PRINT"MINIMUM VALUE = ";V(Z(N))
1640 PRINT"MAXIMUM VALUE = ";V(Z(1))
1650 PRINT"RANGE = ";V(Z(1))-V(Z(N))
1660 PRINT"SUM OF THE VALUES = ";W:PRINT
1670 PRINT"MEAN = ";M
1680 Q=INT(N/2)+1:MD=V(Z(Q)):IF N/2>INT(N/2) THEN 1700
1690 MD=(V(Z(Q))+V(Z(Q-1)))/2
1700 PRINT"MEDIAN = ";MD
1710 PRINT"MID-RANGE = ";(V(Z(1))+V(Z(N)))/2
1720 PRINT:PRINT"STD. DEVIATION = ";SD
1730 PRINT"VARIANCE = ";VA
1740 GOSUB 2900:RETURN
2000 PRINT:PRINT"   IF YOU MAKE A MISTAKE, TYPE"
2010 PRINT B$;"   TO RE-ENTER THE LAST DATUM."
2020 PRINT:PRINT"   WHEN THE LIST IS COMPLETED, TYPE"
```

```
2030 PRINT E$;"  TO TERMINATE THE LIST.":RETURN
2100 PRINT:FOR J=1 TO 38:PRINT"*";:NEXT
2110 PRINT:RETURN
2300 PRINT:PRINT"  WHILE THE LIST IS DISPLAYING, YOU"
2310 PRINT"CAN HIT ANY KEY TO CAUSE A TEMPORARY"
2320 PRINT"HALT.  THE DISPLAY WILL RESUME WHEN YOU"
2330 PRINT"HIT ANOTHER KEY."
2340 PRINT:PRINT"  HIT ANY KEY TO START THE DISPLAY."
2350 GET R$:POKE -16368,0
2360 RETURN
2500 Q=PEEK(-16384):IF Q<128 THEN RETURN
2510 POKE -16368,0
2520 Q=PEEK(-16384):IF Q<128 THEN 2520
2530 POKE -16368,0:RETURN
2700 IF Z(0)=1 THEN RETURN
2710 FOR J=1 TO N:Z(J)=J:NEXT:IF N=1 THEN RETURN
2720 NM=N-1:FOR K=1 TO N:FOR J=1 TO NM:N1=Z(J)
2730 N2=Z(J+1):IF V(N1)>V(N2) THEN 2750
2740 Z(J+1)=N1:Z(J)=N2
2750 NEXT:NEXT:Z(0)=1:RETURN
2900 PRINT:PRINT"HIT ANY KEY TO CONTINUE"
2910 GET R$
2920 RETURN
```

EASY CHANGES

1. The program arrays are currently dimensioned to allow a maximum of 100 data items. The total storage required for the program depends on the maximum dimension parameter, MX, whether or not identifiers are being used, and if so, on the length of a typical identifier. If your system has at least 6K bytes free (see Appendix 1), you should be able to use up to 100 data values with identifiers averaging 10 characters each. If no identifiers are used, this dimensioning would require a system with approximately 5K bytes free. Should your application require more than 100 data values, you will have to increase the value of MX in line 160 accordingly. To accommodate up to 300 data items, make this change

$$160 \ MX = 300$$

Of course, you will have to have enough RAM memory to enable this (about 7K bytes free with no identifiers and 10K bytes free with 10 character identifiers). On a system with 4K bytes free, the program should run under the stringent restrictions of a maximum of 20 data items and no identifiers. To achieve this, use

$$160 \; MX = 20$$

2. Because of possible conflicts with identifiers in your list, you may wish to change the special strings that signal termination of data input and/or the backing up of data input. These are controlled by the variables E$ and B$, respectively. They are set in line 150. If you wish to terminate the data with /DONE/ and to back up with /LAST/ for example, line 150 should be

$$150 \; B\$ = \text{"/LAST/"}:E\$ = \text{"/DONE/"}$$

3. You may wish to see your lists sorted from smallest value to largest value instead of the other way around, as done now. This can be accomplished by changing the "greater than" sign ($>$) in line 2730 to a "less than" sign ($<$). Thus:

$$2730 \; N2 = Z(J+1):IF \; V(N1) < V(N2) \; THEN \; 2750$$

This will, however, cause a few funny things to happen to the statistics. The real minimum value will be displayed under the heading "maximum" and vice versa. Also, the range will have its correct magnitude but with an erroneous minus sign in front. To cure these afflictions, make these changes also:

```
1630 GOSUB 2700:PRINT"MINIMUM VALUE=";V(Z(1))
1640 PRINT"MAXIMUM VALUE=";V(Z(N))
1650 PRINT"RANGE=";V(Z(N))-V(Z(1))
```

MAIN ROUTINES

150 - 180	Initializes constants and dimensioning.
200 - 370	Displays messages, determines if identifiers will be used.
400 - 620	Gets data from the user.
700 - 710	Checks that input contains at least one value.
720 - 820	Command mode – gets user's next option and does a GOSUB to it.
1000 - 1090	Subroutine to list data in the original order.
1200 - 1340	Subroutine to list data in ranking order.
1500 - 1740	Subroutine to calculate and display statistics.
2000 - 2360	Subroutines to display various messages.

MAIN VARIABLES

MX	Maximum number of data values allowed.
D$(MX)	String array of identifiers.
V(MX)	Array of the data values.
Z(MX)	Array of the sorting order.
N	Number of data values in current application.
F	Flag on identifier usage (1=yes, 0=no).
B$	Flag string to back up the input.
E$	Flag string to signal end of the input.
N$	String for a null identifier.
R$	User input string.
NM	N – 1.
R	Continuation option.
NP	Number of positive values.
NN	Number of negative values.
NZ	Number of zero values.
W	Sum of the values.
SQ	Sum of the squares of the values.
M	Mean value.
MD	Median of the values.
VA	Variance.
SD	Standard deviation.
J,K	Loop indices.
N1,N2	Possible data locations to interchange during sorting.
Q	Work variable.

SUGGESTED PROJECTS

1. The sorting algorithm used in the program is efficient only
   when the number of list items is fairly small—less than 25
   or so. This is because it does not do checking along the way
   to see when the list becomes fully sorted. If your lists tend to

be longer than 25 items, you might wish to use another sorting algorithm more appropriate for longer lists. Try researching other sorts and incorporating them into the program. To get you started, try these changes:

```
2720 Q=0:FOR J=1 TO N-1:N1=Z(J)
2730 N2=Z(J+1):IF V(N1)>=V(N2) THEN 2750
2745 Q=1
2750 NEXT:IF Q=1 THEN 2720
2760 Z(0)=1:RETURN
```

If your lists are short, this routine will probably be a little slower than the current one. However, for longer lists it will save proportionately more and more time.

2. Because the INPUT statement is used when entering identifiers, commas cannot be used inside identifier names. BASIC will ignore anything entered past the comma. This can be circumvented if you use quotes around the identifier name, but you may forget to do this. By modifying the input routine to use a series of **GET** commands, you can build up the identifier strings piecemeal and allow embedded commas. Modify the appropriate routine to do this.

3. Many other statistical parameters exist to describe this kind of data. Research them and add some that might be useful to you. One such idea is classifying the data. This consists of dividing the range into a number of equal classes and then counting how many values fall into each class.

Section 6

Miscellaneous Programs

INTRODUCTION TO MISCELLANEOUS PROGRAMS

These programs show how simple programs can do interesting things. All of them have a mathematical flavor. They are short and, as such, would be useful for study for those just learning BASIC in particular or programming in general.

Monte Carlo simulation involves programming the computer to conduct an experiment. (It doesn't involve high-stakes gambling!) PI shows how this technique can be used to calculate an approximation to the famous mathematical constant pi.

PYTHAG will find all right triangles with integral side lengths. A clever algorithm is utilized to do this.

Have you ever looked around your classroom or club meeting and wondered if any two people had the same birthdate? BIRTHDAY will show you what the surprising odds are.

Very high precision arithmetic can be done on the Apple with the proper "know-how." POWERS will calculate the values of integers raised to various powers, not to the Apple's "normal" nine-digit precision, but up to 250 full digits of precision.

BIRTHDAY

PURPOSE

Suppose you are in a room full of people. What is the probability that two or more of these people have the same birthday? How many people have to be in the room before the probability becomes greater than 50 percent? We are talking only about the month and day of birth, not the year.

This is a fairly simple problem to solve, even without a computer. With a computer to help with the calculations, it becomes very easy. What makes the problem interesting is that the correct answer is nowhere near what most people immediately guess. Before reading further, what do you think? How many people have to be in a room before there is better than a 50-50 chance of birthday duplication? 50? 100? 200?

HOW TO USE IT

When you RUN the program, it starts by displaying headings over two columns of numbers that will be shown. The left column is the number of people in the room, starting with one. The right column is the probability of birthday duplication.

For one person, of course, the probability is zero, since there is no one else with a possible duplicate birthday. For two people, the probability is simply the decimal equivalent of 1/365 (note that we assume a 365-day year, and an equal likelihood that each person could have been born on any day of the year).

What is the probability of duplication when there are three people in the room? No, not just 2/365. It's actually

$$1 - (364/365 \text{ times } 363/365)$$

This is simply one minus the probability of *no* duplicate birthdays.

The probability for four people is

$$1 - (364/365 \text{ times } 363/365 \text{ times } 362/365)$$

The calculation continues like this, adding a new term for each additional person in the room. You will find that the result (probability of duplication) exceeds .50 surprisingly fast.

The program continues with the calculation until there are 60 people in the room. You will have to stop the program long before that to see the point where the probability first exceeds 50 percent.

SAMPLE RUN

```
NO. OF     PROB. OF 2 OR MORE
PEOPLE     WITH SAME BIRTHDAY
1          0
2          2.7397261E-03
3          8.20416585E-03
4          .0163559124
5          .0271355736
6          .0404624834
```

PROGRAM LISTING

```
100 REM: BIRTHDAY COINCIDENCE PROBABILITY PROBLEM
110 REM: COPYRIGHT 1980 BY TOM RUGG AND PHIL FELDMAN
120 TEXT:HOME
130 PRINT"NO. OF    PROB. OF 2 OR MORE"
140 PRINT"PEOPLE    WITH SAME BIRTHDAY"
150 Q=1
160 FOR N=1 TO 60
170 PRINT N;TAB(11);1-Q
180 Q=Q*(365-N)/365
190 NEXT N
200 END
```

EASY CHANGES

1. Change the constant value of 60 in line 160 to alter the range of the number of people in the calculation. For example, change it to 100 and watch how fast the probability approaches 1. Or, change it to 20 to end the program before the output rolls off the screen.

MAIN ROUTINES

120 - 140	Displays headings.
150	Initializes Q to 1.
160 - 190	Calculates probability of no duplication, then displays probability of duplication.

MAIN VARIABLES

N	Number of people in the room.
Q	Probability of no duplication of birthdays.

SUGGESTED PROJECTS

Modify the program to allow for leap years in the calculation, instead of assuming 365 days per year.

PI

PURPOSE AND DISCUSSION

The Greek letter pi, π, represents probably the most famous constant in mathematical history. It occurs regularly in many different areas of mathematics. It is best known as the constant appearing in several geometric relationships involving the circle. The circumference of a circle of radius r is $2\pi r$, while the area enclosed by the circle is πr^2.

Being a transcendental number, pi cannot be expressed exactly by any number of decimal digits. To nine significant digits, its value is 3.14159265. Over many centuries, man has devised many different methods to calculate pi.

This program uses a valuable, modern technique known as computer simulation. The name "simulation" is rather self-explanatory; the computer performs an experiment for us. This is often desirable for many different reasons. The experiment may be cheaper, less dangerous, or more accurate to run on a computer. It may even be impossible to do in "real life." Usually, however, the reason is that the speed of the computer allows the simulation to be performed many times faster than actually conducting the real experiment.

This program simulates the results of throwing darts at a specially constructed dartboard. Consider Figure 1 which shows the peculiar square dartboard involved. The curved arc, outlining the shaded area, is that of a circle with the center in the lower left hand corner. The sides of the square, and thus the radius of the circle, are considered to have a length of 1.

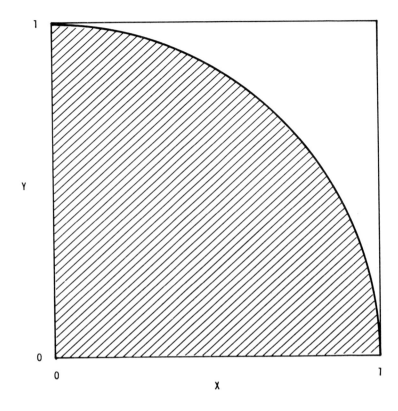

Figure 1. The PI Dartboard

Suppose we were able to throw darts at this square target in such a way that each dart had an equal chance of landing anywhere within the square. A certain percentage of darts would result in "hits," i.e. land in the shaded area. The expected value of this percentage is simply the area of the shaded part divided by the area of the entire square.

The area of the shaded part is one-fourth of the area that the entire circle would enclose if the arc were continued to completely form the circle. Recall that the area of a circle is πr^2 where r is the radius. In our case, $r = 1$, and the area of the entire circle would simply be π. The shaded area of the dartboard is one-fourth of this entire circle and thus has an area of $\pi/4$. The area of the square is s^2, where s is the length of one

side. On our dartboard, s = 1, and the area of the whole dartboard is 1.

Now, the expected ratio of "hits" to darts thrown can be
expressed as

$$\text{RATIO} = \frac{\text{\# hits}}{\text{\# thrown}} = \frac{\text{shaded area}}{\text{entire area}} = \frac{\pi/4}{1} = \frac{\pi}{4}$$

So we now have an experimental way to approximate the value
of π. We perform the experiment and compute the ratio of
"hits" observed. We then multiply this number by four and
we have calculated π experimentally.

But instead of actually constructing the required dartboard
and throwing real darts, we will let the Apple do the job. The
program "throws" each dart by selecting a separate random
number between 0 and 1 for the X and Y coordinates of each
dart. This is accomplished by using the built-in RND function
of BASIC. A "dart" is in the shaded area if $X^2 + Y^2 < 1$ for it.

So the program grinds away, continually throwing darts and
determining the ratio of "hits." This ratio is multiplied by four
to arrive at an empirical approximation to π.

HOW TO USE IT

The program requires only one input from you. This is the
"sample size for printing," i.e. how many darts it should throw
before printing its current results. Any value of one or higher
is acceptable.

After you input this number, the program will commence the
simulation and display its results. A cumulative total of "hits,"
darts thrown, and the current approximation to π will be
displayed for each multiple of the sample size.

This will continue until you press **control C**. When you are
satisfied with the total number of darts thrown, press **control
C** to terminate the program execution.

SAMPLE RUN

       A DARTBOARD PI CALCULATOR

SAMPLE SIZE FOR PRINTING? <u>150</u>

A DARTBOARD PI CALCULATOR

# HITS	# THROWN	PI
113	150	3.01333334
234	300	3.12
351	450	3.12
470	600	3.13333334
587	750	3.13066667
704	900	3.12888889
824	1050	3.13904762
940	1200	3.13333334
1066	1350	3.15851852
1185	1500	3.16
1308	1650	3.17090909
1425	1800	3.16666667

(CONTROL C pressed)

PROGRAM LISTING

```
100 REM: PI
110 REM: COPYRIGHT 1980 BY PHIL FELDMAN AND TOM RUGG
160 T=0:TH=0:Q=PEEK(78)+256*PEEK(79):Q=RND(-Q)
300 GOSUB 600
310 INPUT"SAMPLE SIZE FOR PRINTING? ";NP
320 NP=INT(NP):IF NP<1 THEN 300
330 GOSUB 600
340 PRINT"# HITS    # THROWN";TAB(28);"PI"
400 GOSUB 500:TH=TH+NH:T=T+NP:P=4*TH/T
410 PRINT TAB(2);TH;TAB(13);T;TAB(24);P
420 GOTO 400
500 NH=0:FOR J=1 TO NP
510 X=RND(1):Y=RND(1)
520 IF (X*X+Y*Y)<1 THEN NH=NH+1
530 NEXT:RETURN
600 HOME:PRINT TAB(6);
610 PRINT"A DARTBOARD PI CALCULATOR"
620 PRINT:PRINT:RETURN
```

EASY CHANGES

1. If you want the program to always use a fixed sample size,
   change line 310 to read

   310 NP=150

Of course, the value of 150 given here may be changed to whatever you wish. With this change, line 320 is not needed and may be deleted.

2. If you want the program to stop by itself after a certain number of darts have been thrown, add the following two lines:

```
315 INPUT"TOTAL # DARTS TO THROW";ND
415 IF T>=ND THEN END
```

This will ask the operator how many total darts should be thrown, and then terminate the program when they have been thrown.

MAIN ROUTINES

160	Initializes constants.
300 - 340	Gets operator input, displays column headings.
400 - 420	Calculates and displays results.
500 - 530	Throws NP darts and records number of "hits."
600 - 620	Clears screen and displays program title.

MAIN VARIABLES

T	Total darts thrown.
TH	Total "hits."
NP	Sample size for printing.
NH	Number of hits in one group of NP darts.
P	Calculated value of pi.
X,Y	Random-valued coordinates of a dart.
J	Loop index.

SUGGESTED PROJECTS

1. Calculate the percentage error in the program's calculation of pi and display it with the other results. You will need to define a variable, say PI, which is set to the value of pi. Then the percentage error, PE, can be calculated as:

$$PE = 100*ABS(P-PI)/PI$$

2. The accuracy of this simulation is highly dependent on the quality of the computer's random number generator. Try researching different algorithms for pseudo random number

generation. Then try incorporating them into the program. Change line 510 to use the new algorithm(s). This can actually be used as a test of the various random number generators. Gruenberger's book, referenced in the bibliography, contains good material on various pseudo random number generators.

POWERS

PURPOSE

By now you have probably learned that the Apple keeps track of nine signficiant digits when dealing with numbers. For integers less than one billion (1,000,000,000), the Apple can retain the precise value of the number. But for larger integers the Apple only keeps track of the most significant (leftmost) nine digits, plus the exponent. This means, of course, that there is no way you can use the Apple to deal with precise integers greater than one billion, right?

Wrong.

This program calculates either factorials or successive powers of an integer, and can display precise results that are up to 250 digits long. By using a "multiple-precision arithmetic" technique, this program can tell you *exactly* what 973 to the 47th power is, for example.

HOW TO USE IT

The program first asks you how many digits long you want the largest number to be. This can be any integer from 1 to 250. So, for example, if you enter 40, you will get answers up to 40 digits long.

Next you are asked for the value of N. If you respond with a value of one, you are requesting to be shown all the factorials that will fit in the number of digits you specified. First you will get one factorial, then two factorial, and so on. In case you have forgotten, three factorial is three times two times one, or six. Four factorial is four times three times two times one, or twenty-four.

If you enter an N in the range from 2 through 100,000, you are requesting the successive powers of that number up to the limit of digits you specified. So, if you provide an N of 23, you will get 23 to the first power, then 23 squared, then 23 cubed, and so on.

Finally, after it has displayed the largest number that will fit within the number of digits you entered, the program starts over. The larger the number of digits you ask for, the longer it will take the program to calculate each number. If you ask for zero digits, the program ends.

SAMPLE RUN

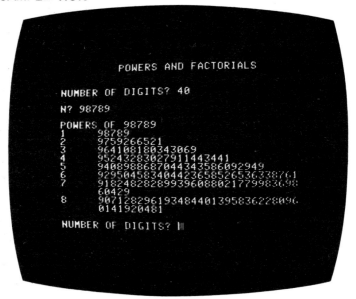

```
                 POWERS AND FACTORIALS

    NUMBER OF DIGITS? 40

    N? 98789

    POWERS OF 98789
    1     98789
    2     9759266521
    3     964108180343069
    4     95243283027911443441
    5     9408988687044343586092949
    6     929504583404423658526536338761
    7     9182482828993960880217799836.98
          60429
    8     907128296193484401395836228096.
          0141920481

    NUMBER OF DIGITS?
```

The operator wants answers up to 40 digits long in the calculations of the powers of 98789. The program calculates numbers up to 98789^8 and then asks for the number of digits again (in preparation for the next calculation the operator requests).

PROGRAM LISTING

```
100 REM: POWERS AND FACTORIALS
110 REM: COPYRIGHT 1980 BY TOM RUGG AND PHIL FELDMAN
```

```
120 TEXT:HOME
130 PRINT TAB(10);"POWERS AND FACTORIALS"
140 PRINT:PRINT
160 DIM N(255)
170 INPUT"NUMBER OF DIGITS? ";M
175 IF M=0 THEN END
180 M=INT(M):IF M>250 OR M<1 THEN 170
190 PRINT:INPUT"N? ";N
200 N=INT(N)
210 IF N<1 OR N>100000 THEN 190
220 PRINT
230 F=0:IF N=1 THEN F=1:PRINT"FACTORIALS"
240 IF F=0 THEN PRINT"POWERS OF ";N
250 T=10:K=1:N(0)=N
260 FOR J=0 TO M
270 IF N(J)<T THEN 300
280 Q=INT(N(J)/T):W=N(J)-Q*T
290 N(J)=W:N(J+1)=N(J+1)+Q
300 NEXT
310 J=M+1
320 IF N(J)=0 THEN J=J-1:GOTO 320
330 IF J>=M THEN 500
340 D=0:PRINT K;TAB(7);
350 N$=STR$(N(J))
360 D=D+1:IF D>30 THEN D=1:PRINT:PRINT TAB(7);
370 PRINT N$;:J=J-1:IF J>=0 THEN 350
380 N=N+F
390 K=K+1:PRINT
400 FOR J=0 TO M:N(J)=N(J)*N:NEXT
410 GOTO 260
500 FOR J=1 TO 255:N(J)=0:NEXT
510 M=0:N=0:PRINT:GOTO 170
```

EASY CHANGES

1. To change the program so that it always uses, say, 50-digit numbers, remove lines 170 and 180, and insert this line:

$$170 \; M = 50$$

2. To clear the screen before the output begins being displayed, change line 220 to say:

$$220 \; HOME$$

3. If 250 digits isn't enough for you, you can go higher. For 500 digits, make these changes:

   a. In line 160, change the 255 to 505.
   b. In line 180, change the 250 to 500.
   c. In line 500, change the 255 to 505.

MAIN ROUTINES

120 - 160	Displays title. Sets up array for calculations.
170 - 240	Asks for number of digits and N. Checks validity of responses. Displays heading.
250	Initializes variables for calculations.
260 - 300	Performs "carrying" in N array so each element has a value no larger than nine.
310 - 320	Scans backwards through N array for first non-zero element.
330	Checks to see if this value would be larger than the number of digits requested.
340 - 370	Displays counter and number. Goes to second line if necessary.
380 - 390	Prepares to multiply by N to get next number.
400 - 410	Multiplies each digit in N array by N. Goes back to line 260.
500 - 510	Zeroes out N array in preparation for next request. Goes back to 170.

MAIN VARIABLES

N	Array in which calculations are made.
M	Number of digits of precision requested by operator.
N	Starting value. If 1, factorials. If greater than 1, powers of N.
F	Set to 0 if powers, 1 if factorials.
T	Constant value of 10.
K	Counter of current power or factorial.
J	Subscript variable.
Q,W	Temporary variables used in reducing each integer position in the N array to a value from 0 to 9.
D	Number of digits displayed so far on the current line (maximum is 30).

N$ String variable used to convert each digit into displayable format.

SUGGESTED PROJECTS

1. Determine the largest N that could be used without errors entering into the calculation (because of intermediate results exceeding one billion), then modify line 210 to permit values that large to be entered.
2. Create a series of subroutines that can add, subtract, multiply, divide, and exchange numbers in two arrays, using a technique like the one used here. Then you can perform high-precision calculations by means of a series of GOSUB statements.

PYTHAG

PURPOSE

Remember the Pythagorean Theorem? It says that the sum of the squares of the two legs of a right triangle is equal to the square of the hypotenuse. Expressed as a formula, it is $a^2 + b^2 = c^2$. The most commonly remembered example of this is the 3-4-5 right triangle ($3^2 + 4^2 = 5^2$). Of course, there are an infinite number of other right triangles.

This program displays integer values of a, b, and c that result in right triangles.

HOW TO USE IT

To use this program, all you need to do is RUN it and watch the "Pythagorean triplets" (sets of values for a, b, and c) come out. The program displays 20 sets of values on each screen, and then waits for you to press any key (except **RESET** or **E**) before it continues with the next 20. It will go on indefinitely until you press the **E** key (for "end").

The left-hand column shows the count of the number of sets of triplets produced, and the other three columns are the values of a, b, and c.

The sequence in which the triplets are produced is not too obvious, so we will explain how the numbers are generated.

It has been shown that the following technique will generate all *primitive* Pythagorean triplets. ("Primitive" means that no set is an exact multiple of another.) If you have two positive integers called R and S such that:

1. R is greater than S,
2. R and S are of opposite parity (one is odd and the other is even), and
3. R and S are relatively prime (they have no common integer divisors except 1),

then a, b, and c can be found as follows:

$$a = R^2 - S^2$$
$$b = 2RS$$
$$c = R^2 + S^2$$

The program starts with a value of two for R. It generates all possible S values for that R (starting at R − 1 and then decreasing) and then adds one to R and continues. So, the first set of triplets is created when R is two and S is one, the second set when R is three and S is two, and so on.

SAMPLE RUN

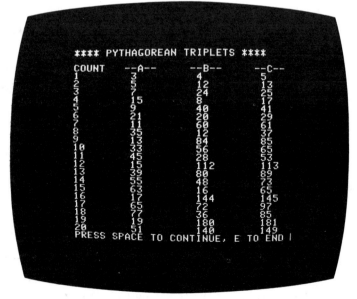

The program generates a screen full of Pythagorean triplets, then waits for the operator to press a key to continue.

PROGRAM LISTING

```
100 REM: PYTHAGOREAN TRIPLETS
110 REM: COPYRIGHT 1980 BY TOM RUGG AND PHIL FELDMAN
130 R=2:K=1:D=0
150 GOSUB 350
180 S=R-1
190 A=R*R-S*S
200 B=2*R*S
210 C=R*R+S*S
220 PRINT K;TAB(10);A;TAB(20);B;TAB(30);C
230 K=K+1:D=D+1:GOTO 400
240 S=S-2:IF S<=0 THEN R=R+1:GOTO 180
250 S1=S:B1=R
260 N=INT(B1/S1)
270 R1=B1-(S1*N)
280 IF R1<>0 THEN B1=S1:S1=R1:GOTO 260
300 IF S1<>1 THEN 240
320 GOTO 190
350 TEXT:HOME
360 PRINT"**** PYTHAGOREAN TRIPLETS ****"
370 PRINT
380 PRINT"COUNT";TAB(9);"--A--";TAB(19);"--B--";TAB(29);
    "--C--"
390 RETURN
400 IF D<20 THEN 240
420 PRINT"PRESS SPACE TO CONTINUE, E TO END ";
430 GET R$
440 IF R$="E" THEN END
450 GOSUB 350:D=0
460 GOTO 240
```

EASY CHANGES

1. Alter the starting value of R in line 130. Instead of 2, try 50 or 100.
2. If you want, you can change the number of sets of triplets displayed on each screen. Change the 20 in line 400 to a 10, for example. You probably won't want to try a value greater than 20, since that would cause the column headings to roll off the screen.

3. To make the program continue without requiring you to press a key for the next screen of values, insert either of these lines:

405 GOTO 450

or

405 GOTO 460

The first will display headings for each screen. The second will only display the headings at the beginning of the run.

MAIN ROUTINES

130	Initializes variables.
150	Displays the title and column headings.
180	Calculates first value of S for current R value.
190 - 210	Calculates A, B, and C.
220 - 230	Displays one line of values. Adds to counters.
240	Calculates next S value. If no more, calculates next R value.
250 - 300	Determines if R and S are relatively prime.
350 - 390	Subroutine to display title and column headings.
400 - 460	Checks if screen is full yet. If so, waits for key to be pressed.

MAIN VARIABLES

R,S	See explanation in "How To Use It."
K	Count of total number of sets displayed.
D	Count of number of sets displayed on one screen.
A,B,C	Lengths of the three sides of the triangle.
S1,B1, R1,N	Used in determining if R and S are relatively prime.

SUGGESTED PROJECTS

1. In addition to displaying K, A, B, and C on each line, display R and S. You will have to squeeze the columns closer together.
2. Because this program uses integer values that get increasingly larger, eventually some will exceed the Apple's nine-digit integer capacity and produce incorrect results. Can you determine when this will be? Modify the program to stop when this occurs.

Appendix I

Memory Usage

Nearly all the programs in this book will run on any typical Apple II, Apple II Plus, or Apple III system. The following chart shows which ones fit, based on the amount of RAM memory and type of Applesoft BASIC you have. Note that an Apple II Plus has Applesoft in ROM.

16K RAM	32K RAM	48K RAM	Type of Applesoft
Note 1	Note 2	Note 2	cassette Applesoft
All	All	All	ROM Applesoft
Note 3	Note 4	All	ROM Applesoft and Disk II (DOS 3.2.1)
(not possible)	Note 5	Note 2	DOS Applesoft and Disk II (DOS 3.2.1)

Note 1: All can run except DECIDE, JOT, WALLOONS, and GRAPH.
Note 2: All can run except WALLOONS.
Note 3: All can run, but DECIDE, GROAN, JOT, WALLOONS, GRAPH, and STATS should be run without DOS software.
Note 4: All can run, but WALLOONS should be run without DOS software.
Note 5: All can run except WALLOONS, but GRAPH should be run without DOS software.

To run a few of the programs, changes will be needed as indicated in the text of the corresponding chapters. Also, some of the chapters mention the limitations of the programs based on the number of "bytes free" in your system. This refers to the memory space available when Applesoft BASIC is in control but no BASIC program has yet been entered. To find out how many bytes free your system has, enter the command

PRINT FRE(0)

after Applesoft gets control. For example, a 16K system using cassette Applesoft shows about 4093 bytes free. If a negative number is shown, it means that more than 32,767 bytes are free.

The programs have been tested using DOS 3.3 as well as DOS 3.2.1. At the time of this writing, we have been unable to test the programs on an Apple III (in Apple II emulation mode). We believe they should work correctly in that configuration, but cannot yet say so for certain.

Bibliography

BOOKS

Bell, R. C., *Board and Table Games From Many Civilizations*, Oxford University Press, London, 1969. (WARI)

Brown, Jerald R., *Instant BASIC*, Dymax, Menlo Park, Calif., 1977. (Self-teaching text on the BASIC language)

Cohen, Daniel, *Biorhythms in Your Life*, Fawcett Publications, Greenwich, Connecticut, 1976. (BIORHYTHM)

Crow, E. L., David, F. A., and Maxfield, M. W., *Statistics Manual*, Dover Publications, New York, 1960. (STATS)

Croxton, F. E., Crowden, D. J., and Klein, S., *Applied General Statistics* (Third Edition), Prentice-Hall, Englewood Cliffs, N.J., 1967. (STATS)

Gruenberger, Fred J., and Jaffray, George, *Problems for Computer Solution*, John Wiley and Sons, New York, 1965. (BIRTHDAY, PI)

Gruenberger, Fred J., and McCracken, Daniel D., *Introduction to Electronic Computers*, John Wiley and Sons, New York, 1961. (MILEAGE, PI, PYTHAG, WARI as Oware)

Hildebrand, F. B., *Introduction to Numerical Analysis*, McGraw-Hill, New York, 1956. (CURVE, DIFFEQN, INTEGRATE, SIMEQN)

Kuo, S. S., *Computer Applications of Numerical Methods*, Addison-Wesley, Reading, Massachusetts, 1972. (CURVE, DIFFEQN, INTEGRATE, SIMEQN)

McCracken, Daniel D., and Dorn, W. S., *Numerical Methods and FORTRAN Programming*, John Wiley and Sons, New York, 1964. (CURVE, DIFFEQN, INTEGRATE, SIMEQN)

Shefter, Harry, *Faster Reading Self-Taught*, Washington Square
    Press, New York, 1960. (TACHIST)

PERIODICALS

Feldman, Phil, and Rugg, Tom, "Pass the Buck," *Kilobaud*, July
    1977, pp. 90-96. (DECIDE)
Fliegel, H. F., and Van Flandern, T. C., "A Machine Algorithm
    for Processing Calendar Dates," *Communications of the
    ACM*, October, 1968, p. 657. (BIORHYTHM)

All of the programs in this book have been tested carefully and are working correctly to the best of our knowledge. However, we take no responsibility for any losses which may be suffered as a result of errors or misuse. You must bear the responsibility of verifying each program's accuracy and applicability for your purposes.

If you want to get a copy of an errata sheet that lists corrections for any errors or ambiguities we have found to date, send one dollar ($1.00) and a self-addressed stamped envelope (SASE) to the address below. Ask for errata for this book (by name). In addition to any errors we can tell you about, we'll send you an entertaining new program for the Apple.

If you think you've found an error, please let us know. If you want an answer, include a SASE.

Please keep in mind that the most likely cause of a program working incorrectly is a typing error. Check your typing *very* carefully before you send us an irate note about an error in one of the programs.

If you don't want to type all of the programs into the Apple II yourself, here is an alternative. You can send us $29.95 (U.S.) at the address below and we will send you a disk (DOS 3.3) containing all 32 programs in this book, plus the new one mentioned above (California residents add sales tax, please.)

Tom Rugg and Phil Feldman
Errata – 32 Programs for the Apple
P.O. Box 24815
Los Angeles, CA 90024